P9-AEZ-918

Battle for Hue

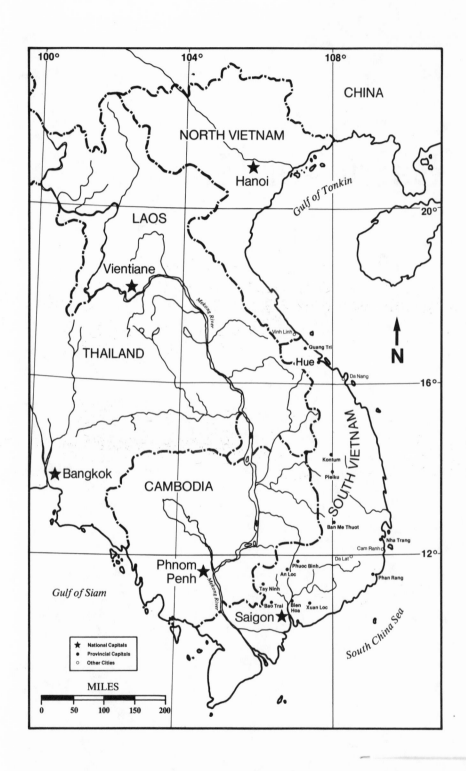

DEDICATION

*This book is for
my father, William; my mother, Ulla;
my brother, Erik;
and every Vietnam veteran—
especially those who made the
supreme sacrifice for America*

Sometimes I lie in bed at night and things come back to me, but I've forgotten a lot of it. I think your mind represses a lot of it. It has to.

Josef Burghardt, Marine sergeant in Hue

Contents

Preface

If it had been a popular war like our involvement in World War II, the Battle for Hue would today still be a familiar name. More importantly, the men who survived to return home would have been greeted as heroes; those who had fallen would have been remembered. But that was not to be. Those Americans who fought in Hue became part of the unfortunate generation whose own nation could not separate the war from the warriors, who were shunned for not turning their back on the job at hand. However unpopular the Vietnam War, the American people seemed to forget that their soldiers were enduring the same hardships and privations as their much-praised forerunners in World War II. The Battle of Hue was a focal point of those hardships — a brutal, month-long, house-to-house battle fought, primarily, by three understrength U.S. Marine infantry battalions.

I was three years old when the Marines were fighting in Hue. When I was growing up, the Vietnam War was some vague, distant thing which was treated like a dirty word. It was this silence — compounded by the flip remarks of my liberal teachers in school about My Lai, drug addicts, and psychotic Vietnam veterans — which sparked my interest in the subject. It bothered me that so many of our countrymen could have suffered so greatly, and so few care about it. It bothered me that those who deserted to Canada and elsewhere were lauded for their humanity, while those who didn't run, but faced the year of hell in Vietnam were dismissed as baby-killers, junkies, and suckers. I began to research the subject and I went to the only source that really mattered, the men who were there.

This book is, of course, the product of that interest and those interviews. It is history in the sense that it covers the dates, tactics, units, logistics, and the rest that made up the Battle of Hue. But, with the great input of those veterans, it tries to tell a bit more. It describes the day-by-day existence of the combat Marines in that month-long battle, the fears, victories, lost friends, comradeship, the weariness. I was fortunate in being able to talk with some of the Marine commanders in Hue; I was even more fortunate in being able to talk with the combat infantrymen — the grunts. This book is mostly about them, the battle as seen through the eyes of the grunts.

I will always have a fond memory of those veterans who helped me in this work. I talked to many who were not in Hue, and the spirit of those conversations is in this book; the Hue vets I had the opportunity to interview number thirty-four. Some of them, particularly those among the general officers, were forced by their busy schedules to assist mostly by reviewing rough drafts and suggesting other avenues of securing information. Others, particularly those among the junior enlisted, began helping with this project at the beginning and carried through with it over the years. I am grateful for each one's help, and feel gratified and thankful that their assistance and faith has come to a solid conclusion. The veterans who lent specific help to *The Battle for Hue* were: Gen. William C. Westmoreland, USA (Ret.); Lt. Gen. Foster C. LaHue, USMC (Ret.); Lt. Gen. John J. Tolson, USA (Ret.); Col. Frank Breth, USMC; Col. James J. Coolican, USMC; Col. Marcus J. Gravel, USMC (Ret.); Capt. Robert H. Hamilton, USNR, (Ret.); Col. Myron C. Harrington, USMC; Col. Edward J. LaMontagne, USMC (Ret.); Col. Wayne R. Swenson, USMC; Col. Robert H. Thompson, USMC (Ret.); Lt. Col. Gordon D. Batcheller, USMC; Lt. Col. Terry Charbonneau, USMCR; Lt. Col. William Harvey, USMC; Lt. Col. Ralph J. Salvati, USMC (Ret.); Maj. James V. DiBernardo, USMC (Ret.); Maj. Harold Pyle, USMC (Ret.); Capt. Dale A. Dye, USMC; CW04 William Dickman, USMCR; Sgt. Maj. Frank Thomas, USMC; MSgt. Joseph L. McLaughlin, USMC (Ret.); MSgt. Paul Thompson, USMC (Ret.); SSgt. Josef Burghardt, USMC (Ret.); SSgt. Richard W. Carter, USMC; SSgt. Edward F. Neas, USMCR; Cpl. Dan Allbritton, USMC (Ret.); Sgt. Steve Berntson, USMC (Ret.); Peter Braestrup; Cpl. Bill Jackson USMC (Ret.); Cpl. Edward Landry, USMC (Ret.); Cpl. Lewis C. Lawhorn, USMC (Ret.); Lt. Richard Lyons, USN (Ret.); Cpl. Brian Mayer, USMC (Ret.); Lt. Patrick Polk, USMC (Ret.); PFC George Schamberger, USMC (Ret.); Don Webster.

A special note of thanks should go to Brig. Gen. O. K. Steele, USMC (a graduate of the same 1956 Basic School class as my father, William

F. Nolan). When he was a colonel commanding the Marine Barracks, Washington, D.C., in the summer of 1981, Steele invited me to spend two weeks with his family at their on-base residence. It was a fabulous visit. General Steele not only provided his own memories of Hue, but pointed me in the right direction at the USMC archives, and arranged for me to meet and interview Bill Harvey and Harold Pyle.

Another important thank-you must go to the U.S. Marine Corps Historical Center in Washington, D.C., for providing numerous documents and other such material pertaining to the Marines in Vietnam. Two members of the staff, retired Brig. Gen. Edwin H. Simmons and CW04 Robert Skidmore, were extremely helpful and encouraging during the many years of research.

Keith W. Nolan
August 1983

Foreword

Hue, like Saigon, was not attacked until the second night. Like Saigon, too, it was unprepared despite a full day's warning. Hue's defenders, though, were not able to beat off the city's assailants. Communists, gaining a firm foothold, accomplished their aims there.

Hue is actually two towns. The interior city, called the Citadel, is a walled fortress patterned after the Imperial City at Peking. A rough square, about two miles on a side, built on the banks of the Perfume River, the Citadel once served as the residence for Annamese emperors. It contains many ancient and revered structures, including the imposing Palace of Peace. One of the few cultural shrines the Vietnamese have, the Citadel is protected by an outer wall sixteen feet high and varying in thickness from sixty to over two hundred feet.

Brigadier General Ngo Quang Truong, commander of the ARVN 1st Division, held a special flag raising ceremony at his headquarters in the Citadel on the morning of 30 January to mark the arrival of the Year of the Monkey. Right afterwards, he received the disturbing news of the first wave of attacks elsewhere in the country. Cautiously, but not showing undue concern, General Truong heightened his division's alert status and decided he and his staff would sleep that night in the Citadel headquarters. That precautionary step saved Hue by keeping intact Truong's command setup and by preventing the 1st Division from being surprised. The general did not know it, but sappers were already inside the city. Having sneaked in two days earlier, they were anxiously awaiting the arrival of two Viet Cong regiments.

Those regiments, the 5th, commanded by Lieutenant Colonel Nguyen Van, and the 6th, commanded by Lieutenant Colonel Nguyen

Trong Dan, were moving stealthily toward Hue even while General Truong was holding his New Year's ceremony, In all, the eight battalions of the two regiments had seventy-five hundred men, including both Viet Cong and North Vietnamese soldiers.

About 2:00 A.M. Colonel Dan's men, aided by dense fog and guided by accomplices inside the city, slipped undetected into the outskirts and headed directly for their objective, the Citadel. At 3:40 A.M. they surged into one section, surprising sentries and gaining an immediate bridgehead. Colonel Van's 5th Regiment, meanwhile, having been delayed by a South Vietnamese ambush, hurried to join unexpectedly ferocious ARVN opposition, the two regiments had occupied only a portion of the Citadel when dawn came. They found themselves sharing the sturdy fortress with General Truong's stubbornly resistant ARVN troops. Perhaps two full Viet Cong battalions held the crucial central part of the Citadel. As they consolidated their newly conquered position, other battalions fortified sectors of the outer city, particularly the area south of the Perfume River. At 8:00 A.M. unhappy Allied officers saw a huge Viet Cong flag fluttering defiantly from the main flagpole in front of the Palace of Peace.

Straightway, Allied forces counterattacked. American marines, South Vietnamese paratroopers, and South Vietnamese armored troops tried to root out the invaders. They failed. That first attempt set the pattern. Day after day Allied units endeavored to shove the obstinate communists out of the Citadel and to loosen their bulldog grip on the adjacent part of the outer city. But they found the positions too tough to take without absorbing prohibitive casualties. They were extremely reluctant, also, to damage the highly valued cultural center by bringing heavy weapons to bear on the entrenched foe. As a result, the fighting was largely house-to-house, hand-to-hand, bloody, and quite drawn out.

reprinted from *Summons of the Trumpet* by
Dave Richard Palmer. Presidio Press, 1978.
pages 192–93.

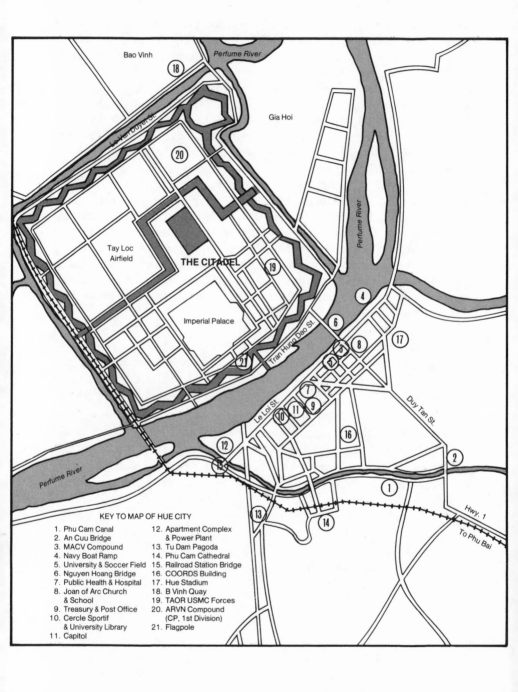

KEY TO MAP OF HUE CITY

1. Phu Cam Canal
2. An Cuu Bridge
3. MACV Compound
4. Navy Boat Ramp
5. University & Soccer Field
6. Nguyen Hoang Bridge
7. Public Health & Hospital
8. Joan of Arc Church
   & School
9. Treasury & Post Office
10. Cercle Sportif
    & University Library
11. Capitol
12. Apartment Complex
    & Power Plant
13. Tu Dam Pagoda
14. Phu Cam Cathedral
15. Railroad Station Bridge
16. COORDS Building
17. Hue Stadium
18. B Vinh Quay
19. TAOR USMC Forces
20. ARVN Compound
    (CP, 1st Division)
21. Flagpole

Chapter 1

Call to Battle

From Phu Bai to Hue

The Marine was dead. His body, its head bouncing, hung over the side of the jeep driving past the column of grunts on the dirt road called Highway 1.

Rich Carter stood there watching as the jeep disappeared into the darkness down the road. The enemy had ambushed the front of the company, killed the point man, wounded three others, and now they were gone, blended back into the jungle and the night. It was always like that. Since Carter had joined the company three months before, they had rarely found the enemy. What they did find were the mines and booby traps and snipers and ambushes; they found frustration. It wasn't exactly what Carter had expected. He'd joined the Marine Corps a week out of high school in Carteret, New Jersey, because his father had been a Marine, his uncle had been one, he believed in the war — and he was eighteen years old and wanted a piece of it.

He went to Vietnam all full of the piss and vinegar and nervous excitement of a new infantryman. But then it came — the sweating patrols in the sun-baked paddies and treelines of the An Hoa River basin, the relocation operations where they had to load the people into amtracs — the women crying and the children screaming at them — and then burn down the thatch hootches. The Viet Cong were omnipresent, but rarely to be seen. Carter had spent one night patrol sitting in a black, steaming jungle while some invisible phantom shouted at them, "Ma-line, tonight you die!" Once, his night ambush team surprised a VC on a trail and gunned him down; in the morning, the body was gone. Another time they searched a hootch and found the ring of a dead Marine in it. And there were the booby traps. God, the booby traps. Grenades fixed with tripwires, rigged C ration cans, wired duds, thirty-pound mines. They seemed to be everywhere. In the jungle one day, Carter heard a deafening roar, and then the terrible cry, "All corpsmen up!" It had been a rigged 155mm artillery shell, and eight Marines were blown away. The day after that, the grunt in front of Carter stepped onto a path through a treeline. The ground suddenly erupted, something thudded against Carter's head, and when he shook his brain clear, he could see the man's frayed jungle boot lying beside him, burnt and smoking, with the foot still inside. The grunt was on the trail, screaming horribly at the sight of his bone jammed into the dirt like a stake. Both his legs were gone below the knee.

The jeep with the body was gone, and the column of Marines went back down the road and started setting up. They dug their fighting holes, wired in the claymore mines around them, and divided up the watch. Then, Lance Cpl. Richard Walter Carter, of the 3d Platoon's machine gun section, and the rest of the grunts of Fox Company, 2d Battalion, 5th Marines, 1st Marine Division, settled in their holes, trying to get some sleep among the mosquitoes and the night sounds.

It was the night of January 30–31, 1968.

The Battle of Hue City was a few hours away.

———————

That day, a U.S. Army radio intercept field station set up at the Phu Bai Combat Base, south of Hue on Highway 1, had picked up enemy radio transmissions indicating an attack on Hue City. Following standard operating procedure, the telltale message was not sent directly to Hue, but to high command in Da Nang for posting and analysis. By the time it was to be sent to Hue via teletype, it made little difference.

———————

Capt. James J. Coolican, the capable U.S. Marine advisor to the all-volunteer Hoc Bao ("Black Panther") Company, 1st ARVN Division, was worried. The day before, January 29, his unit had taken a convoy to Hue from combat operations north on the DMZ. It was Tet, the Vietnamese lunar new year — 1968 was the Year of the Monkey — a holiday which to an American would be like, as the cliché goes, having your birthday, Christmas, and the Fourth of July all rolled into one. As was the custom throughout the war, Tet cease-fire truces had been declared by both sides. But, as they drove south towards Hue for their standdown, Coolican saw that there were no throngs of holiday travelers on the roads, none of the hustle and bustle typical of the Tet holiday. Something uneasy was in the air. And Captain Coolican knew it meant the enemy was going to attack.

But when? And where?

Inside Hue, at the 1st ARVN Division Headquarters, Brig. Gen. Ngo Quang Truong, the division commander, also knew something was in the wind. The traditional cease-fire had been cancelled that day by Gen. William Westmoreland's high command in Saigon, when eight cities came under communist attack. Truong, who was one of the best South Vietnamese generals, took the precaution of gathering his division staff inside the walls of his HQ compound, putting them on 100-percent alert, and issuing more alerts to his units outside Hue. Nevertheless, half of the men in the division were given holiday leave; most of the ARVN soldiers in that unit had family in Hue. But, intelligence reports indicated an enemy force, the size of two regiments, building up forty kilometers west of the city. South of the city, enemy forces had been harassing the Phu Loc area. And that's where Truong expected the enemy to strike — an attack at Phu Loc and an attempt to cut Highway 1, leading up to Hue. The division commander had his battalions deployed accordingly.

Although an attack could be seen in the offing, there was no reliable indication that Hue was the target. Hue City was something sacred to the Vietnamese, both North and South, because it had been the imperial capital when there was only one Vietnam. During the hundreds of years of bloodshed in the country, Hue had only twice been a victim. The first time was in 1883 when French warships bombarded the city before a colonial takeover. The last time was when communist guerrillas tried unsuccessfully to wrest it from the French. That had been in 1945. Hue was so peaceful, in fact, that South Vietnamese officers were known to offer bribes for assignment there.

Hue was the third largest city in South Vietnam, with a population of about 140,000. Located ten kilometers west from the coast of the South China Sea, and one hundred kilometers from the battle-scarred DMZ, Hue was the seat of government in Thua Thien Province. Actually, it was two cities, separated by the Huong Giang, the "River of Perfumes," which flowed out into the ocean.

On the northern bank was the Citadel, a three-square-kilometer section surrounded by the huge walls that the French military and the Vietnamese emperor had built in the 1800s. Around those walls were deep blue moats, dotted green along the edges by lotus plants, and lined with acre upon acre of thick green treelines. It was from inside those walls that the emperors had ruled in the dynasties of previous centuries. Across from the Citadel, on the southern bank of the Perfume River, was the South Side, a newer, residential district. It was about half the size of the Citadel and shaped roughly like a triangle, with the wide Perfume River on the northern edge, and the Phu Cam Canal flowing down from the river, then moving back up, forming a loose "V" around the South Side.

Militarily, Hue was important; a railroad and Highway 1 passed through, over the Perfume River, bringing supplies from Da Nang to the DMZ, and it was the unloading point for Navy supply boats moving from the mouth of the river out to the ocean. But the city was hardly secure. In the Citadel, tucked inside the northern corner of the massive walls, was General Truong's ARVN HQ. There were no combat units stationed there, only staff and garrison troops. Across the river, on the South Side, was a U.S. Navy boat ramp, maintained by the Hue Ramp Detachment, U.S. Naval Support Activity. Several hundred yards down Highway 1 from the ramp was the Military Assistance Command Vietnam compound, supervised by Col. George O. Adkisson, U.S. Army, the senior advisor to the 1st ARVN Division. The MACV compound consisted of several two- and three- story buildings, including a converted hotel, surrounded by high walls. The men of Advisory Team 3 assigned there lived comfortably.

While Hue historically had never been a military center, it was renowned for something else. It was the cultural center of Vietnam, a place of learning, a remembrance of the traditions and values of the past. Hue was known for the Citadel, with its great walls and old imperial buildings with names such as the Imperial Palace, the Forbidden City, the Palace of Perfect Peace. It was known for its lush gardens and flowing moats, its beautiful red-gold-and-blue palaces with their intricate stonework. And there was the South Side, with the University, the French-style province capitol building, the country club, Cercle Sportif, with its wide green lawns stretching down to the river, verandas, and 1930s furnishings. Hue was tree-lined streets, the gonging of Buddhist bells, the delicate French-Vietnamese architecture, the beautiful schoolgirls with their flowing *ao dai* dresses and silky black hair. In the Buddhist myth, Hue was the lotus flower growing from the mud; it was the serenity and beauty of a city at peace in a nation at war.

Captain Coolican was six feet five, a big man from the coal country of Carbondale, Pennsylvania, and out in the field, he towered over his tiny Vietnamese soldiers. That was about the only visible difference between them; in his nine months with the 1st ARVN Division, he had become one of them. He spoke Vietnamese, he wore their uniform, ate their food, and when he was sick or injured, he was treated by an ARVN medic. He understood their culture and he respected the fighting ability of their soldiers; Coolican liked the South Vietnamese.

He knew sadly that he was in the minority among his peers; the American military as a whole held a condescending view toward the Vietnamese in general, and the ARVN in particular. As far as Coolican was concerned, that was mostly the result of the Americans trying to judge everything and everybody by American standards, without knowing anything of Vietnamese history and traditions. For example, a young grunt could repeatedly see Vietnamese men holding hands, and conclude that he was fighting for a nation of perverts, not knowing that holding hands for the Vietnamese was like shaking hands to an American. Or, Coolican reckoned, an American convoy might go through a village and see the local part-time Popular and Regional Force militia troops sitting around lazily, many not even carrying weapons, and conclude that the South Vietnamese were miserable soldiers — without ever having seen regular ARVN units in action. Such stereotypes, garnered from limited personal experience, bothered Coolican deeply; he saw great courage and fighting skill among his South Vietnamese soldiers, and they always did the job at hand.

At first, culture shock had affected Coolican. During a midnight-to-dawn battle south of Quang Tri when he had been with the 2d Battalion, 3d ARVN Regiment, the brave and popular battalion commander was killed. In the morning, Coolican had the ARVN bodies lined up along the side of the road waiting for the helicopters. He was shocked to see the other Viets sitting nonchalantly nearby, eating rice, drinking tea, and joking. He commented to one of the officers that it was strange no one seemed to care about their dead commander, and the ARVN said to him, "Well, why should we be sad? He was a good man, he was a good person, he lived a good life. He died very bravely so his family will be proud of him. And because he lived a good life and died a good death, now he will have his destiny and be very happy for it. So instead of being sorrowful in a situation like this, we're happy for him." Coolican also had to learn that the Vietnamese placed high priority on proper burial for their dead; during firefights, he had his dead soldiers medevacked right after the seriously wounded, instead of last as did the U.S. military. It took four months, but then Coolican was thinking like a Vietnamese. They might do things differently, he mused, but the end results were always the same.

Because he had a feeling for Vietnamese culture and knew how important the Tet holiday was to his soldiers, Coolican felt it would be an imposition for him, a foreigner, to be with them when the festivities began. Coolican knew several of the U.S. staff officers, advisors, and radiomen of Advisory Team 3 who worked across the river in Colonel Adkisson's MACV compound, so he decided to spend Tet with them. He gathered his gear, said good-bye to his men set up in the ARVN HQ, and took a jeep.

He drove alone through the Citadel, the jeep's headlights cutting a swath in the darkness, and stopped before going across the span bridge over the Perfume. He got out and stood silently, just looking. It was a beautiful, peaceful night, the moon high and bright, the trees across the river reaching up in black silhouettes. There seemed to be no one else around.

Down below, the river flowed black and gold in the moonlight, quietly lapping against the sampans that bobbed along the piers.

Down the river, about four kilometers southwest of the city, sat 1st Lt. Nguyen Thi Tan, commander of the Reconnaissance Company, 1st ARVN Division; his Australian Army advisor, W02 Terry Egan, and thirty-six of his soldiers. They were set up near the river banks on a surveillance mission. They sat quietly, watching, waiting, cloaked by the night. Suddenly, at 10:00 P.M., firing erupted to the east — a North Vietnamese unit was attacking a Regional Force militia company. They listened to the exchange of gunfire, and then they could see figures moving among the trees. Lieutenant Tan and W02 Egan got on the radio to General Truong's division headquarters and sent word of enemy positions, numbers, and equipment. Then the ARVNs sat even stiller in the dark and watched the North Vietnamese filter past their position. There were at least two battalions of enemy troops, all headed toward Hue.

One hour and forty minutes after Lieutenant Tan reported the enemy troop movement, at 3:40 A.M., on Wednesday, January 31, 1968, the North Vietnamese Army and the Viet Cong brought the war to Hue City. The rockets and mortars began falling from the mountains to the west. Flares popped and glowed above the rooftops. The infantry followed, moving across the bridges into the city. Already inside Hue, other Communists who had infiltrated the civilian Tet traffic became soldiers by simply changing their clothes and breaking out the stockpiles of weapons and supplies that had been smuggled into the city.

At the MACV compound on the South Side, they had just opened the main gate. An Air Force pilot, who had left his observation plane at the Citadel airstrip, drove his jeep in — and then the NVA hit. A dozen 122mm rockets whooshed in from the dark, blowing eight-foot craters. One caved in the roof of the sector TOC building, killing and wounding the staffers inside, while another exploded inside the compound, destroying a jeep. The others luckily either fell short or overshot the target. At the first explosions, the men inside the compound rushed for their battle stations.

The rockets stopped falling. For some reason, there was a five-minute delay before the NVA ground troops attacked the compound.

Those five minutes gave the Americans time to grab weapons and ammo and take up positions on the walls. Then perhaps forty North Vietnamese emerged from the buildings around MACV, firing wildly, and running towards the wall with satchel charges. A young Army enlisted man up in a twenty-foot wooden observation tower on the wall opened up with his machine gun. He killed a half-dozen NVA and delayed the attack for perhaps five minutes, until a B-40 rocket-propelled grenade hit his tower. Badly injured in the legs, he called for help. Captain Coolican crawled to the tower and, under heavy fire, climbed up and brought the man down.

The NVA assault platoon continued until they got to the main gate. Marines of a Da Nang security unit manning a bunker at the gate, opened up, holding off the attack for another few minutes until they were silenced by another B-40. More men were firing from the wall, including Coolican, who was laying down a barrage with an M-79 grenade launcher.

The delay provided by the observation tower and the bunker allowed Marine Maj. Frank Breth, his Australian Army roommate, and an Army major to get to the top floor of a building with weapons and grenades. Breth had already been wounded — the rocket that had blown up the jeep brought the roof down on his head while he was sleeping, gouging his forehead — but he had cleared his head and was ready. Forty feet down and across, they could see the survivors of the NVA assault platoon — about sixteen men — trying to get through the main gate. They were carrying satchel charges. Breth had a staff job at MACV as liaison officer from the 3d Marine Division to the 1st ARVN Division, but before that he had served at Con Thien and been wounded as a company commander with the 9th Marines. He knew how to fight. He aimed through the dim light with his M-16 rifle and sprayed the NVA coming through the gate, while his companions hurled grenade after grenade. Below them, the North Vietnamese sprawled dead around the entrance to the compound.

That was the end of the enemy ground attack.

The North Vietnamese began moving into buildings near the MACV compound, setting up machine guns in windows, and putting the inhabitants under heavy fire. More B-40 rockets were fired. So were mortars.

The staff inside the compound was no unarmed garrison. Besides the Americans, there was a tough crew of Australian warrant officers, and they all stored the weapons and supplies they used on field operations inside the compound. By now, everyone was fully equipped and ready. They could hear firing around them in all directions, but the North Vietnamese made no more direct attacks against the compound. Captain Coolican, who had no immediate way to get back to his ARVN troops in the Citadel, proved to be a powerhouse in organizing the security of the compound. He got together a ragtag group, and with the help of Lt. Steve Lampo, USMC, and Lt. Fred Drew, U.S. Army, they moved about, guarding the walls and pulling back casualties to the MACV dispensary.

The Army doctor stationed at the compound, Capt. Stephen Bernie, was doing a tremendous job. But evacuation to better facilities was needed for the seriously wounded. There was a U.S. Army communications center down the street, a block south on Highway 1; for some inexplicable reason, the NVA had not seized it. Thus, communications were still open with the outside. Requests for medical evacuation helicopters were sent to the I Corps advisory headquarters in Da Nang, relayed to the III Marine Amphibious Force, and sent down to 1st Marine Division. The result of this garbled, meandering route was: no results.

The troops in the compound also began requesting immediate aid. They were isolated and their cable to the ARVN HQ had been cut, so they did not know what was happening in the Citadel. The result was that their requests for aid contained little intelligence information. They didn't know that the Tet Offensive was erupting throughout the country; they didn't even know if all of Hue was falling, or if they were experiencing a tough, but limited, sapper attack. They didn't know it, but in most of the city, NVA and VC soldiers were roaming at will, passing dead ARVNs, and starting to dig in, setting up machine guns and mortars in people's homes. Most of the citizens of Hue stayed behind locked doors and closed shutters, scared and confused. Over the walls of the Imperial Palace in the Citadel, near the Perfume River, a huge red-blue-and-gold Viet Cong flag went up.

The takeover had taken only a few hours.

Lance Corporal Carter was being shaken awake in his fighting hole. "We're on a hundred percent alert," the man said.

Carter sat up, irritated. "You gotta be shitting me, I just got to sleep!"

A squad leader said word had come that the gooks were attacking everything — everywhere. Rumor was that Hue City had fallen. Carter peered down in the valley from the company's hilltop position. He could see red and green tracers blipping back and forth in the black where the CAP units held the villages. And further away, he could see the flashes of exploding rockets hitting the Phu Bai Combat Base.

Holy shit, he thought.

The principal command at the Phu Bai Combat Base was Task Force X-RAY, more formally called the 1st Marine Division Forward Headquarters. It had been established on January 13 as a result of the Division's large tactical area of responsibility, which extended from south of Da Nang to slightly north of Hue. X-RAY had been given responsibility for the area from Hai Van Pass to the northern boundary of the TAOR (tactical area of responsibility), with the mission of protecting the base at Phu Bai, screening the western approaches to Hue, and keeping Highway 1 open between the Hai Van Pass and Hue. Elements of Army divisions had recently moved into the area, freeing up 3d Marine Division units, which then moved north to their TAOR below the DMZ. Under X-RAY control, units from the 1st had been moving to replace the 3d Marine Division area; in fact, Task Force X-RAY Headquarters physically occupied the space vacated by the Headquarters, 3d Marine Division.

In command of X-RAY was Brig. Gen. Foster C. LaHue, Assistant Commander of the 1st Marine Division, a World War II veteran with the Silver Star and Purple Heart. At Phu Bai, LaHue had the regimental headquarters of the 1st and 5th Marines, control of four infantry battalions, and the full quota of supporting arms, including armor, artillery, motor transport, engineer, and medical. LaHue was under the administrative control of Division (Maj. Gen. Donn J. Robertson) and under the operational control of the III Marine Amphibious Force (Lt. Gen. Robert E. Cushman). The entire area of operations, I Corps, was under South Vietnamese control, directed from Da Nang by Lt. Gen. Hoang Xuan Lam.

At Phu Bai on that morning of January 31, radio reports kept pouring into LaHue's command post. Enemy activity was reported throughout his TAOR: hamlets were under attack, enemy forces were striking at the bridges along Highway 1, Marine positions were being mortared, CAP units had North Vietnamese and Viet Cong storming their perimeter wire. Intelligence had known some sort of enemy attack was coming, and the Marines under LaHue's command had been in the field to meet the threat — but no one had imagined the scope and magnitude of the communist strikes. It was the beginning of the nationwide Tet Offensive; the enemy seemed to be everywhere at once. And word was also coming from the "open city" of Hue. The calls for assistance from MACV followed the meandering route of I Corps to III MAF to 1st MarDiv to X-RAY. By the time LaHue got the message, it had been so diluted it was hardly discernible what exactly was happening in Hue.

Orders from III MAF were to send reinforcements to Hue. Almost all of his command was already committed in the TAOR, so LaHue decided to send one company that was readily available.

No one had any way of knowing it, but in Hue the enemy had assembled the 804th, K4B, and K4C Battalions of the 4th NVA Regiment; the 800th, 802d, and 806th Battalions of the 6th NVA Regiment; the independent 810th NVA Battalion; and the 12th and Co Be Sapper Battalions. It was a division-size force and they controlled virtually everything except the isolated MACV and ARVN HQ compounds.

Going against that was A Company, 1st Battalion, 1st Marines, 1st Marine Division. They were to go straight up Highway 1, called "The Street Without Joy" because so many Frenchmen had died there in the years past.

Alpha 1/1 was an outstanding fighting outfit, and much of that was because of the company commander, Capt. Gordon D. Batcheller, a big man, modest, intelligent, rugged, who — in the gung ho atmosphere of Vietnam — took to shaving his head.

Twenty-eight years old, Captain Batcheller was born in Boston, the second of three sons to a Navy admiral. As a young boy, he had grown to dislike military life with its frequent moves and disruptions, and had never seriously considered enlisting. But by the time he was at Princeton making his football reputation, something inside said he owed something to his country. He tried to get in a Marine officer program — he had never considered any service except the Marine Corps — but a bad knee disqualified him. He promptly dropped the idea, but by his senior year, his conscience tugged at him again. He passed the physical this time and in 1960, he was commissioned. And after two years as a lieutenant, the boy who'd been fed up with military life decided to make a career in the Corps.

When the Marines first landed at Da Nang, Batcheller immediately put in requests for combat duty. It took two years, but in August 1967 he got his orders, said good-bye to his wife and two children, and left for the war. He ended up with a staff job, intelligence officer of 1/1, a frustrating position for one anxious to command a rifle company. Finally, on Christmas Day 1967, he got it — Alpha Company. "The all-time great Christmas present," he called it.

And he was good. As one of his lance corporals said, "Captain Batcheller was a big dude who was always up in front when the shit hit the fan."

Batcheller was sleeping in a tent inside the Phu Bai Combat Base, when he was awakened and told to get his company organized. He was given no real information; all he knew was that "something was up." His orders were to take Alpha Company and link up with an ARVN unit outside Phu Bai.

He had another problem besides the lack of good intelligence; his company was seriously undermanned. The executive officer was rotating home in three days, and the leader of Third Platoon was at school in Da Nang. The company had choppered to Phu Bai from Quang Tri only several hours before (part of the battalion's shift south under X-RAY control), and a helicopter mix-up had left part of First Platoon and the First and Second Platoon lieutenants stranded at Quang Tri. That morning of the 31st, Batcheller did have with him Gunnery Sgt. J. L. Canley, his slow-talking company gunny, a giant Southern black with a reputation for incredible courage under fire; and his company radioman, Cpl. Larry Williams, a young, blond, all American kid from California. What remained of First Platoon was under Staff Sgt. C. D. Godfrey. With Second Platoon, there was the acting platoon sergeant, Cpl. Bill Jackson, a tough nineteen-year-old New York City boy, a six-month platoon vet with a Purple Heart from Con Thien. Running Third Platoon, in the absence of the lieutenants, was the platoon sergeant, Sgt. Alfredo Gonzalez, a quiet, twenty-one year-old Mexican-American, from the border town of Edinburg, Texas.

Batcheller had faith in them; they were all fine Marines.

Batcheller and his two-and-a-half platoons loaded onto trucks from C Company, 1st Motor Transport Battalion, under 2d Lt. Jerome Nadolski. A U.S. Army truck mounted with four .50-caliber machine guns pulled to the front, while another Duster drove behind the last truck in the convoy to provide rear security. They got moving at first light, bouncing out past the perimeter wire, headed south — away from Hue — to rendezvous with the ARVN unit. They drove along in the cold, gray morning, uneasy because no one knew what was going on or what to expect. After two edgy but uneventful hours, they reached the rendezvous point and the column came to a halt, waiting for their South Vietnamese reinforcements.

The ARVN never showed.

Captain Batcheller got on the horn to Phu Bai, and his instructions were revised: turn the convoy around, retrace the route up Highway 1, and link up with another ARVN unit north of Hue. Batcheller checked his map; it ended halfway through the city. Coincidentally, as they neared the southern outskirts of Hue, they happened upon another group on the road: four M-48 tanks from the 3d Tank Battalion, 3d Marine Division; a jeep, and a Bay City Crane, under the direction of Lt. Col. Edward J. LaMontagne, the embarkation officer of the 3d Marine Division. He had been making a routine trip up Highway 1, escorting the equipment to the Navy ramp on the South Side for transport to his division on the DMZ. But near the Phu Cam Canal, they had come upon a startling sight — several wrecked ARVN tanks with dead crewmen. LaMontagne was a gruff man and a fine officer with three years as a Navy corpsman and a stint as advisor with the Vietnamese Marines under his belt. He had quickly organized his force for whatever they might run into. The arrival of Alpha Company was most fortuitous; the two forces joined up and continued on.

Batcheller's radio crackled again; this time his orders were to relieve the MACV compound inside Hue. LaMontagne correctly pointed out that they had to move faster. The convoy clanked through a village on the fringes of the South Side. Suddenly snipers opened up. First contact. Several Marines were wounded. The grunts poured fire back at the buildings and trees, and the tanks and trucks kept going.

A little farther down the road they crossed the Phu Cam Canal over the An Cuu Bridge. There were several holes blown through the concrete of the bridge, as if the enemy had been trying to knock it down with shaped charges. In fact, they had tried; if they could destroy the bridge, it would tie up the expected relief force along the Phu Cam for hours, and by the time they got across, MACV would have fallen. But the NVA failed, and the Marines effected a crossing without difficulty. Batcheller ordered a halt across the canal. Ahead of them, the highway ran between a cluster of buildings. It reminded Batcheller of an Old Western town — two-story wooden houses, the buildings packed one right next to the other, and no sidewalks.

Nothing moved in the street.

Batcheller gave the word for his men to leave the trucks and climb onto the tanks. Then he and his radioman, Corporal Williams, left their jeep and hoisted themselves beside the turret of the lead tank. He said go, and the tanks hauled ass down the road, raising dust and an incredible roar, everyone firing into the wooden buildings as a precaution.

But, suddenly, fire started pouring back.

A B-40 rocket flashed from nowhere and Batcheller's tank shuddered under the impact. There was another explosion with a spray of AK-47 automatic rifles from the houses. The tank driver moved as fast as his vehicle would go, finally emerging from the gauntlet of buildings and coming to a stop in a traffic circle, with a gas station on the left. The Marines began carrying their casualties to cover in a ditch. Batcheller was afraid that the B-40 had left him with a ruptured eardrum in addition to minor shrapnel wounds. He became aware suddenly that Corporal Williams was gone — the rocket concussions must have cleared him off the deck. And then he saw his corpsman, a New Yorker nicknamed Doc Brooklyn, leaning motionless against the tank turret. Both his legs were gone at the knees. There was little blood, and Batcheller stared, thinking it was like sliced baloney; Brooklyn died.

Down the road the firing was still heavy as the Marines and tanks struggled to get through the gauntlet to continue recovering their casualties.

Corporal Jackson went down on the side of the road, ducking flat in the gutter, trying to keep his head from getting blown off. Jesus, Jesus, this was bad. He could see NVA up on the roofs ahead, in the windows, darting among the alleys. Rounds ricocheted all around. Other Marines were firing back furiously. Civilians were caught in the cross fire.

Suddenly Jackson saw Sergeant Gonzalez hustling up to him, bleeding from shrapnel wounds, but still dragging another wounded Marine to cover. Jackson looked at the man — it was Williams, the skipper's radioman. Most of his leg was a bloody mess. A corpsman quickly patched him up. The firing went on forever — a few minutes — then the tanks were moving forward again and the grunts ran behind, firing as they went, dragging their wounded with them; NVA fire splattered all around them.

Finally, they pulled into the traffic circle next to Batcheller.

A wide, open field of rice paddies stretched ahead of them, with rows of houses and trees at the far end. The highway cut across the paddy on a raised road and halfway through, there were two large buildings, one on each side of the road. Automatic weapons fire began snapping from the houses across the field. A few mortar rounds exploded near the Marines. Capt. Batcheller and Lt. Col. LaMontagne brought their firepower to bear. The 90mm cannons of the tanks boomed, and quad-fifty gunners fired furiously, spilling empty brass and links on the ground.

The NVA kept up their fire. The pop-pop-pop of M-16 rifles continued from the Marine line.

They had a long way to go to MACV, so the tanks started down the raised road in the paddy, the grunts following in trace behind the lurching machines. Trees and telephone poles lined the street; brown leaves covered it. Batcheller, crouching along behind the lead tank, couldn't raise anybody; all the radio frequencies were jammed with Vietnamese voices. He couldn't tell if they were North or South, or both. Around him the Marines were pouring fire at the two large buildings. Plaster and dust flew.

They had killed the NVA in the buildings, and were moving past when an NVA machine gun opened up. A Navy man with the column sprawled wounded in the street. Batcheller bolted from behind the tank and tried to drag him back. Then the machine gun raked again, and Batcheller felt the wounded man tugged out of his hands, killed by the blast. Batcheller was suddenly flying ass over teakettle. He came down hard on the left side of the road, sprawled in a roll of concertina.

He looked himself over. There were gaping holes on his right forearm, right thigh, and left knee. Blood was splattered on his fatigues and flak jacket. He was sure he would bleed to death. He could hear rounds smacking by, and hollered to his Marines to stay back. He lay there, snagged in the wire, and gazed up through the branches of the tree above him. He saw that the early morning overcast had burned off into a beautiful blue sky.

He began to pray.

It was around noon when news that Alpha Company was being hit hard was relayed to Phu Bai. Lt. Col. Marcus J. Gravel, the commander of 1/1, organized a hasty reaction force: himself, his operations officer, Maj. Walter M. Murphy; some others from his battalion command group, and the attached Golf Company 2/5.

Lt. Richard Lyons, USN, the 1/1 Catholic chaplain, was just back from visiting the battalion wounded at Da Nang and was walking off the Phu Bai helo pad, when a jeep pulled up. Sitting inside were several Marines, including Gravel and Murphy. Lieutenant Colonel Gravel called to him, "Do you want to go into Hue City for an afternoon of street fighting?" Lyons, who in nearly a year in Vietnam had earned the reputation as a field chaplain — including firing to cover casualties being evacuated — climbed aboard. They jeeped to the battalion area where they joined the assembled Golf 2/5. Gravel had no time to make plans for his reaction force. It was just, "Get on the trucks!" and they were moving north on Highway 1.

Across the damaged An Cuu Bridge, they ran into a traffic jam of tanks, trucks, and stalled Alpha Company grunts. With Gravel pushing, they dismounted and moved around the mess. Chaplain Lyons glanced to his right as they went by, noticing several dead civilians off the road. One of them, a woman, was already stiff with rigor mortis, her hand reaching skyward. It was eerie, Lyons thought, and he forgot about the heat and his thirst.

A bit ahead, more Alpha Marines were still holding on the road.

Chaplain Lyons kept crawling forward with some of the grunts, huddled low along the right side of the road berm. On the left side, he could see the supine figure of his friend, Captain Batcheller. On the road between them were two dead men. He bellied through the dirt and leaves on the road, giving last rites over their bodies. Crawling closer, he saw Batcheller clearly, lying there, shot to hell; looking near death. In his fury, Lyons grabbed an abandoned M-16 and loosed off a burst at the treeline far away across the paddy.

Then Lyons heard Batcheller shouting to him to cease fire, that it would only draw a torrent of return blasts. He shouted for Lyons to get back.

Behind them, the battalion jeep hauled up. The driver, Cpl. Don Schultz, braked to a stop in the street and piled out — the jeep made too good a target. Lieutenant Colonel Gravel tried to quickly appraise the situation. Staff Sergeant Godfrey of First Platoon was down with a leg wound, and the ranking NCO, Gunny Canley, was in command of Alpha. Canley was still very much in control despite shrapnel wounds and the constant firing from ahead. That wasn't surprising; Canley was known as an outstanding sergeant, something of a legend in the battalion. The Marines started to drag their wounded back towards the relief force, and Batcheller was carried across the road and behind the jeep. Corporal Jackson and a couple of others made a hasty splint on their skipper's shattered leg with a broken shovel and some bandages.

Captain Batcheller, Staff Sergeant Godfrey, Corporal Williams, and a good number of others needed fast evacuation. Gravel, crouched down with them, made the decision to send all the casualties back on one truck — without any escort aboard. It was incredibly risky, but there was no choice; he couldn't spare the men. The Marines hustled the wounded through the fire into the truck bed. One kid jumped up to the cab to drive and tumbled down, shot in the ankle. He was patched up and thrown in the back with the rest of the wounded. Someone shouted, "Somebody get up there!" and another Marine jumped behind the wheel. In the midst of the firing, the truck sped away. Gravel, Jackson, and the rest stared after it. The truck made it out of sight.

By early evening, the truckful of wounded were at C Company, 1st Medical Battalion in Phu Bai. After surgery, Batcheller lay in a bed in post-op. His radioman, Corporal Williams, was in the adjacent bed, cleaned up and sleeping. Under the sheets, where his left foot should have been was only a hollow space. Batcheller admired the young Williams; he was a tall, handsome, athletic kid. And, more than that, he was a young man who had joined not because he was drafted or wanted to prove how tough he was, but because he felt a commitment to his nation and couldn't stand to sit safe at home while others his age were fighting and dying on the other side of the world. Yes, Batcheller thought, Larry was one fine, fine young man.

Cpl. Larry Williams died on that fresh hospital bed that evening in Charlie Med. Batcheller watched them pull the sheets over his face.

The NVA fire kept pouring across the highway from the flanks. Corporal Jackson and two other Marines got up and took off, running off the road. They crouched among the brush and thatch hootches, then spotted it — a small concrete building. AK-47 automatic rifle fire snapped from it. The three Marines opened up with their M-16s, and ran toward it. They tossed grenades, blew the door down, and jumped up and ran through before the enemy had a chance to react. Two North Vietnamese soldiers were standing inside, shaken by the explosions. The grunts blew them away in a heartbeat.

At the front of the Marine column, Lieutenant Colonel LaMontagne had taken charge. He had come across an ARVN tank, the survivor of the demolished armored unit they had seen around the Phu Cam, and had shepherded it into the Marine column. Heavy fire continued to rake the area and the grunts were pinned down in ditches and against the road berm. LaMontagne grabbed some Marines and two of the tanks and started to cross the paddy field to ward MACV.

Inside the compound, the surrounded garrison could hear the wild firing down the road. Then came the sound of tanks. Some of the soldiers cheered. "Super! Here come's the Army!"

Then Major Breth saw who was headed for their front gate. He recognized LaMontagne — short, squat, and ugly as ever, with a big cigar in his mouth and two tanks beside him. "Take a look," Breth shouted at the cheering soldiers, "that's Marines!"

LaMontagne got to the main gate, and calmly announced he needed some help. First, though, Breth pointed to the NVA positions — directly across the street — and the tanks blasted them. Then they organized to rush back down the road and help the pinned-down 1/1 column. Maj.

Breth and Maj. Wayne R. Swenson, liaison officer from Task Force X-RAY to the 1st ARVN Division, organized a group of volunteers in one civilian truck. Capt. Coolican and Lt. Lampo gathered another truckful and they prepared to move out. Col. Adkisson insisted they stay inside the compound, but the order was ignored and the trucks hauled back down Highway 1. One of the tanks followed, then stopped short because it couldn't maneuver on the raised paddy road. It boomed out cover fire.

They reached the pinned Alpha grunts, and LaMontagne directed the evacuation of the wounded. He was with Breth and Swenson, giving instructions and pointing, when a round suddenly creased down his finger. It hardly fazed him.

The casualties were finally loaded into the trucks, and started back towards the compound.

Back down the road, near the end of the 1/1 column, Lieutenant Colonel Gravel and Major Murphy were working their way forward. Gravel left his jeep on the road, and ordered Lyons to stick with the CP group. The chaplain tagged along reluctantly. Gravel was a good leader, Lyons thought, and for that reason, he was just that much more dangerous to be around. He was totally selfless, concerned only about his men. There he was in the thick of it, his radioman alongside, the radio aerial waving above them. It was like showing a red flag to a bull, and Lyons tried to edge away.

Golf Company, under Capt. Charles Meadows, moved to the front and the battered Alpha followed them. They were strung out along both sides of the road, in clear sight of the enemy, and occasional fire cracked past them. Suddenly, a group of NVA popped up on their left front and began running away through houses that had been a school.

Gravel marvelled. Six months in Vietnam and it was the first time he'd ever seen the enemy in action.

Anxious to reach the MACV compound, and not knowing what might be in those houses, he ordered his men to keep going without engaging the NVA around the school. A couple hundred yards more up the highway, they came to an intersection. A North Vietnamese machine gun dug in on the right side of the road opened up and everyone ducked behind the tanks again. Then Gravel saw Sergeant Gonzalez, the wounded First Platoon leader, run out from behind a tank. Gonzalez scrambled into the roadside ditch and crawled forward, throwing grenades. They exploded right on top of the machine gun.

The firing stopped. The column continued.

Gravel looked back down the road, saw his jeep sitting there, and realized the NVA might get to the radios. He shouted at one of the tank commanders, pointed, and the tank cannon flashed out a shell. The jeep blew up. Another stretch down the road, and they were moving up with LaMontagne's people near the MACV compound. It was around three in the afternoon. To augment the brave and hard-pressed staff, there were now tanks, Dusters, and best of all, two companies of Marine infantrymen. As Major Swenson would later say, "I have little doubt that many of us would not be alive today, had those Marines not arrived."

Around the MACV compound, there was still sporadic enemy fire. The tanks boomed out in return. The Marine grunts of Alpha and Golf companies took up positions around MACV and the Navy boat ramp on the river. They also secured the base of the Nguyen Hoang Bridge, the Highway 1 route across the Perfume River into the Citadel side, where there was a shoreline park suitable for a landing zone adjacent to the Navy station.

Inside the compound, Breth introduced Gravel to Adkisson. Breth was surprised when Adkisson responded rudely, telling Gravel that he didn't care what his orders were, his Marines were going to stick there and defend his compound. Adkisson was a tall, handsome, gentlemanly officer who had taken over his post only about a week before. Breth thought he was responding exactly like a noncombat staff officer. He seemed to Breth to have no common sense, was worried about the trivial, and was acting defensively because he really didn't know what was going on. The introduction put Gravel on edge about the man he had just helped save.

There were scores of wounded men gathered in the compound, and the MACV doctor, Captain Bernie, did his best with them, while calls were made for medevacs. This time, word came that they were on the way. Major Murphy and Gunny Canley organized some infantrymen to bring the casualties to the park LZ near the Navy ramp. Breth and Swenson knew the area and came along to help set the Marines in; Coolican also came to aid Murphy in calling in the choppers. Some of the Marine and ARVN tanks set up in the LZ to fire cover. A Marine CH-46 Sea Knight from Phu Bai came in, unloaded some ammunition, and took off with a load of wounded. A second batch of casualties were also evacuated.

There was a lull. While the Marine grunts stayed low in position around the landing zone, Majors Breth, Murphy, and Swenson; Captain Coolican, and Lieutenants Drew and Lampo stood talking in a circle behind one of the tanks. Then came the shuddering crack of a recoilless rifle. Breth jerked his head just in time to see the backblast dust rising across the Perfume River. The round flew at them like a big black dart. It flashed chest-high through the group, miraculously missing them and the tank, and smashed into a building behind them, blowing away one corner. They went for cover. Firing erupted from NVA positions at the base of the bridge on the opposite bank and the Marine grunts around the LZ responded in kind.

Major Breth and his driver, Lance Cpl. Robert Hull, from 3d Mar-Div, jumped on the back of the ARVN tank hunkered there, and manned the externally mounted .50-caliber machine gun. Breth fired across the river and Hull fed in the heavy ammunition belts. They ran out and pounded on the top of the tank for more. The terrified ARVNs inside refused to open the hatch.

Two U.S. Navy PBR gunboats appeared on the river and hosed down the opposite bank with their twin-fifties. A third medevac chopper was able to swoop into the LZ and depart with another fuselage full of wounded men. And then it was all quiet again.

Before long, the X-RAY staff at Phu Bai contacted Gravel over the radio. General LaHue's orders — dictated down to him from III MAF in Da Nang — were to take Alpha 1/1 and Golf 2/5 across the Perfume River into the Citadel. There they were to effect a link-up with General Truong in the ARVN HQ which, like the MACV compound, was under heavy attack.

Gravel was incredulous. With all the NVA troops in the city, it would be hard enough just to hold the compound. A concentrated attack would threaten their already precarious foothold. He saw absolutely no reason to risk what had been gained in an ill-conceived foray across the river. There was no intelligence on enemy strength or disposition; no one knew what to expect. Gravel wanted to consolidate their position at MACV, and that is the message he sent back to General LaHue. Task Force X-RAY radioed back: "Proceed."

Gravel could only shake his head; LaHue had no idea of what was going on in the city. They must have the idea this is a small village of straw huts, he thought, instead of a modern city of concrete and steel. It would prove to be another example of a distant headquarters being out of touch with battlefield realities.

Gravel left the Marine tanks at the LZ near the Navy ramp because he thought they were too heavy to cross the Nguyen Hoang Bridge, the Highway 1 route into the Citadel. When they tried to get the lighter ARVN tank to accompany the force, the South Vietnamese refused.

Gravel left his undermanned, bloodied Alpha Company at the compound, and sent Captain Meadows's Golf Company onto the bridge. Meanwhile the Marine and ARVN tanks hunkered along the shore, firing across the river. The lead platoon of Golf got halfway across the bridge, when a machine gun erupted, toppling ten men dead or wounded in their tracks. The gun was dug in at the far side, and the Marines poured fire toward it. One of the Golf grunts, Cpl. Lester A. Tully, simply charged forward, jumped beside the gun pit, and killed the five NVA inside it, an act that earned him the Silver Star. The bridge was secured and Gravel and his battalion staff came across with the rest of Golf. Gravel looked down at the riddled gun pit and the five men slumped inside — dying like worms in a can, he thought. One North Vietnamese was still breathing. Gravel's interpreter, a Marine corporal, kneeled beside him, talking to him in Vietnamese, pumping for information. The man didn't say anything. He just stopped breathing.

The wounded were put aboard a truck and, accompanied by Chaplain Lyons, returned to the MACV compound. By then, it was late afternoon and the sun was in the eyes of the men still on the Citadel side. The Marines turned left through the houses and trees outside the Citadel, then swung up a street that led through the imposing wall and north to the ARVN HQ. The lead squad went up the street — and was ambushed. The fire poured from the houses ahead — B-40 rockets, AK-47 automatic weapons, machine guns, and recoilless rifles. Rounds ricocheted in the street, concrete shards flew, Marines ducked and dived for doorways and alleys. They started shooting back. The dead and wounded lay where they fell. A navy corpsman with Golf, HM3 Donald A. Kirkham, ran forward to drag back those he could reach. He was hit, but ignored the wound and kept helping, patching up the injured. He was running to another position on the street — and an AK burst blew him dead to the concrete.

Captain Meadows's company could go neither forward nor back. The firing went on for two hours. It seemed an eternity.

Of the 150 Marines in Golf Company, fifty were dead or wounded. Gravel knew it was impossible to continue; the casualties were simply unacceptable. Without consultation with Task Force X-RAY, Gravel gave the order to pull back across the river. The grunts popped smoke grenades and the street filled with yellow clouds. The NVA fired blindly through the smoke as the Marines inched away down the block, dragging their dead and wounded with them.

Gravel got on the radio to Colonel Adkisson at the MACV compound, to send men and equipment across to assist with the evacuation of the casualties. Since the compound was under fire and could still be

overrun, Adkisson chose to disregard the request because he had prac-
tically no resources to spare.

Back on the other side of the bridge, Gravel waited. Nothing showed
up. Gravel was infuriated. That goddamn doggie colonel seemed to
think the compound was his own private property, the way he seemed
unwilling to help or share with anybody else.

He took his radioman and the Marine interpreter, and they ran back
across the bridge, got to the compound, and asked Adkisson where in
the hell the help was. Adkisson stood there, saying nothing. Gravel
fumed. Finally, some of the young officers and enlisted men in the
compound spontaneously piled into vehicles and drove back across the
bridge, taking Gravel with them. Some street-wise grunts there had
hot-wired several Vietnamese cars parked in the street. The wounded
and dead were loaded aboard.

The NVA fire was still heavy. One of the U.S. Army trucks took off
from the relatively safe side of the river, stopped on the other side of
the bridge, and started hosing down the enemy positions with its quad-
fifties. Breth was watching from the LZ across the river, admiring the
crew's bravery, when he suddenly saw two North Vietnamese break
from a house. The sappers sprinted a dozen yards and hurled two
satchel charges in the back. The truck and men went up in a hellish
explosion. The evacuation continued.

Major Murphy moved to the vehicles to direct the removal of the
casualties. Chaplain Lyons, who had come back across in one of the
trucks, was hustling past him, helping a Marine carry a wounded man.
There was a sudden concussion and roar and Lyons felt himself being
lifted up and knocked down a few feet away by a B-40 rocket. He
landed, scrambled across the street, and dove for cover. Then he
realized there was blood soaking his leg. Shrapnel had dug into his
thigh and hand. A corpsman bandaged him up, and Lyons limped
back to help with the rest of the casualties. Then he saw Murphy lying
there, badly wounded by the rocket fragment, but still conscious.
Lyons kept hauling men to the trucks until his bandaged leg swelled up
so that he couldn't walk. Some grunts, deeply concerned about their
chaplain being hurt, ushered him into a truck. Lyons shared the ride
back to MACV with Major Murphy.

It was obvious that more firepower was needed across the bridge.
The day was saved by Pfc. Nolan J. Lala, one of the truckers with
Charlie 1st MTB, which had ferried the troops to Hue. Lala was a
black-haired, nineteen year old, 8th-grade dropout from Denver,
Colorado. He was a wildman, a troublemaker, a professional private,
bright, brave, and unwilling to listen to his sergeants and officers,

especially after he won the Silver Star for what he did in Hue. Lala was near the LZ, watching the hell across the river, and on his own volition, he got some Army volunteers in a truck and hauled across the bridge. When he stopped, the men in the back jumped out to help with the casualties, and Lala slid from the driver's seat into the truck's .50-caliber ring mount. Despite all the firing, he stood in place, raking the powerful weapon back and forth over the enemy positions.

Everyone else was getting geared up to get the hell out, when a young Vietnamese man came out of one of the shops facing the street. He was wearing an ARVN uniform, and through the interpreter, he told Gravel he was an airborne lieutenant, a doctor, home on Tet leave. There was no way to verify the story. But with so many men dying, Gravel thought, God knows we need a doctor, let's take a chance. He told the interpreter to stick with the doctor, and they got him aboard one of the vehicles.

The trucks and Marines hauled back across to the South Side, with Private First Class Lala firing cover. He was one of the last men — if not the last man — back across the Perfume River.

At the LZ, Major Breth watched stunned as they came back. The bridge looked like a Fourth of July sparkler, he thought, with all the firing.

Inside the compound, Gravel was having another verbal battle with Adkisson — all of this right in the middle of the battle.

Adkisson didn't like the ARVN doctor, thought he might be a VC infiltrator. "Who is he?"

"He's a doctor."

"How do you know?"

"Because he says he is."

Gravel was tired and didn't have time for such petty problems. He was getting sick of the colonel acting as though the Marines were not welcome in his area. When Gravel tried to set up a command post inside one of the buildings, Adkisson said there was no room and left the Marines out in the courtyard. Finally Gravel told him to knock off the cheap bullshit or he would take his men and move out of the compound.

Down the block from MACV, there were several U.S. personnel trapped in the CORDS building. Adkisson informed Gravel that they needed immediate evacuation back to the compound. A Marine squad started down the street towards them and was mowed down. A tank was sent and came under heavy fire, with a score of B-40s suddenly exploding against it, blowing off the aerials, fenders, mufflers, gas tanks, and gear. It belched smoke, and those who could see from the MACV compound watched in horror. They were sure the crew had been killed. But, the tank suddenly switched to reverse and came hauling back to the MACV compound. The hatch popped open and all Major Breth could see was the big smile of the Marine crewman inside. It was a beautiful sight.

That tank and another revved up and went back down the street to evacuate the decimated Marine squad.

To assist in the removal of the casualties, Major Breth and Swenson organized about twenty volunteers — Marines, Army, and Australians — to move and fire on the flank of the tanks. Another tank blew a hole in the wall for them, and they moved out until they got into a beautiful church area. There they discovered about twenty nuns and forty children. They were still taking fire, and the civilians were utterly terrified. Breth assigned a couple of the younger men to escort them back to the compound.

The group kept moving parallel to the tanks and Marines. Breth walked into the corridor of one building with the most unlikely of volunteers, a truck driver from the 1st Air Cavalry Division who happened to get stuck in Hue on the wrong night. They entered a room and Breth suddenly saw from the window an NVA standing atop a wall just outside. Breth swung up his M-16 and squeezed the trigger. Nothing happened. The truck driver pointed his rifle. It also jammed. And then the North Vietnamese let go with a grenade at them. It bounced off the roof, and they watched as the explosion boomed back at the man, hurling him off the wall. Breth cleared his M-16 and ran to the window, firing. Four more North Vietnamese suddenly broke from behind the wall, about fifteen feet away, and tried to run away. Breth and his partner braced, firing from the hip. The four men collapsed.

They were running out of ammunition, so the group started pulling back to the compound. By then, the tanks and Marines had brought back the gunned-down squad. The CORDS building, which they had been sent to secure, fell to the North Vietnamese soldiers.

The wounded were gathered inside a room at the MACV compound and Doctor Bernie pitched back in to help. Lyons lay on a stretcher near Murphy. One young wounded Marine sat there, miserable in his pain and fear, crying out, until Murphy called from his stretcher, telling him to be quiet, that everything would be okay. Lyons was impressed — Murphy was hurt badly, but he was still in control, still encouraging the other casualties. Like Gravel, he thought, Murphy's only concern was the men.

Not far away, Captain Coolican was on the radio trying to arrange another medevac helicopter for the wounded. There were many who would die without immediate attention — including his farm boy radioman, Frank Dozerman, and his old friend, Walt Murphy, who was bleeding internally, Finally, they all knew it was too late. Swenson and Breth lifted Chaplain Lyons on his stretcher and carried him to Murphy. He administered the last rites, and then Murphy was dead. They put a poncho over his body and put him in a safe place. Breth, Coolican, and Swenson had all served with Murphy before Vietnam; it was a bad time for everyone. When Gravel was told, he could feel something drain from him. He and Murphy had been close, enjoying each other's humor, spending Thanksgiving at Con Thien, Christmas at Quang Tri, and looking forward to their post-Vietnam assignments in Washington, D.C.

A short time later, word came that a medevac was enroute.

The wounded were put on trucks and they started towards the LZ on the river. They took fire on their way down and by the time they made it, their sixteen seriously wounded had become twenty. It was night-time by then, pitch black and foggy as the chopper came beating overhead. Corporal Chisler, a tall, bright, and brave black Marine with 1/1, got on the radio to the pilot. He talked and coaxed and brought the pilot in through the shroud for a perfect landing right at his feet.

"Where are you," the pilot asked, "I can't see."

Corporal Chisler just raised his hand and rapped on the nose of the bird.

The pilot asked how many casualties there were.

"Twenty, sir."

"You only called with sixteen."

"Yes, sir," Chisler said, "but a funny thing happened on the flight to the LZ . . . we know you can make it." They got the casualties aboard the chopper, a Sea Knight, and the pilot roared out of the landing zone. One of those aboard was Frank Dozerman. He died in the air, enroute to the hospital.

The Marines at the LZ fought their way back to the compound.

That night, all they held was MACV, the LZ, and the Navy ramp. They were still getting organized and set up for night defense, when the NVA opened up again. Tracers, shouts, curses, and return fire filled the air. The NVA stopped shooting. The Marine grunts, nervous and exhausted, fired all night.

Lt. Col. Mark Gravel sat by his radios. He'd never felt so empty or hopeless. His friend, Gordon Batcheller, was shot to pieces and lying in a hospital someplace; only a miracle could save him. The young Marine he much respected, Larry Williams, was gone — dead or saved he didn't know yet. Walt Murphy was dead. And fifty other Marines had been shot up across the bridge. Goddamn it, he thought, what a waste. Why? Just so senseless — that goddamn worthless venture across that stupid bridge — to do what? Go have coffee with General Truong, see how he's doing, pay my respects? With only two undermanned companies, Gravel reckoned, shouldn't Truong and his division have come to make contact with me?

The only thing he could be thankful for was that the North Vietnamese had opened fire on Golf Company too soon after starting their way into the Citadel. If they had held their fire and sucked all the Marines into the maze of streets, they could have cut them off, killed or captured everyone — and then there wouldn't have been anything between them and the MACV compound. It would have made Custer's Last Stand look like a walk in the woods, he mused. Maybe, Gravel thought, maybe the North Vietnamese soldiers who had opened up on them too soon were just young, inexperienced kids. Or maybe their officers had ordered it. Either way, someone on their side had screwed up too.

It had been a long, long day. Gravel was beyond exhaustion, but somehow, sleep would not come.

Chapter 2

Second Day in the Imperial City

February 1, 1968

On the second day of the battle, Thursday, February 1, 1968, the Marine command at Task Force X-RAY was separated from Hue by eight miles of road and by a wall of optimism, disbelief, and misinformation. Add to that the inherent problem suffered by field commanders in Vietnam — pressure from Washington to say what they wanted to hear — one can understand why General LaHue, interviewed by a UPI reporter that second day of fighting, said, "Very definitely, we control the South Side of the city. I don't think they [the NVA/VC forces) can sustain. I know they can't. I don't think they have any resupply capabilities, and once they use up what they have brought in, they're finished." LaHue was not alone with his misinformation: press releases from the Saigon-based MACV headquarters said the enemy was being "mopped up"; the advisory team at I Corps headquarters in Da Nang said that the allies were "pushing VC out of Hue this morning"; and the ARVN Corps commander, General Lam, said that the enemy had been defeated except for a "platoon" holding out in the Citadel.

In Hue, the Communists were in control. In the Citadel, General Truong and his men still hung on in their ARVN HQ; on the South Side, Lieutenant Colonel Gravel's force held "the Alamo" compound. Throughout the city there were isolated bands of American and South Vietnamese soldiers holding out in buildings that had been bypassed

27

and surrounded by the enemy. At that point, nobody had the strength or support to mount a meaningful counterattack against the invaders.

The NVA/VC had done a superb job of infiltrating and seizing Hue. They had moved with speed and stealth — and most importantly, they had the capability of support themselves inside the city. Ideally, the Americans and South Vietnamese would have deployed units around the entire city, cutting off the enemy lines of resupply and rein- forcement, while the Marines mopped up the underfed, under- manned, casualty-ridden enemy units that would be trapped in Hue. But the situation was far from ideal. This was the Tet Offensive — the attack on the American embassy was just over, the battle of Saigon was only beginning, the siege of Khe Sanh was continuing, and cities in the Mekong Delta had fallen. Hue City, albeit the longest and bloodiest action of the Tet Offensive, was not something that could be given the undivided attention of the allies. The overall strain of Tet, plus the fact that X-RAY had just been in the process of shuffling its 1st Marine Division units, allowed only a relatively few units to be committed to Hue. To seal off the eight-mile perimeter effectively around Hue would have required, according to one estimate, sixteen infantry battalions. Such troops simply weren't available.

In an effort to disrupt enemy movement in and out of Hue, Maj. Gen. John J. Tolson, the hard-charging and highly-decorated com- mander of the 1st Air Cavalry Division, was directed to send forces out- side of Hue. The Air Cav was heavily committed to fighting in Quang Tri and elsewhere, so on February 2, only the 2d Battalion of the 12th Cavalry was deployed from Camp Evans, north of Hue. They air- assaulted into an LZ about ten kilometers northwest of Hue on High- way 1, and began pushing down towards the city, with the Perfume River on their right flank. Before the battle was over, three additional Cav battalions were helicoptered into what the Army called Operation Jeb Stuart. They encountered miserable weather (the ceiling kept most chopper missions at twenty-five feet); resupply problems (parachute drops were sometimes the only way to get supplies in, even at the main base at Camp Evans); and utterly intense jungle fighting (at least one NVA regimental-counterattack was launched against the Cav peri- meter). Progress was creepingly slow.

As a result, the enemy in Hue — under the control of the 6th NVA Regiment — were able to maintain their forces. Besides capturing numerous U.S.-made weapons of all types in the ARVN armory, they had continuous resupply coming in from the west. And the same open routes which allowed the beans, bullets, and bandages to reach the NVA/VC forces, also allowed for reinforcement. To augment the nine enemy battalions which invaded Hue on the first day, an additional five were able to move in; the 416th Battalion, 5th NVA Regiment; the 4th and 6th Battalions, 24th NVA Regiments; the 7th and 8th Battalions; 90th NVA Regiment. Around six thousand NVA were facing the Marines and ARVN. (These reinforcements, it would prove, were simply not enough for a communist victory. A scenario discussed after the battle suggested the NVA would have been wise to shift one of their ten-thousand-man divisions from their mountain lairs around the besieged Marine base at Khe Sanh, and send it into Hue — a possibility that prompted Gen. Creighton Abrams to tell a reporter in January 1969, "We'd still be fighting there.")

The weather, too, was on the side of the enemy. It grew cold, an unusual fifty degrees, and the constant misty drizzle of the monsoon season occasionally turned into a cold drenching rain. The cloud cover and ground fog, along with the rain, severely hampered helicopter and jet support for the Marines. The allies also put themselves at a disadvantage by following ARVN Corps commander General Lam's request that to spare civilians and reduce destruction to the historic city, no artillery, bombs, or napalm be used.

For all their advantages at the outset of the battle, the North Vietnamese leaders in Hue made some serious mistakes and miscalculations. The Communists, believing their own propaganda, had expected the citizens of Hue to rise up, greet them as liberators, and fight alongside them. This never happened. Although a small number of sympathizers rallied to the invaders — mostly young university students who acted as guides — the vast majority of civilians quite naturally spent most of their time trying to avoid the shifting combat zones and stay alive.

The enemy were also unsuccessful in defending the city once they had captured it. They failed to blow up the An Cuu Bridge over the Phu Cam to cut off traffic between the South Side and Phu Bai, then failed to stop the Marine reaction force when they came across the bridge. They also tried, and again failed, to capture any one of the several bridges along Highway 1 between Hue and the Marine base. The NVA had expected to seize Hue in one night and then defend it from counterattack; their defenses were structured from the outside in. But the MACV compound and the ARVN HQ offered unexpected pockets of resistance — they allowed the Marines to counterattack from the inside out — and the enemy, so well respected for their maneuverability and improvisation in the rice paddy — jungle war, failed to respond aggressively. They didn't attempt to seize those two positions after the influx of Marines. Instead they fell back, dug in, and went on the defensive.

And that is what killed them. From their foothold in the compound,

Gravel's Marines were able to get across the street to the University compound. There, they secured a soccer field. The Americans controlled the air, and the choppers began bringing in reinforcements.

Lance Corporal Carter and the rest of the grunts in Fox 2/5 had spent a nervous night atop their hill, watching the explosions and tracers blip down in the valley. In the morning, a convoy of trucks pulled up to their position. They loaded up and the drivers roared down the road at what seemed like sixty miles per hour, everyone scared of being ambushed. Luckily, there was no firing.

They began passing the villages along the route and they saw what hell had been let loose the night before. People were crying and wailing, squatting on their haunches next to the bodies of husbands and mothers and sons, all of them wrapped in white burial cloths. They rumbled past one village and could see CAP Marines behind the perimeter concertina. Dead enemy were plastered in the wire and flies hung above them in buzzing packs. One Viet Cong lay dead near the road, his body shot up, and his head blown off and lying there. Carter couldn't believe it when the truck ahead of him swerved to run it over.

The head exploded like a ripe pumpkin. Carter grimaced, "Man, that was really gross!"

They secured themselves inside the wire and bunkers at Phu Bai, and resupplied, getting mail, hot chow, and even a chance to visit the PX. They spent the night in the troop tents and the next morning, February 1, they were assembled outside on the airstrip. Their orders were for Hue. The company commander, Capt. Michael P. Downs, was there. Carter didn't know what to think about their captain. He was a competent officer who performed with icy professionalism. But it was just that coldly precise exterior that repelled Carter; maybe the skipper had to push personal feelings to the side and present an insensitive front to get the job done, he thought, but sometimes it seemed like he just didn't care about them. But, Carter trusted Captain Downs. The man knew what he was doing in combat.

In a few minutes, the CH-46 Sea Knight choppers came in, looking like giant locusts from above, and Fox Company was on its way to Hue City.

Ron Christmas was a twenty-seven-year-old captain from Yeadon, Pennsylvania, married to the daughter of Col. David Lownds, the hero of Khe Sanh. Captain Christmas was in command of Hotel Company 2/5 when Tet broke on the 31st. The North Vietnamese attacked the bridge on Highway 1 that his men were guarding. The shooting went on for hours. By daylight, the enemy had been driven down the river bed.

Captain Christmas was getting ready to lead the counterattack against them, when one of his radiomen said word had come to cease fire.

"What!" Christmas yelled. "You must be kidding me!"

"No sir. The CO wants us to withdraw to Route 1 and await further orders."

The grunts trudged up the road and Christmas made contact with the commander of 2d Battalion, 5th Marines, Lt. Col. Ernest Cheatham. The colonel filled him in on the unit's situation: Hue had been attacked and Chuck Meadows' Golf Company was going in with elements of 1/1, and Mike Downs's Fox Company was on its way to Phu Bai for transport to Hue.

"You will probably be next," Cheatham told Christmas. "In fact, we'll probably all end up in Hue." Then the colonel muttered, "Why must they always piecemeal us into a battle?"

Carter sat back in the canvas webbing of the chopper with the rest of the grunts, feeling that lump in his stomach, those rubbery pregame, prebattle jitters: oh shit, here we go again.

The Sea Knights dropped low on the approach to Hue, to avoid anti-aircraft fire, and skimmed in. Carter peered out the round fuselage window. He could see the Perfume River, the big span bridge, roof-tops, puffy treelines — and muzzle flashes. Rounds smacked into his chopper. Tiny holes suddenly appeared in the thin skin and two Marines jerked in their seats, hit in the legs. The two door-gunners pounded out bursts on their .50-caliber machine guns.

Then the chopper hit the ground in the university soccer field, with the back ramp already down. The two grunts who'd been shot in the leg stayed on board, while the rest ran out of the bird, hunkered over like football players with their helmets and flak jackets and packs. Fire snapped overhead. Carter crouched down behind a two-foot high cement wall, huddled against it with the others while rounds came buzzing by. They were told to rush in groups of three to another wall leading inside the university building, then head down the street to the right and get into the MACV compound. Someone gave the word and the first three Marines took off. Carter was with the last group to go. They got up and started running, Carter noticed a reporter kneeling across the field with a minicam over his shoulder, filming them. He turned his head to smile at the camera so his parents would see — but, he tripped in a shell hole and went sprawling, his pack flipping over his head, his helmet and M-16 bouncing away in different directions. By the time Carter and his two buddies got inside the building, the platoon was gone.

They ran into the street, not knowing where they were, getting spooked. They jogged past a Marine tank sitting in the street, ducked under the barrel — and just at that moment the cannon roared. Carter staggered to the sidewalk, his ears ringing, his head rattled. A Marine popped out of the turret hatch, looked down at them, and said flippantly, "Sorry about that. If you want, you can go by now."

Fifty more yards down the street they found their platoon going into the MACV compound.

At first light on that morning of the second day, civilians began to trickle and then stream in to the compound from the southeastern quadrant of the city. They were mostly women, children, a few old men, and a number of ARVN soldiers home on leave. For a hopeful moment, Gravel had the notion that the battle was over, that the enemy had withdrawn during the night and released the people. It soon became obvious that this was not the case. Gravel turned the refugees over to the Army advisors, took control of the battle situation, and tried to organize his position.

So far, he had Alpha 1/1, Golf 2/5, and the newly-arrived Fox 2/5. Task Force X-RAY contacted him with another mission: send Fox Company to secure the prison building west of his position before the VC could release the prisoners there. The prison was several blocks away through NVA territory, and according to common sense and what sketchy information Gravel could put together, the enemy had turned the prisoners loose on the first day. He radioed back that the prisoners had been freed. This time, X-RAY reconsidered. The orders were cancelled.

With the casualties building up, it soon became apparent to Gravel that a more expeditious route was needed from MACV to the Navy ramp and LZ. Fighting house to house to the evacuation point, as they'd done the first night, was an unacceptable alternative. Finally Gravel directed a tank to "walk" its way to the LZ. The tanker did just that, knocking down walls and any other obstacles in the way. Colonel Adkisson was livid over the destruction. But that didn't really matter, because the scheme worked and Gravel was able to get his seriously wounded to the LZ along that route without any more major problems. Gravel was, however, to have another, more trivial confrontation with Adkisson. Within a few days, the Marines had run out of cigarettes. The Post Exchange was full of cigarettes, but the Marines didn't have any money, and Adkisson was unwilling to give them away free and write it off as a combat loss. Finally, perhaps realizing the consequences of having a large number of angry grunts, the colonel did open the doors of the PX.

On the back of his flak jacket, Cpl. Jim Soukup had drawn a big bull's-eye with the inscription Try Your Luck, Charlie. That was part of the bravado of being a twenty-year-old combat Marine. But, as far as Soukup was concerned, he didn't want to see another Vietnamese the rest of his life. He'd already done ten months in the field, and had just returned from an Australian R&R six days before the battle started. After the respite with round-eyed women, clean sheets, and cold beer, Soukup came to the decision that he "didn't want any more of that stinking, blood-soaked shithole we were fighting for." He wanted to sit out the last two months of his tour in a rear job, but Tet blew away those plans. Then, on February 1, the orders came, "Saddle up, full load." And there he was at the Phu Bai airstrip with his old job as squad leader, recoilless rifle section, Headquarters & Service Company 1/1.

He kept his griping to a minimum; he was a Marine and, besides, the men in his squad were all buddies.

They loaded up a Sea Knight, lugging aboard their 350-pound 106mm recoilless rifle, and took off, the helicopter crammed full of men and equipment. Soukup had no idea where they were going until they dropped low near Hue and zipped in for the university LZ. Fire started popping around them, rounds zipped through the floor, and fuel and hydraulic lines gushed fluid around their feet. Soukup tensed up — oh, come on baby, make it, don't crash! The chopper careened into the LZ, and then the rear ramp malfunctioned and only opened halfway. The Marines quickly scrambled up over the lip, jumped ten feet to the ground, and went running for cover. NVA fire from across the Perfume River peppered the landing zone.

Other Marines, already in the LZ, were shouting and pointing. Soukup could see quick muzzle flashes in windows across the river. He opened up with his M-16.

The firing kept up, and one of the guys in the squad came unglued. He started hollering, firing wildly, aiming at nothing. Marines, crouched down behind the trees and lawn fountains, shouted at him. He didn't hear. Finally some grunts grabbed him and held him to the ground. They threw him on the first chopper going out, and Soukup never saw him again. The NVA fire slacked off.

Soukup and his squad ran back to the waiting chopper, managed to get the ramp wrenched down, and carried the 106 out. From there, they started humping it down the streets to the MACV compound, their rifles slung because they needed both hands to carry it — everyone scared about snipers. They got inside and Soukup began looking for an officer. He didn't know the streets; he didn't know what his squad was supposed to do; he didn't have a Mechanical Mule to haul the 106 and ammunition crates. He didn't even know where his battalion, 1/1, was set up. He decided to hook up with the first grunt platoon he found, and play it by ear.

He thought the Marines said they were with Fox 2/5. He wasn't sure. Everything was mass confusion. And it was tough — before the battle was over, Soukup's ten-man squad would lose two men killed and seven wounded. But, the reinforcements kept coming. For some, the reinforcements came too late.

Lt. James V. DiBernardo was a thirty-three-year-old, up-from-the-ranks Marine journalist from Fulton, New York. He was in charge of Detachment 5, Armed Forces Radio and Television Station, set up on the South Side. He had a mixed bag of Marines, Vietnamese, and civilians living in a house several blocks from MACV. The day before the attack, Majors Breth and Swenson had been visiting with him and DiBernardo had laughed about what great accommodations they had, and how good it was to be his own boss. The two majors suggested he move into the MACV compound but DiBernardo said no, his place was pretty secure. Then the Communists invaded.

DiBernardo and his staff waited for two days, isolated, cut off, listening to the shooting in the streets. Then, on the third day, he was walking up to the front room when one of the guards at the windows came running back, shouting that they had company. DiBernardo ran to the window. About seven NVA were crouched along the wall outside, getting ready to charge the house. He rushed back to the living room, and everyone bolted to position. He grabbed a carbine and ran back to the window. The lead North Vietnamese was drawing back to throw a satchel charge. DiBernardo cracked off a fast shot. The man exploded.

All hell broke loose. The Americans opened up, the North Vietnamese opened up — it went on for hours. DiBernardo caught some shrapnel in his hand; all of them had at least one wound. Finally, some NVA crawled up and set fire to the roof. The flames came down, smoke filled the rooms, and the occupants ran from the house, firing from the hip. Enemy fire greeted them and a civilian technical advisor tumbled dead in the street.

DiBernardo and six survivors ran down to the end of the block. Ahead of them was a hundred yards of open paddy. How do we get out of here? Then he realized something — the NVA had let them get this far. The firing started up again from all sides. Two men were killed. A round grazed DiBernardo's arm. There was nowhere to go. Looking around he saw at least fifty enemy soldiers in the houses around them. He only had four men left, and they'd all been wounded again in the cross fire. The Americans surrendered.

It was later in the battle when Sergeants Steve Berntson and Dale Dye, two 1st Marine Division combat correspondents, came upon the shot-up house. They knew the staff members there, and they found one of them, Sgt. Tom Young, lying in a ditch. His hands were bound behind his back, and the back of his head had been shot off. Berntson and Dye tore off a door and carried their friend back to MACV on it. They cried a little because they knew Tom hadn't had a chance, and they figured Lieutenant Di must have been killed, too. They had no way of knowing that DiBernardo was on his way to Hanoi.

The Battle of Hue City was not the usual place for a French woman, but Cathy Leroy was an unusual woman. Born and raised in France, she left her studies at the Conservatory to become a war correspondent. A small, vivacious blonde, she arrived in the Vietnam battle zone in jeans, pigtails, and combat boots; cameras hanging around her neck. In the line of her duty, she had jumped with the U.S. Army airborne, photographed the brutal DMZ hill battles of the summer of '67; was wounded two weeks later during a mortar barrage on a Marine unit. Of her time with the U.S. Marines, she wrote in an article for *Life* magazine*, "The Leathernecks will always remind me of what we call the Foreign Legion . . . big mouths with hearts of gold."

When Cathy heard that the Marines were fighting in Hue, that is where she went, accompanied by Francois Mazure, a fellow correspondent. Having heard that the Marines were guarding the road, they hitched a ride with a convoy going up Highway 1, and didn't find any Marines, but they did encounter a French-speaking Vietnamese and, for a few piasters, rented his bicycle. Riding tandem, they rode off along the empty highway.

Obviously, the inhabitants were all inside their houses with the shutters closed. This made the reporters nervous. Whenever they noticed anyone peering out, Mazure would shout "Bonjour," loudly, anxious they not be mistaken for Americans.

When they reached the South Side, the popping of bullets made them realize what they had ridden into: the communist-controlled section of Hue. They stood around nervously with the people clustered in the open market, listening to the shooting and watching South Viet-

Life, February 16, 1968. PP. 22-29.

namese planes bombing the Citadel. Nobody spoke to them and whenever any Vietnamese approached them directly, they quickly said, in
Vietnamese, that they were French reporters from Paris. The Vietnamese were hostile and Cathy and Francois were scared. They sweat-
ed it out for two hours. Finally, one man walked up to them, pointed in
the direction of the Catholic church and suggested they join the
refugees who had taken sanctuary there.

There were thousands of refugees on the grounds of the church. The
crowd did not make way or help them. Children pushed against them
and stared at them silently.

Thankfully, an elderly priest saw them and in fluent French welcomed them, showing them around as if he were a tour guide. He told
them that the last Vietnamese emperor had taken refuge in this Cathedral twenty years before, during the Viet Minh revolution. People
— mostly women and children and old men — were packed everywhere
among the polished wooden pews, around the altar, and a mother and
her newborn infant were resting against the confessional.

The noise was overwhelming: children crying, people talking, priests
praying loudly. The firing outside went on all night.

The two reporters tried to sleep in the priest's small room. In the
morning they were told that the Vietnamese resented their presence
and were afraid that, as Caucasians, they might provoke an NVA
attack. The priest told them to try to get to the American section and a
young boy who had been in the priest's care volunteered to lead them
to the MACV compound. Cathy and Mazure left all their military gear
in the church, even their boots; pinned identification tags on themselves and made a white flag out of a priest's robe. The priest even
wrote a letter explaining their neutral, civilian status.

They followed their guide down a dirt trail and, in a few minutes,
were at the entrance of a large villa surrounded by bright green
garden. They stopped, realizing that several men in green fatigues,
with AK-47 automatic rifles were looking at them. The boy waved the
white flag furiously. Three other North Vietnamese soldiers in khaki
uniforms came up to them. They seemed hostile but not angry and
Cathy relaxed a bit. Mazure handed them the priest's letter but they
made no move to read it. When he reached instinctively to protect his
cameras, the soldiers took them and motioned the three into the
garden. They bound the reporters' hands with parachute cord, calmly
but thoroughly. About fifteen NVA were sitting in spider holes under
the trees in the garden. Cathy and Mazure were left alone for approximately forty-five minutes. Mazure talked a lot in French, not wanting
to appear frightened. The NVA soldiers just stared.

Finally another soldier came and they were led towards the back of the villa. A white man, possibly French, sat at a table.

"Are you French?" Mazure asked.

He was, and very happy to meet the reporters. He even managed to go around to shake their bound hands. He and his family were prisoners in their own home but were not being treated badly. The Frenchman explained who the reporters were to a young NVA officer who had come in to interrogate them. The officer, about twenty-five who, under other circumstances, might have been a Vietnamese university student in Paris, said they could go. Their hands were untied, belongings returned. The officer said that the Communists held the city and they were liberating all of Vietnam.

Cathy and Francois, their courage restored, asked for permission to take photographs. The officer was delighted, escorted them back out to the garden. The other NVA soldiers were happy to pose for pictures. They were so young and confident.

It was not a peaceful atmosphere, however, and Cathy and Mazure noted that the NVA were prepared to fire through slits in the walls. If any Marines suddenly charged the villa, they could all be in the midst of a firefight. The NVA were well armed with AK-47 and SKS rifles, B-40 rockets, captured U.S.-made weapons and radios, and plenty of ammunition.

After taking some photographs, Mazure went back to the villa and announced nonchalantly that they had to get back with the story. No one objected.

The Frenchman produced some cigars, shook hands and wished them luck. Cathy and Mazure picked up their guide and went back out of the gate. They decided that it would be safer to go back to the church and try to get to the American compound from another direction.

The people at the church seemed to know immediately about their encounter with the NVA, and the boy was proud to fill them in on the whole experience. The reporters were laughing with relief and excitement and the refugees joined in their emotion. They offered them food. The priest led them to the gate and waved them off.

Cathy and Mazure were alone in the street. They wandered cautiously through no-man's land, headed, they hoped, towards the MACV compound. They crouched for a time in an ARVN compound, sat out a firefight, but they made it, just as the sun was going down.

Fox Company 2/5 had gotten itself organized in MACV, when Captain Downs was ordered to send his men across the street, west past the university LZ, to reconnoiter the NVA positions. Third Platoon moved out, and as they neared the end of the street, they could see Marines from Alpha 1/1 and Golf 2/5 up in the windows. At the intersection they stopped in a huddle. Lance Corporal Carter crouched along the wall with one of the M-60 machine gun teams. Up ahead, two grunts and a sergeant named Mahoney stood nearest the end of the wall. The Marines were jungle fighters, new to street fighting. They didn't know that to walk upright was to invite death; they didn't know to prepare every move with a grenade or M-16 burst. They were inexperienced. That's why the two Marines with the sergeant simply strolled past the wall to get to the next street.

Sergeant Mahoney suddenly lunged past the wall and shoved the two Marines back to cover. Just then — as Carter stared open-mouthed — an AK-47 roared from up ahead and the sergeant, a big man, came flopping down beside Carter like a sack of stones. He'd been shot in the face, killed instantly. Carter grabbed his arms to pull him back, but could hardly budge him; he couldn't believe how heavy the body was. He shouted for someone to help him, a couple of Marines ran up — and a fusillade abruptly started pouring down from the houses across from their corner. Rounds sprayed around the men, riddling the wall, and they all scrambled for cover. Carter got behind a wall, breathing hard, wondering why he was still alive.

The Marines returned the fire. Several grunts ran up and dragged Mahoney's body back with them. Then they got word to return to the compound. They'd paid dearly to learn that the North Vietnamese were dug in one block outside the MACV compound.

That night, the NVA hit the MACV walls again. Like the other attempts they made, their attack was met by a fusillade of fire and buckled. Fox Company didn't fight that night. They were assigned a building in which to sleep and lay strewn around the floor with their gear, trying to get some rest, while the firing chattered outside the windows. Their first day in Hue had been rough and one of the Marines, a young man new to Vietnam, finally flipped out. He got up, shouting over and over that he couldn't take it, sobbing, stumbling around among the sleeping forms of his platoon. Some of the grunts grabbed him and held him down, for evacuation out of Hue. The firing outside the walls died away, and the grunts slept as best they could.

The morning of Friday, February 2, saw the Nguyen Hoang Bridge over the Perfume River suddenly explode. (The Marines took to calling it the Silver Bridge because it was painted metallic silver.) There was a roar, the hiss of metal splashing deep into the water, and when the smoke and mist cleared, it could be seen that the center span had been dropped. Traffic between the South Side and the Citadel was cut, and there were no engineer units available to repair the bridge. Reports came that enemy sappers had been seen near the bridge. They were described as large men, bigger than the average Vietnamese, and wearing uniforms not seen on NVA or VC. The initial guess was that the sappers were from a Chinese Communist platoon. It was a suspicion that could be neither confirmed nor denied.

For Carter, the morning came too quickly. The grunts ate a cold breakfast of C rations, then headed out, moving down the main street on another patrol. Carter was in the middle of the column with his Third Platoon, back near Captain Downs and his radiomen, as they walked down the tree-lined road. Up ahead, snipers in palm trees fired at the lead platoon. Marines also were firing furiously, blowing away trees and men. Wounded VC tumbled from the branches, only to be gunned down as they tried to stagger away. They moved farther along past a demolished jeep in the road. Several NVA bodies lay in the mud and wire.

The lead platoon located the city's police headquarters two or three blocks from MACV, and much to the Marines' amazement, several South Vietnamese police officers emerged from the loft. They were crying and shaking, grabbing the Marines' arms, falling to their knees to give thanks. The ARVN interpreter came up and the policemen explained they'd been hiding in the house for days while NVA soldiers occupied the bottom floor. The place was bullet-riddled. Carter looked inside. There was blood smeared on the walls, dead Vietnamese lying among the debris. Some grunts went in and dragged the bodies out to the front courtyard. Carter couldn't tell if they were ARVN or NVA or VC or civilians or what. Who cares, he thought, they all look the same anyway.

More sniper fire cracked by, most of it coming from around the Catholic church. The Marines gathered behind the police headquarters on a dirt trail that led toward the church grounds. An Ontos antitank vehicle came clanking up and Carter watched the gunner sight in all six 106mm recoilless rifles mounted on the vehicle. They roared all at once, the tremendous back-blast kicking up dust and leaves. The church's ten-foot high cross shattered into a thousand pieces, the stained glass blew away, and the back of the building blew out. Smoke rose in the air. Swarms of people came pouring out.

Carter glanced at the Ontos gunner. The kid stared at the civilians, shocked and hurt, no one wanted to kill the innocents.

Cathy Leroy, who had been taking photographs nearby, ran toward the Marines. She grabbed the first officer she saw and shouted, "There are four thousand refugees in there! They aren't VC! They are just people!" The Marines stopped shooting while enemy snipers ahead continued to fire occasional rounds. The refugees clutched bags and babies, some of them carrying white rags on sticks, and wearily started up the road towards the compound.

Corporal Soukup had his 106mm recoilless rifle set up on a sidewalk a couple of blocks from the MACV compound. Everything in front of them was North Vietnamese. The crew worked the gun perfunctorily, sliding another long shell in, slamming the breech, punching the firing knob, raising a cloud of back-blast dust with each shot. The rounds exploded in little puffs down the street. Soukup was standing in a doorway with a bunch of grunts he didn't know, waiting for some word about what he should do with his gun.

There was a sudden crack in the air, and something sliced just above Soukup's head and went thunking into a wall inside the house. When he strolled inside, he saw that a bullet had gone through a watercolor hanging on the wall. The painting would make a good souvenir, and he stuffed it in his pack with a grin. Then the grin turned to numbness with the realization that a North Vietnamese Army soldier had just lined up his head in his sights. Someone had actually tried to kill him. That hadn't been a wild spray of rounds, but a deliberate aim. Inches lower and he'd have been just another piece of meat. He felt like crawling away into a crack.

Chapter 3

The House to House Begins

Treasury/Post Office Complex

When colleagues said that Lt. Col. Ernest C. Cheatham, Jr., was the finest Marine officer they had served with, they meant it.

He was a big man, standing well over six feet, an ex-professional football player, with the aggressiveness, skill, and personal bravery of a real military leader. Although he was a hard-charger in the Patton style (complete with goggles on his helmet), he displayed deep concern for the young Marines under his command. He was known in his battalion as Big Ernie.

And Big Ernie was frustrated. Three of his four line companies — Fox, Golf, and Hotel 2/5 — were fighting in Hue, while he was stuck at Phu Bai with no idea of what was going on. He kept pestering the regimental commander, Col. Robert D. Bohn, and finally, on February 3, he received instructions to go take charge of his battalion. They organized a convoy: Cheatham and his sergeant major in a jeep, the battalion staff crammed in radio jeeps, replacements and Headquarters & Service Company clerks-turned-riflemen in trucks. An Army Quad-50 truck drove up front for security. Aboard a truck with them was Col. Stanley Smith Hughes, newly-appointed commander of the 1st Marine Regiment, who had been charged with taking command and control of the Hue City Task Force.

The convoy started north up Highway 1 in the early morning. It was the same old story; nothing but gray skies, no sign of the enemy, no sign of anybody. They went across the Phu Cam Canal, toward the compound — and then the NVA hit. AK–47 fire sprayed from the buildings. Marines from 1/1 were off to the side, firing back. The convoy kept moving. An Ontos on the street suddenly shuddered as a B–40 rocket clanged against it. More firing was coming from their right, back near the Catholic church.

They arrived at the compound about 1:00 P.M.

Colonel Hughes took over from Gravel, and immediately set up his command post in the MACV officers' club. Hughes was a good choice for commander of the operation. A New York state native, he was stocky and dark complexioned — part Indian — and a quiet, friendly man. As a young platoon leader in 1944, he had won the Navy Cross for taking over two additional platoons after their officers were killed during a brutal attack across a stream on Cape Gloucester. As an older regimental commander, he led through mutual respect.

At the CP, Hughes and his regimental staff laid out their maps and tried to work out exactly what was happening in Hue — and what to do about it. General LaHue and the people at Task Force X-RAY had no solid intelligence; in fact, no one really had. About the only thing Hughes was sure of was what he had with him to fight the battle. On that afternoon of February 3, they consisted of:

F, G, H Companies 2/5, under Lieutenant Colonel Cheatham.

Most of A Company and a HqCo platoon 1/1, under Lieutenant Colonel Gravel.

Mortar and recoilless rifle crews from the battalion H&S Companies; Ontos from the Anti-tank Company, 1st Tank Battalion; the four stranded tanks from 3d Tank Battalion, 3d Marine Division; the U.S. Army Quad–50's from D Battery, 1st Battalion, 44th Artillery, I Field Force Vietnam Artillery.

Personnel of Advisory Team 3 at the MACV compound; sailors of NSA at the boat ramp; a number of clerks who had been sent up from the rear as reinforcements; Marines from the 1st Motor Transport Battalion who were making the convoy runs between Hue and Phu Bai.

A small number of ARVN units.

Colonel Hughes' orders were to clear the South Side. The other half of the battle in the Citadel was under the control of General Truong and his South Vietnamese, without U.S. Marine infantry assistance. With that in mind, Hughes quickly laid out his plan. To the hard-charging Cheatham went the enormous task of pushing west from MACV along the Perfume River, down to where the Phu Cam branched from the river. The main axis of advance for his 2/5 would be roughly along Le Loi Street, which paralleled the river (and which it turned out, was the location of the NVA headquarters and most of the enemy troops). Gravel and his 1/1 were to move with 2/5, but down along the Phu Cam, with the mission of keeping Highway 1 open to the compound. This was considered the easier of the two missions and Gravel got it because his force was seriously undermanned and bloodied. Also, in comparison to Cheatham, Gravel was a more cautious commander. In fact, before the arrival of the reinforcements — before the Marine command knew what was happening in Hue — Task Force X-RAY had been pressing him to hurry up and get the job done; they thought he was hedging.

The ARVN troops under Hughes's control were to sweep behind the Marines, mopping up any snipers and such who might have been missed, and handle the flow of civilian refugees and casualties which were sure to occur in the close-in, house-to-house fighting.

Cheatham and Gravel stood in the CP while Hughes gave them their marching orders. Cheatham hesitated for a moment, waiting for more. Was that it? Wasn't there any more intelligence, something?

Hughes answered his thoughts. "If you're looking for any more, you aren't going to get it." Like everyone else going into Hue, Hughes had only the sketchiest information. Then he added, "You do it any way you want, and you get any heat from above, I'll take care of that."

Hearing that, Cheatham put his helmet back on, picked up his M-16 rifle, and went out to fight the battle. Within a few minutes, the 2d Battalion, 5th Marines was on the counterattack.

Lieutenant Colonel Cheatham set up his CP across the street from the MACV compound, in the semisecure university building complex. Fox, Golf, and Hotel Companies were in and around the building — that was all they held. The NVA were up ahead; every now and then, shots broke out. To their right was Le Loi Street and the Perfume River. On their left was 1/1. Right in front, the enemy held the streets, about eleven blocks across and nine blocks deep. Every single alley, street corner, window, and intersection harbored potential death. It had to be taken block by block, house by house, brick by brick. They were able to scrounge some detailed city maps from the Shell station, police headquarters, and the Army people at MACV. Among Cheatham, his three company commanders, and their nine rifle platoon leaders, there were three maps. The first objective was to the front — the treasury building and the adjacent post office. The North Vietnamese soldiers were dug in deep. And they had no intention of fading away or retreating, as they did back in the rice paddies and jungles.

Corporal Dan "Arkie" Allbritton was a twenty-year-old, four-month-veteran squad leader in Third Platoon of Fox Company. He was a short man with glasses, an Arkansas twang, and some Purple Heart shrapnel scars in his back from a booby trap three months before in An Hoa. When they first got to Hue, Allbritton heard a sergeant say they were there to clean out a few snipers.

Within a couple of days, his response to that was: Bullshit!

The Third Platoon had mostly been holding its own around MACV and the university those first days. There was an ARVN tank there, parked up against the wall, and Allbritton would watch, amused, as a little South Vietnamese soldier would scurry up the back of the tank, fire a couple of rounds from the turret machine gun, then jump back down before a sniper could zero in — grinning ear to ear at the Marines.

Finally, the word came to move out — they were going to attack. But Corporal Allbritton, Lance Corporal Carter, and the rest of the Third Platoon grunts were lucky; it was Second Platoon that was picked to advance as point. They watched the Second Platoon Marines go around a wall, then disappear up the first street on the left, headed for the treasury/post office complex. In a few minutes, the whole street came alive with gunfire.

2d Lt. Donald A. Hausrath, Jr., the leader of the Third Platoon, was ordered to move up the street and help Second Platoon pull back. A pair of Marine tanks drove ahead of them, and they started inching down the wide, tree-lined road. NVA fire poured from the rooftops ahead, clanging and thunking around them. The grunts followed the tanks in a tight huddle, hunched over, inching forward on their toes and knees and hands, keeping their heads down. Carter could see a black Marine lying on the sidewalk. Fire kept raking around them. My God, Carter thought, Second Platoon was almost wiped out.

The tanks opened up with their .50-caliber machine guns and 90mm cannons. Some grunts joined in the firing from behind the tanks, and Lieutenant Hausrath and others started grabbing the bodies and dragging them back. Survivors from the platoon, crouched in doorways and alleys, started bolting back. Somebody threw a young, unconscious grunt on the back of the tank, above Carter's head. Suddenly, a B-40 rocket hit the turret and glanced over the wounded Marine in a spray of shrapnel. The kid came tumbling off the tank, wide awake and screaming. His foot was gone.

They got all the wounded and dead on the tanks, then backed down the street, firing and taking fire the whole way. Mortar rounds from the battalion CP exploded ahead of them as cover. It had been a short, bloody ordeal; Captain Downs himself had taken superficial shrapnel wounds from a B-40 rocket.

The casualties were moved back to the American dispensary, and the Marines crouched among the houses and walls, right back where they started. Carter was standing there when Lieutenant Hausrath grabbed him.

"Carter, is it true that you're a rocketman, that you're qualified in rockets?"

"Yes, sir," he said, "I'm an expert in rockets. That's my MOS."

"Okay, you're our rocketman."

A 3.5-inch rocket launcher, akin to the old bazooka, was brought up. Carter was told to move up the street where they'd just been mauled, and blow a hole in the courtyard wall on the right side. The plan was to get Fox Company into the courtyard ahead of them, then advance house to house up to the treasury, thereby staying out of the open streets. One of the tanks started clanking slowly down the street and Carter moved beside it, crouched low between it and the wall, the 3.5 over his shoulder with a round in the tube. He aimed, fired, and the iron gate on the wall blew open.

The rest of the company moved forward and ducked through the hole in the wall. They started moving through the houses, Carter blowing open the doors with the 3.5, the grunts tossing in grenades, then moving inside to check. There was no enemy fire. That lasted about fifteen minutes.

Carter was crouched down, reloading, when he saw some grunts from the decimated Second Platoon huddled along another courtyard wall. (Every yard had a wall.) They boosted one guy up over to the next yard — and just as his head popped over the wall, a sniper's AK roared from nowhere. The grunt came flopping back down, shot in the face. He cried out, "Momma!" and then he was dead.

Carter blew open the doors of the next house, and he and another lance corporal rushed in. No one was there. They slid up to the opposite wall, and Carter slowly opened the shutters and looked out. His heart stopped. Standing on the second floor balcony of the building on the left were three North Vietnamese soldiers. They were wearing pith helmets with red stars in front. He was close enough to see their faces.

He hesitated, unsure if he should fire and give his platoon's position away. He called to the lance corporal, "Hey, look at this, Tom. There's a couple of gooks up there!"

"What the hell you talking to me for? Shoot 'em!"

It was an easy shot. Carter unslung his M-16 and brought it to his shoulder. He lined up a khaki shirt in the peep sight and squeezed the trigger. The man went flying back. He got off a second quick shot. Another man bounced against the balcony wall. The third NVA disappeared.

Carter grinned at the lance corporal, spit on his fingers, and smacked the barrel of his M-16.

The sun went down. The shooting continued, off and on, all night. That night, Cheatham called up his company commanders. In the morning, he said, the whole battalion was going to make a concentrated assault across the line towards the treasury/post office. Captain Downs's Fox Company was to make the actual assault on the building complex. Captain Christmas's Hotel Company was to seize the public health building in front of the university, on Fox's right flank, and support their attack by fire. Captain Meadows and his Golf Company, which had one-third of its complement killed or wounded on the first day, was to be in reserve.

In an attempt to preserve the history and beauty of Hue, General Lam and the Saigon government had persuaded the Marine command to restrict the use of supporting arms. That meant no bombing runs, no offshore Naval bombardment, no artillery prep fires. The Marines were facing an enemy force, superior in numbers which was well dug in, had planty of cover, and was well-armed with automatic weapons, recoilless rifles, mortars, and rockets. About the only thing the Marines had which the North Vietnamese didn't were tanks — but there were reports that the NVA were using the cannons of captured ARVN tanks.

It was one hell of a situation for every Marine there, from the thirty-eight-year-old battalion commander, down to those eighteen-year-old grunts who had to charge across the street. As Cheatham told his captains at the briefing, "You must dig the rats from their holes."

The dawn of Sunday, February 4, was overcast, cold, and gloomy. The firing cranked up in the streets again.

Captain Christmas, with his company gunnery sergeant, Frank A. Thomas, Jr., directed Hotel's advance. First Platoon fought its way into a house adjacent to their target, the public health building. Third Platoon tried to get across the street into the building, but an NVA machine gun opened up from down the street. They fell back with a couple of men wounded. The grunts tossed smoke grenades into the street for cover, but the flanking gun fired blindly through the smoke. Marines from Golf Company in the university building started shooting down from the windows. Captain Christmas and Gunny Thomas quickly conferred with the platoon leader, then decided to bring up a 106mm recoilless rifle to cover the street crossing. They popped smoke, sighted in on the muzzle flash, and the 106 crew went into action. Christmas watched, amazed, as the young kids rolled their 106, atop a Mechanical Mule, halfway into the street and calmly sighted in. The round flashed down the street, the back blast blew smoke onto the road, and the NVA ducked their heads for a few seconds. The platoon got across the street.

They went into the public health building. Firing broke out. In a few minutes, one Marine and a dozen NVA were dead.

The Hotel grunts climbed to the rooftop, took positions in the windows, and started firing to their left at the treasury/post office. On their left, Fox Company was taking a hell of a beating.

Lieutenant Hausrath's platoon was in front. Carter blew a hole in the courtyard wall around a two-story Catholic schoolhouse, and the grunts quickly scrambled through and ran for cover along the opposite wall. The treasury building was directly in front of them across the street. NVA fire poured down from it, splattering the wall and the lawn and the schoolhouse. The treasury was built like a treasury is supposed to be: two stories high with a loft; thick concrete construction; an eight-foot wall around the tree-dotted courtyard.

The North Vietnamese were buttoned up tight inside.

Captain Downs and his radiomen got inside the schoolhouse. The captain wanted a fireteam to rush into the treasury, and called Carter to open the walls for them. He took his 3.5, and since there was no gate in the school courtyard wall, he blew a hole in it, spraying concrete and bricks into the street. Then he blasted a small hole in the treasury courtyard wall, careful to aim at a spot fifteen feet away from the front gate, at a place where the NVA fire from the building would be partially blocked by some trees and a stone marker. It was a wasted effort.

As soon as the team ran into the street, the NVA opened up with a fury. The Marines threw themselves against the wall, the rounds passing over their heads and bouncing in the street behind them. A young man named Washburn edged up to the hole and started to wiggle through. Suddenly, he jerked violently and sagged — the enemy had shot him in the head. The others quickly yanked him out of the hole. He was still breathing shallowly, but they couldn't get him back across the street without being gunned down.

Along the schoolhouse wall, Corporal Allbritton and his squad were firing like hell, trying to give the pinned-down team some support. The NVA also kept shooting.

The team's squad leader, Cpl. Thomas R. Burnham of Pennsylvania, crouched along the wall near Allbritton, visibly distressed. "Bernie" Burnham was something of a legend in the battalion. First of all, he was thirty-one years old. He had joined originally to fight in Korea, but the war ended while he was in boot camp. He did his time, got a job as an electrical engineer, then reenlisted when the Vietnam War heated up. Four months before Hue, during a VC attack at Nong Son, Burnham had thrown himself on a grenade. It failed to explode and he lived to vomit in realization of what should have happened — and to see his Navy Cross recommendation. He was something of an idol to the eighteen-and nineteen-year-old kid Marines in the platoon; he was the kind of guy you could always count on.

Corporal Burnham was about to prove that again.

He edged up to the hole in the wall — then bolted straight into the street. Everyone poured down cover fire. NVA fire spattered around him. Burnham flattened himself against the treasury wall, then hoisted Washburn over his shoulders and ran back across the street. The fireteam got up and followed him at a dead run. Burnham made it through the torrent of fire and came tumbling through the school wall with Washburn. The grunts would have cheered if they'd had the time. Washburn died on the grass before they could get him back to MACV.

Burnham had just made it back when Allbritton saw a reporter and his cameraman packing up to leave. They said they were going back to the CP since nothing interesting was happening. Allbritton knew they were civilians and didn't have to be there, and it wouldn't have bothered him if they'd just admit it was too hot and they were bugging out. But their BS story about nothing going on bothered him. The grunts asked an Australian correspondent there why he didn't go back like the Americans. He admitted he was too damn scared to go by himself.

Carter hunkered down behind the wall with his 3.5-inch rocket launcher. He knew he had one hell of a weapon and had to do something with it. He figured if he could get back into the schoolhouse, he could fire from the second floor right down the throats of those damn gooks.

He shouted to Hausrath, telling him what he wanted to do.

Lieutenant Hausrath, crouched along the wall with the rest, yelled back, "Give it a try, and don't get hit!"

"You really expect a lot, Lieutenant!" he joked back.

Carter and his assistant gunner started crawling and ducking and running toward the schoolhouse. Rounds blew up dirt and concrete around them. They stayed behind cover. The firing slacked off. They got up again. More firing. It took them twenty minutes just to get across the lawn. Then they rushed through the door. Carter was amazed he wasn't hit. They went past Captain Downs and his radiomen, and started up the steps to the second-floor hallway. It was long, with French doors on one side and a row of about fifteen windows facing the treasury on the other. Carter bent with the launcher on his shoulder and the A-gunner slid a round in. Then he stepped to the window, squinted through the rubber sight piece, and fired.

The round flashed down and exploded against the treasury.

Carter ducked down, the A-gunner reloaded, and they worked their way down the hallway, popping shells out of each window. Marines with an M-60 machine gun pounded up the stairs and joined them in the hallway. They propped their M-60 on a windowsill and started putting tracer bursts on the muzzle flashes they saw in the treasury, pinpointing targets for Carter. More grunts came up, dumping ammunition on the floor, then taking off to get more. Carter kept shooting; he didn't know how many, maybe a hundred rounds. The NVA fire ricocheted outside and Carter was scared, but he was also happy. As the Marines crudely put it: "Payback is a motherfucker."

Allbritton squatted behind some concrete pillars, firing his M-16 like hell across the street. Suddenly, a round blew up against the pillars, spraying shards in his face. He jumped to a new position, holding his helmet down, spitting concrete crumbs out of his mouth. He looked up to see an old buddy down behind some cover, looking at him with a small grin. The grunt drawled, "You know, Arkie, a fella could get a second Purple Heart like that."

Cheatham was moving about in the buildings, directing fire, trying to figure out how to crack the treasury. He got on the radio, called up one of the tanks, then pointed it towards the target. The tank poked its nose out between the buildings and before it could even get a round off, a B-40 exploded against its front. The driver threw the tank in reverse and hauled backward, only to get a tread tangled in a spool of barbed wire. Cheatham swore at the tank, then got on the radio for a recoilless rifle crew to come up. The kids came up on the Mechanical Mule and opened up with their 106. The rounds barely dented the wall.

Captain Harold "Ernie" Pyle was upset. Before the convoy to Hue with the 2/5 command group, the 1st Marine regimental air liaison officer had briefed him on the Rules of Engagement for Hue. He was told that when calling in jet strikes, he could only use 7.62mm and 20mm guns, and 2.75-inch aerial rockets. Hell, he thought, the guys on the ground have bigger stuff than that. What they needed were 500-pound bombs and napalm. When they'd gotten to Hue, he had watched old Skyraiders from the Vietnamese Air Force dropping bombs in the Citadel, but the Marines still wouldn't allow it. And all it would take — if the weather was good enough — were a few Phantoms working over the treasury to soften it up for the grunts.

But that was not to be. Captain Pyle found himself, along with Capt. Tom Fine, the battalion's out-of-work forward air controller, joining in the battle as infantryman. They got to the second floor of the university and made their way to a corner room facing the treasury. They opened the French door to the veranda and started firing their M-16s at the treasury.

They could see an NVA machine gun firing from inside a building down the street. It was the position that had opened up on Hotel's advance, and it was playing hell with Fox Company. Captain Pyle took off to find Cheatham.

Cheatham and his executive officer, Maj. Ralph J. Salvati, showed up. Cheatham took a look and ordered up a 106. The crew pulled up in their Mule, and Major Salvati helped them manhandle the gun up the stairs into the corner room. They sighted in on the machine gun position and fired a few spotter rounds from the .50-caliber mounted on the tube. Then the gunner unwound the lanyard and they all backed up into the hallway. The kid yanked the cord, the weapon roared, and the whole place shook from the back blast. When the dust settled, they went back in the room. The ceiling had caved in and the 106 was buried under the plaster and debris. But, Cheatham's plan had worked. Down the street, the NVA machine gun was silent.

Major Salvati picked up his Thompson machine gun and took off to see how Fox was doing. He found Captain Downs in the schoolhouse. He was frustrated: most of the Marine fire was bouncing off the treasury walls, the NVA had excellent fields of fire, and although the battalion 81mm mortar teams dug in in the university courtyard were dropping shells on the roof, it seemed to have little effect. Salvati knew he couldn't do much around the battalion CP, so he rounded up a couple of Marines and a 3.5 and stayed with Fox Company. The team got behind a wall and started sending rounds into the treasury.

Carter fired another shell from his perch, the A-gunner reloaded, and he popped back up in front of the window. Then Carter noticed his partner hadn't put up the contact latch so the 3.5 would fire. He ducked down, turned to flip up the latch — and the B-40 rocket whooshed through the window. The corridor erupted with shrapnel and flying glass and concrete and metal.

Carter went crashing through a French door. Then he was lying very still. He couldn't feel his body. He couldn't hear or see; everything was gray. All he could do was think, and he said to himself. "Oh my God, I think I'm dead." He felt as though he were spinning through a tunnel with a light at the end. He kept telling himself that if he could shake his arm, shake his head, maybe he wouldn't be dead. He started shaking his head, coming out of it. There was a shout, "Let's get him out of here, I think he's dead!" and somebody grabbed his wrists, dragging him away. He thrashed, shook his head, sat up. His arm stung from shrapnel. The whole corridor was smoking and strewn with rubble. Marines were moving up and down the steps with the wounded.

Someone behind Carter was screaming and he jerked around. It was his A-gunner. He was sitting in the rubble, blood on his cheeks, and glass in his eyes. Carter didn't know what to do, he couldn't touch the man's eyes. He found a C ration cardboard box and gingerly wrapped it around the man's head. Then he carried him downstairs with the rest of the seriously wounded.

The grunts who'd been slightly wounded started going back upstairs. The M-60 team opened up again. Carter stepped through the rubble, found his 3.5, and started putting out rounds.

Earlier in his tour, when he'd been the commander of a headquarters company, Major Salvati had used the E-8 tear gas launcher. It was a small contraption, about two feet high, which would hurl gas capsules up to 250 meters. The smoke grenades they'd been throwing at the treasury didn't produce enough smoke and dispersed too quickly. He thought the E-8s might help, and remembered seeing some stacked in the MACV compound, unused.

He left the schoolhouse, hunted up Cheatham, and told him his idea. The colonel said it was worth a try. Salvati got his driver, jumped in a jeep, and drove back to MACV. There were some ARVN soldiers standing around near the E-8s. They stared blandly at Salvati as he threw the launchers in the jeep trailer.

Back at the schoolhouse, Salvati and a couple of Marines slipped on their gas masks and ran into the courtyard with one of the E-8s. They set it up, pointed it at an angle over the wall towards the treasury, then ran back behind a wall.

Salvati yanked the lanyard. Nothing happened. What the hell?

The E-8 could also be triggered with an electrical charge, so Salvati took off to scrounge up a power-cell battery. He found one — somewhere, he didn't know where — then ran back into the courtyard and wired it up. The capsules exploded from the launcher and sailed into the treasury compound. The nonlethal tear gas started floating up around the building, through the windows and gun slits. The North Vietnamese soldiers didn't have gas masks.

Captain Downs was yelling to Carter to come down, that the company was attacking, that he should use the 3.5 for support fire. Carter picked up the launcher and some shells and ran into the open courtyard to make a good shot. He dropped to his knee and aimed. No enemy fire came at him; he figured the enemy was waiting to let the company charge and mow them down in the street. His first shot hit the treasury-wall gate, then whooshed into the doorway, blowing down one of the big oak doors. His second shot blew the other side of the door away. He fired a white-phosphorous round through the door, then ran up to the schoolhouse wall and fired a smoke round down the street. The wind blew the smoke back over the treasury. In the courtyard, Downs was preparing his men for the attack.

Allbritton and his squad were up against the wall, wearing gas masks, clutching their M-16s, waiting. Someone shouted to go. They climbed one at a time through the hole in the wall, and they were up and running like hell across the street. Move!Move!Move! Through the blown-down gate, across the courtyard, up around the door of the treasury, sweating hard into their gas masks. Allbritton and the rest tossed in a barrage of grenades, then ran in, firing from the hip.

They made it to a hallway, with a room on the left and one on the right. Allbritton shouted at two men to cover the rooms, then started toward the door at the end of the hallway. It was blocked by rubble. There was some scurrying from behind the door, the sound of men coming down stairs, Vietnamese voices. Allbritton yelled, pointed, and a machine-gunner wheeled around and hosed down the door with his M-60. They threw more grenades, blew in the door, then stormed up the stairs, firing wildly. Allbritton jogged to the staircase leading up to the loft, pitched a grenade up, then ran up the stairs, firing his M-16. There was no one there.

AK-cartridge brass littered the floor of the loft, and Albritton could see an E-8 gas capsule lying in the debris. He stepped to the windows. The walls were two-foot-thick concrete and had little bunker-style firing slits in them. He looked through the slits. They looked directly down on the street and on the schoolhouse. It was a perfect field of fire. Allbritton stepped back. "Son of a bitch," he mumbled, "Son of a bitch."

Corporal Burnham had gathered what was left of his squad into the first floor of the treasury. The North Vietnamese were gone, having run out the back among the other houses and courtyard walls. Wild firing followed after them. Burnham came into a hallway — and there he was, a wounded NVA crawling nowhere. Burnham emptied his M–16 into his chest. Payback. In a few minutes, the treasury/post office was secured.

The Marines started coming across the street, counting the NVA bodies crushed amongst the rubble, and searching through the debris. Some grunts from Hotel Company busted into the treasury and stuffed their packs with gold bars and wads of piaster notes. Nobody said much about it. Carter helped patch up some wounded Marines who'd stumbled back across the street after a departing grenade from the NVA hit them. Then he walked over to the buildings. He found a broken B–40 rocket launcher and a bunch of letters and packets scattered on the floor. Upstairs, a couple of dud rockets were sticking in the wall. In one office room, there were paintings on the wall, a wedding photo of two Vietnamese, and toys scattered among the rubble. Lance Corporal Carter pulled a couch from the debris and fell asleep on it.

In the morning, some Marines came and woke Carter, telling him to get his 3.5-inch rocket launcher and hurry over to the post office. A dozen NVA had been found hiding in a shed, and they wouldn't come out. The door of the shed was about fifteen feet from the post office, so Carter couldn't fire from there — his own shrapnel would have sprayed right back at him. So he got up on the post office roof, walked up to the edge, and aimed in, dead zero on the sight, right down on the NVA. His rounds still exploded back at him, superficial shrapnel wounds scraping his face. Three shots and the door was twisted like a pretzel. A grunt from Second Platoon tossed in a CS tear gas grenade. In a few seconds, the North Vietnamese came running out, coughing and crying. The machine-gunners opened up.

When it was over, Carter climbed off the roof. One of the sergeants told him he'd done a great job, and asked if he'd been aware that snipers were firing. Yeah, Carter said, he had heard the shots, but he had to concentrate on his own firing. The sergeant said he was going to put him in for a Bronze Star, and Carter felt pretty good.

He never heard anything more about the medal. Carter never saw the sergeant again. Someone said he'd been hit, killed. The street fighting continued.

Chapter 4

The House to House Continues

Joan of Arc School and Church

Back during the booby-trap war, the Marines who'd been slightly wounded expected a two- or three-day vacation at the aid station before heading back to the field. But during the Hue street war, the doctors and corpsmen at the MACV aid station had a hard time convincing wounded men they couldn't go back to the fighting. Some kids with injuries would walk to a house, sit around for awhile, then go back to their unit and tell the CO the corpsmen said they were okay. Lt. Ray Smith, the commander of Alpha 1/1 after Batcheller's evacuation, wrote to his former captain a few weeks after the battle ended: "A man couldn't have been with these Marines in Hue and not love them. I had several men who had shrapnel in legs and arms and hobbled around and begged me not to medevac them. They did a tremendous job against real odds and I never heard a complaint." So, there it was — the morale of the Marines in Hue City.

One of the biggest factors in that was the aggressive attitude drummed into Marines from the day they got off the bus at boot camp. They saw themselves as fighters, as winners, as The Best. They had faith in their leaders — from the battalion commanders down to the young platoon lieutenants and sergeants — all of whom were right beside them in the streets, doing their share of the fighting and taking their share of the casualties. The young Marines also took special pride

55

in the fact that they were infantrymen, a perverse sense of pride that no one had it worse than a combat grunt. In addition, they had their fundamental pride in the United States Marine Corps and their country.

But pride only explains part of it. The "noble cause of freedom for South Vietnam" didn't propel a Marine to run through enemy fire to pull a wounded man to cover. A politician at home praising "our boys overseas" wasn't the reason a man would refuse evacuation to a safe hospital after one or two wounds. "Mom, dad, and apple pie" had only a little to do with a grunt keeping his sense of balance in the midst of one of the ghastliest actions in the Vietnam War. What caused many of these things to happen in Hue was simple comradeship.

There are few human experiences comparable to the camaraderie and brother-love of a Marine infantry unit in combat. It doesn't matter what your background is, what color your skin is, how much schooling you've had, how much money your father makes. All that matters are the men in your squad or platoon. The whole world revolves around helping them, sharing with them, trying to keep your ass and their asses alive when the shooting starts. The Marine grunts slept in the same holes at night, suffered under the same broiling sun and freezing monsoon rains, slogged through the same muddy paddy fields, and fought the same enemy. And when it came to fighting, the individual Marine did his best because he couldn't let his buddies down. Nothing else mattered. This was true in World War II and Korea and was true again here in Vietnam.

But in Hue, there was one particular twist: revenge. Before the battle, many of the young Marines had never seen a North Vietnamese or a Viet Cong soldier in combat. What they knew was the impersonal killing and horrible maiming done by the booby traps; they had tasted fear with nothing to strike back at. They had known the frustration of patrolling in circles over the same patch of ground without finding anything, only to be sniped at that night from villages and not allowed to return fire because of the civilians. But in Hue, they saw some sense in what they were doing. They could see the enemy face to face — and they could kill him. As Captain Pyle said, "The Marines in Hue were high. It was payback time for An Hoa."

High morale was another good reason for the Marines' success. Said Battalion Commander Gravel, "Probably the greatest attribute is the fact that people, regardless of their rank, performed at levels that you would seldom see. For instance, second lieutenants commanding a company, sergeants leading platoons, corporals and Pfc.'s taking responsibility. I had some men that were doing things, performing in ways that you wouldn't expect from men of much greater age and maturity; doing things correctly in high risk situations. . . I had little or nothing to worry about because they just knew, sensed what was needed to be done and worked extremely well with very little direction."

Dale Dye, the 1st Marine Division correspondent with an eye for detail, pretty well summed it up: "Nearly all of us had bandages or rags tied around one minor wound or another. We were filthy dirty and I guess we looked like a bunch of Mexican bandits. But the Marines were magnificent in their squalor. The morale was typical of Marine Corps morale during any rugged fight. They bitched, they moaned, and they cussed everything from the Commandant to the NVA and the miserable weather. But I think morale is really the wrong word. It was more a sort of bitter tenacity and a determination to see the fight through no matter what. We had been so beaten, so strung out by the constant pressure, that we all had a sort of weary resignation. I don't think any of us thought we would live through the fight, and I don't think any of us gave a shit one way or the other."

Besides comradeship, the Marine grunts in Hue had one other trait in common — a hatred for the North Vietnamese and Viet Cong. It had nothing to do with politics. It was much more personal; it was having their friends blown away and mangled. So, they were the gooks, the dinks, the slopeheads. And they were to be killed without regret, and maybe with a joke afterwards. That is something that cannot be ignored, or denied. But there was one other feeling for the enemy — grudging respect. That skinny little Vietnamese fought hard and rarely gave up. Sergeant Dye summed that up well also: "The NVA in Hue were mean, motivated bastards. They fought a defensive fight while we were moving during the day, and moved over to the offense during the night. We'd constantly find ourselves retaking real estate we had fought for the previous day, because the NVA moved back in at night and we didn't have enough Marines to occupy all the ground. I suppose there were both zealots and cowards among the NVA we fought. As far as I'm concerned, there were entirely too damn many zealots. But, the plain fact is, we were better."

Lt. Com. Robert C. Hamilton, a Navy doctor in charge of Bravo Company, 1st Medical Battalion, 1st Marine Division, had seen Hue before the battle started. The Sunday before Tet, he'd rounded up his Marine jeep driver and a young regimental civil affairs lieutenant, and they'd made a tourist trip to Hue. They drank in the outdoor cafes;

took pictures of the imperial Palace in the Citadel until some guards chased them out; and downed some rounds in the MACV officers' club with Capt. Stephen Bernie, the Army doctor running the dispensary in the compound.

Everything felt perfectly normal. Dr. Hamilton spent the first night of Tet in the Phu Bai bunkers with the rest of his Marines and Navy corpsmen while the rockets exploded.

Later, he got a call from General LaHue, telling him to report to his command post. It was around midnight, and a blackout was in effect. But Hamilton found a daring American-Indian Marine who jeeped him to the CP in the pitch darkness. Since Hamilton was also the Medical Officer of Task Force X-RAY, LaHue explained to him that there was some trouble up in Hue, but none of the units had their doctors with them. By odd coincidence, they had all been to a medical conference in Da Nang when Tet started, and were unable to get back. He asked what Hamilton could do.

Hamilton responded that they had the option of mobilizing a 20-man Medical Support Team from the 1st Med at Da Nang. But since it didn't sound too serious, he said, he could just go up there with a few corpsmen and help Dr. Bernie at the MACV dispensary until the battalion surgeons could make it to Hue. The general agreed.

Hamilton went to the transportation officer to arrange to catch a convoy, then returned to his unit's compound to pick a few corpsmen to accompany him. Much to the man's disappointment, Hamilton ordered his chief corpsman to stay at Phu Bai and handle the place in his absence. Hamilton then went into a bunker to talk to the young corpsmen. He explained the situation and one corpsman asked if Hamilton was going. Hamilton said he was and was very pleased when the young man responded with, "Well, then I'm going, too." Hamilton picked him, two other young corpsmen, and the company old man, a veteran HM2 named "Pappy" Reinhardt.

In the morning, February 4, they checked in at the base motor pool. There were two convoys scheduled for Hue, and they climbed aboard the first one, about thirty trucks stacked with supplies and ammunition. A few cooks and clerk-typists had been handed M-16s and were aboard as security. That was not an unknown occurence; the Marine Corps axiom that every Marine is a rifleman no matter what his specific job, often was put into practice. Hamilton found himself sharing the ride up Highway 1 in the back of a truck with cartons of M-26 hand grenades.

They'd just crossed the Phu Cam Canal and were driving through an open market when the NVA opened up from the buildings. Hamilton hunkered down next to the stacks of grenades, while the cooks and clerks fired back from the railings, and the drivers pressed the accelerators. They got to the MACV compound, pulled inside, and Hamilton and his corpsmen jumped down from the trucks. Dr. Bernie greeted them and they stood talking in a loose circle, Hamilton feeling very relieved to be inside the walls.

Then the rocket-propelled grenade hit.

It shot over the wall, blew up on the roof of a building, and the shrapnel and concrete sprayed the men. There hadn't been time to do anything but stand there in shock. When Hamilton looked around, only he and one of his young corpsmen were unscathed. Bernie had minor shrapnel wounds in his arm. One of the men, a civilian government worker, was almost scalped by a piece of flying tile. He stood there, dripping blood, and they quickly got him into the aid station.

It was some welcome for Hamilton, thirty-four years old and drafted out of his Chicago medical practice only six months before. But the day was just beginning. Hamilton, Bernie, and the rest of the Navy corpsmen and Army medics patched up the wounded Marines already there and during a lull, Hamilton drifted over to Colonel Hughes' officers' club CP. Word came there that the afternoon convoy — the one after Hamilton's — was being hit hard.

The afternoon convoy was being led in by 2d Lt. Terry Charbonneau, a twenty-five-year-old from Detroit, the leader of Second Platoon, Charlie Company, 1st Motor Transport Battalion, 1st Marine Division.

He had been stranded at the 1st Cav's Camp Evans with a platoon of trucks from a different company, when an Army general told him to find out what plans his battalion had for the lost truckers. Charbonneau hitchhiked on Army helos to the 1st MTB rear at Gia Le, then got stuck at Phu Bai. There really wasn't much for him to do — in the Tet rush, his platoon had been mixed in with others and was stuck in Hue — so he wandered around. Some trucks came by from the base supply area with a number of new replacements aboard. They weren't wearing helmets and Charbonneau asked why they only had soft covers. The answer: supply had run out of helmets and other nice-to-have items. Charbonneau told the new kids to scrounge some helmets from an aid station when they got to their destination.

Charbonneau recognized the captain of the battalion's Alpha Company, who was organizing a convoy with men from A and B Companies, and some of his own Second Platoon Marines. He walked over to say hi to the captain, and asked where they were going. Hue. Charbonneau wanted to go along, but the captain asked if he realized there was fighting there. He knew — his man Lala was already in for the Silver Star — but he still wanted to go. The captain looked at him as if he thought, Is this guy gungho or what? "Fine", he said, "you'll be my trail officer" [responsible for securing the rear of the convoy]. Charbonneau took over the post from a gunnery sergeant and boarded the second-to-last truck, sharing the ride with a driver, a gunner in the fifty-mount, and a radio. Behind him, the gunny and his platoon corpsmen rode on the last vehicle, a wrecker (towtruck). About twenty trucks were filled with ammunition, food, medical gear, and such. An Army Duster and another batch of clerks-, cooks-, mechanics-, supply-men-turned-grunts were provided for security.

They pushed out a little after noon, the captain up front in his jeep. As they bumped along the highway, they saw no one; all the civilians were buttoned up inside their houses. Only one little Vietnamese boy stood along the side of the road, all alone, giving the Americans the thumbs-up sign as they came by. Charbonneau thought that was pretty impressive — the kid and his family were taking a big risk if the VC saw him. The Marines looked down from the truck beds — most of them not smiling because they knew what was waiting up ahead — and waved back at the boy.

They got to the Phu Cam Canal, then the convoy slowly bumped to a halt in front of the An Cuu Bridge. Charbonneau waited anxiously — a stopped truck was a sitting duck — then jumped down. He walked to the side of the road and peered up front. The lead vehicles were moving slowly. What's the problem? he wondered. He got back in his seat and picked up the radio to call the captain. Suddenly there was a tremendous explosion. The captain's jeep was on fire. Small-arms fire erupted.

The voice of the battalion executive officer (he'd been monitoring the net from 1st MTB headquarters) suddenly cut in on the radio. He told Lieutenant Charbonneau that he was in charge, and to keep moving.

Up ahead, the trucks were starting to haul across the bridge at top speed and Charbonneau followed. He had his driver stop past the burning jeep, then jumped from the cab to look for the captain and his driver, while the fifty-gunner pounded out cover fire. Charbonneau couldn't see anybody. The convoy was getting way ahead of them, so he jumped back inside and they rushed to catch up. The trucks got through the traffic circle which had the Shell station and were moving through the paddy field. And then — Charbonneau couldn't believe it — North Vietnamese soldiers were running through the field, firing at the trucks. Everyone with a weapon opened up, the gunner above

Charbonneau hammering away, the "rear" Marines popping their M–16s, the Duster crew roaring with their twin-40mm cannons. The paddy exploded with flying mud and water. The NVA threw themselves into gullies and trenches, ducking their heads and not firing.

The convoy shot past, firing to the front, the sides, then behind.

Charbonneau had driven through Hue only days before, when the people had been celebrating Tet and giving them wine and candy. Now, the city was deserted and the familiar storefronts had been reinforced with logs to make NVA bunkers. They made it up the road to the compound, then got bottlenecked outside the gate. Charbonneau looked back. The wrecker that had been following them wasn't there. He ran to the Duster and shouted that they had to go back and find the lost vehicle.

The soldier in charge balked; he didn't want to run the gauntlet again.

"C'mon!"

The man was looking for excuses. "We're an antiaircraft weapon!"

"We see any airplanes, you can shoot 'em. Let's go!"

The Duster maneuvered out of the stopped convoy, got turned around, and just then, the wrecker came bouncing toward them. The captain, with shrapnel in his back, was hanging on the back. His driver had a foot dangling by a few threads of skin just above the ankle. The gunny was there too, a graze wound under his cheekbone, and the corpsman, a gung-ho guy with a big handlebar mustache and a Thompson machine gun, crouched with them, patching them up. They were all splattered with hydraulic fluid from the shot-up wrecker. A few ARVNs came bearing a stretcher for the casualties — then departed after stealing a Marine's M–16 in the confusion. The Marines unfolded the stretcher, gingerly laid the driver on it, and slowly and carefully walked towards the MACV aid station.

"C'mon," urged the man on the stretcher, "it's gone already. Hurry up!"

Carbonneau burst into the dispensary with the driver. Dr. Hamilton checked the wound and gave the driver a shot. The Marine stared unemotionally at his foot. Hamilton took a pair of surgical scissors and amputated it with one snip.

Carbonneau went back out in the compound to check on his men and trucks. Some of the Marines kept asking when the convoy was going back to Phu Bai; no one knew. A few of the trucks were being driven on blown-away tires and the hydraulic systems of some were full of holes. The Marine mechanics were just getting to work on them when the first mortar round came whooshing down. It exploded in the courtyard and they all went for cover, Charbonneau rolling under the truck before wondering if that would do any good since mortars explode at ground level. A few more rounds dropped in, not hurting anyone, but riddling another truck with shrapnel.

By the time it was dark, Charbonneau, the wounded captain, the corpsman, and a number of Marines carried the wounded through a hole in the compound wall into the first floor of a building, to wait for the medevac choppers. The corpsman asked the driver with the blown-away foot if he wanted some more morphine.

The man was in obvious pain, but he shook his head. No, he said, he didn't want to get hooked, he'd have to get used to the pain.

Charbonneau thought it was ironic. The man had been found asleep on guard duty before, and was a legal hold in Vietnam for smoking marijuana, but he was responding bravely to his wound.

Finally, word came that helos were coming in to the boat ramp LZ on the river. The wounded were taken there, down a dark road in the rainy mist. Two Sea Knights came in, lights off, flying low from the direction of the Phu Bai, and taking fire. They came in, one at a time, and departed with the wounded. The Alpha captain, although himself a casualty, elected to stay. He returned to the MACV compound with Charbonneau to organize the truckers.

In the morning, they were back to running casualties to the LZ. The choppers came in every now and then, but only took out the most seriously wounded. A grunt, bandaged in four places, hobbled up and waited with them among the palm trees and packed earth. The air officer said another helo was on its way. When Charbonneau saw that it was a U.S. Army chopper that was coming toward them down the Perfume River, he started razzing the air officer. The man responded that with so many Marine choppers having been shot out of the sky, there was no other choice. The chopper landed and the grunt with four bandages was already crammed aboard with the rest, when a lieutenant with a bandage around his head approached to board. The crew chief yanked the grunt out and ushered the lieutenant aboard in his place. Charbonneau locked eyes with the lieutenant for a moment, and he saw a look of: screw the women and children, me first! Mostly it was a look of embarrassment and fear.

The bird flew off. Charbonneau realized he'd just seen a bad example of rank having its privileges: the lieutenant hadn't seemed too badly hurt. The man on the radio said it would be a couple of hours before the next chopper would arrive, and the grunt said he'd wait at the compound instead. Charbonneau offered to get him a ride. The grunt said no thanks and limped away.

Several days later, Lieutenant Charbonneau was ordered by the wounded captain to get back in touch with their battalion. He left in a Navy Mike boat, sharing the ride with some Vietnamese civilians, dead Marines, and the driver's foot in its own body bag.

Up until February 4, Lieutenant Colonel Gravel remained in the MACV compound. He didn't have much choice; his whole battalion in Hue consisted of little more than his staff and the undermanned, bloodied platoons of Alpha 1/1. On February 2, two of his lieutenants — Smith and the Alpha forward observer, Perkins — had tried to rejoin the battalion on the convoy bringing Hotel 2/5. They came under fire across the Phu Cam. One of the trucks hit a hole and Perkins fell off the back ramp, the ammo boxes on the truck sliding out on top of him. He was crushed to death. The other officer, 2d Lt. Ray L. Smith, the leader of Second Platoon, took over Alpha Company from the able leadership of Gunny Canley.

On the morning of the 4th, Gravel decided it was time to get moving.

Their target was the Joan of Arc school and church, only about a hundred yards from the compound. Gravel knew the North Vietnamese were in there in force. On the morning of the 1st, when the refugees had come streaming to MACV, there had been several Vietnamese Catholic nuns among them. Gravel had talked to them in his fractured high-school French. The small women in black and white habits and sandals had said the NVA had invaded their church grounds. There were at least a hundred enemy soldiers, they'd said, quartered in the classrooms and in their living chambers. Going against that force were the two-and-a-half platoons of Alpha, under Smith and Canley.

The Marines moved toward the target and the NVA fire poured down on them. Men were getting hit whenever they went around corners or through doors, and the Marines had to start using C-4 explosives and LAWs to blast holes through the buildings and courtyard walls. It was a laborious effort; progress was slow. Finally, they made it through the enemy fire to the target. The school was a big square complex with a courtyard in the center; the church sat alongside it among the houses and trees.

Lieutenant Smith and Gunny Canley got their men up, pouring fire at the positions. The two ran from point to point, shouting, talking with Gravel on the radio — leading from the front. Corporal Jackson lay with his squad, terrified at all the B-40 rocket explosions whirling shrapnel around them. He'd never heard so many rockets. God, it was a horror show, he thought. Marine mortar fire started pounding in. A couple of shells fell short, went through a roof, and wounded some grunts. To the north, where 2/5 was fighting for the treasury, there was the sound of more battle — then 2/5's tear gas started blowing down over Alpha Company. Guys started choking, the momentum of the attack stalled.

Gravel got on the radio to his friend, Big Ernie Cheatham. "Hold the gas."

"Roger old buddy, sorry about that."

The platoons attacked, rushing into the church, and suddenly grenades were exploding around the lead fireteam. Several Marines were killed or wounded. The grenades had come from the roof — the enemy soldiers were in the rafters!

The Marines scrambled back to their starting point.

Smith got on the radio to Gravel, "What do we do?"

Gravel thought of the gracious Vietnamese nuns who had lived there, but he didn't have much choice. "Take the roof off."

Smith brought a tank up and it started pounding rounds. A recoilless rifle team joined in the cacophony. The church shuddered, tile and wood blowing off the roof, the pillars and windows in front crumbling into a heap of rubble. The enemy in the rafters died. The grunts attacked again, blowing holes through the walls inside, cleaning out the NVA in the classrooms and in the humble cells of the nuns. The enemy fought for every foot. It was a bloody mess. There was no order — just fireteam rushes into rooms, mad firing, bursting grenades. Smoke, shouts, flying plaster, bodies. Then the Marines discovered they had captured one wing of the school, and they exchanged volleys with the NVA across the courtyard. Sergeant Gonzalez, who'd been hit by shrapnel the day before but was still on the line, kicked in the door of one room and rushed in with several Marines from his Third Platoon. There were B-40s flying at them from two windows ahead, and Gonzalez sighted in with some LAW rockets. He fired at least ten rockets, and the NVA positions belched smoke and stopped firing. Gonzalez had saved the day again.

The enemy was gone from the church and school and the Marines moved in. Two grunts had been killed, another twenty wounded.

Corporal Jackson moved into one of the rooms with some of his men. They were getting set when a huge, shuddering explosion shook the adjacent room. The enemy across the street had fired a last, departing B-40. Jackson and several Marines ran into the smoking corridor and rushed into the room. The grill over the window was blown in. Two grunts were down with shrapnel — and Jesus no, Gonzalez was plastered to the floor, his guts hanging out. He must have taken the rocket in his belly. Jackson didn't want to leave him in the rubble — he didn't want the NVA to have a chance to touch his body — so he and a couple of others lifted Gonzalez onto a blown-down door. Then they ran out the back of the school and through a little chapel building where Gravel had set up his hasty CP.

Gravel looked up, aghast. Sergeant Gonzalez, the perfect Marine, was dead. They laid the body out in back of the chapel with the casualties. Two reporters were standing there, taking pictures of the dead and wounded Marines. They talked funny, Jackson thought, maybe they were French. He didn't care. He ran back toward his platoon.

Gravel started moving up to the secured position, when he saw Marines with the two priests who ran the Joan of Arc Church. The priests had been liberated from the NVA. Gravel was surprised they made it through alive — the grunts usually automatically shot anyone wearing black. But they had white faces. One was French, the other Belgian. The priests were furious; one seemed to be in shock from the battle and he screamed at Gravel over the blown-down church.

All Gravel could do was quietly apologize. But he knew there hadn't been any choice. He continued through the rubble and looked up through the shattered roof. The North Vietnamese soldiers were smashed in the wooden eaves — they were hanging there like spaghetti, Gravel thought. It had been a long, costly afternoon. And Sergeant Gonzalez had been a fine, caring man.

In the afternoon, while the two-and-a-half platoons of Alpha were fighting around the Joan of Arc School, the rest of First Platoon, which had been stranded at Quang Tri, made it to Phu Bai. There they joined Bravo Company 1/1 and were put on a convoy going up Highway 1.

Sitting in one of the trucks, which was loaded with so much ammo he could barely stand up, was Lance Cpl. Edward F. Neas of the First Platoon machine gun section. If there were such a thing as the typical Marine infantryman of the Vietnam War, Neas would have fit the bill. He was a tough, dark-haired nineteen-year-old from Queens. He had dropped out of school at sixteen because he was tired of hassles with his parents; joined the Marines the day he turned seventeen; and volunteered for Vietnam the day he turned eighteen because he wanted a piece of the action. He had the eagle, globe, and anchor tattooed on one biceps, and the initials D.T.K. (Down to Kill) on the back of his flak jacket. He hated the NVA because they were the ones shooting at him and his buddies, and he did his best in combat because he was a Marine. And when they pulled to the rear, he turned up the oldies on the radio and drank some beer and smoked some grass with his friends.

Near the Phu Cam Canal, the convoy ran past U.S.-made tanks, destroyed and crashed into buildings, the cannon blown off one and lying beside it. It looked like they'd been hit by B-40s. Neas and the rest quieted down, tensed up, and stared outboard, weapons ready. Suddenly there were explosions, then the crack of small-arms fire from the buildings. The Marines shot back, and the truckers hit top speed, Neas thinking they were going on two wheels when they made the turn towards MACV. They pulled into the compound, piled out of the trucks, and stood spread out along the compound walls. All around the compound were North Vietnamese dead, draped over fences, sprawled on courtyards, twisted in barbed wire, getting stiff and bloated.

Jesus, Neas thought, it was like a damn movie.

Then they got the word: Captain Batcheller was seriously wounded, Lieutenant Perkins was dead, Sergeant Gonzalez was dead, Doc Brooklyn was dead. Neas was in shock; the enemy had blown away some of their best people. But, he consoled himself, at least they still had Gunny Canley, shrapnel wounds and all.

Only six weeks before, the company had been making an attack on an NVA trenchline at Con Thien. Neas was crouched behind a tank as they moved forward, taking AC and mortar fire. One of his machine gunners took a burst in the chest. The corpsman ran for him, got shot in the butt, and fell in the open. Then, Neas saw Canley run past him, pick up the wounded corpsman like a rag doll, and come storming back like an unshakeable redwood tree, taking fire the entire time and not receiving a scratch.

Neas had a lot of faith in the people running 1st Platoon. The lieutenant, William R. Donnelly, was a wiry, blond guy, just commissioned from Annapolis. Because Neas and the other eighteen-and nineteen-year-old grunts thought he was young looking, they nicknamed him The Kid. And then there was the platoon sergeant, Sgt. Josef Burghardt, twenty-one years old, stocky, handsome, and bright. He had emigrated to America from Yugoslavia when he was five, and hoped to make his career in the Marine Corps. He had a big USMC emblem tattooed on one biceps. He'd been to Vietnam before, a 1966-67 tour with the 9th Marines. He'd been awarded a Bronze Star for, as he put it, "a bunch of little crap," — which included getting his fireteam out of a Viet Cong ambush after taking a shrapnel wound.

Neas liked Burghardt; he was a good Marine, a friend, the kind of guy you could trust with your life. And that's exactly what the men in First Platoon had to do.

Lieutenant Donnelly and Sergeant Burghardt didn't have much time to rest after getting their people organized inside MACV. The lieutenant was instructed to take his platoon, a platoon from Bravo Company, and two Dusters, and recover the bodies of two Marines killed east of the compound, around the Hue stadium. They had been left lying in the streets. (The Marine Corps has a tradition that none of its dead will be left behind.)

The Marines moved out, winding down the streets and alleys, no one sure what to expect. They'd never fought in a city before, and everyone was keyed up. Suddenly there was movement up front; some Vietnamese popped out of a ditch to one side of the road. In an instant, the two Marines on point dropped to their knees and opened up, the lead Duster opened up, and the figures were mowed down. When the Marines moved up, they found a puzzling scene. Crumpled at the bottom of the ditch and on the road were the bodies of several Vietnamese in civilian clothes. They might have been NVA infiltrators in disguise (1/1 had had some problems with that), or they might have simply been refugees trying to surrender.

Few of the grunts could have cared less either way.

The patrol kept going, and then an AK erupted ahead of them. At the first shot, Burghardt and Neas threw themselves belly-flat beside the lead Duster. The Duster swung toward a little house sitting in a paddy and pummelled it. The house blew apart. More fire came in, and Neas shouted at his machine gun team to set up and put out rounds. The whole line came alive with fire, and Lieutenant Donnelly quickly led them to cover in buildings nearby.

Somebody spotted the bodies they'd come to recover and four grunts ran out to get them. There was another abrupt explosion of AK-47s and B-40s, and three of the would-be rescuers went down in the street, wounded. Rushing toward them went Donnelly and 1st Sgt. James R. Bresnahan and HM2 Glen J. Dagley, both of Bravo Company. The grunts fired furiously to cover them. Enemy fire was raking around them from positions a mere fifty yards away. Donnelly took some rocket shrapnel, but the three grunts kept ducking and running and they managed to drag all the wounded with them to cover.

The platoons gathered their casualties and shot their way back down the street. From MACV, Lieutenant Donnelly took his platoon west to join the remainder of the company. They set up in a large building, and Donnelly discovered he was ahead of the line. He got on the radio with Lieutenant Smith, who wanted him to pull back. But it was already nighttime and it would be too risky to move in the dark. So the platoon holed up. There were only nineteen men left. Donnelly radioed Smith to plot the 60mm mortars on top of their heads. Just in case.

Sergeant Burghardt spent the night staring out a window at the paddies and treelines on their flank. An occasional flare burst overhead and came floating down on its parachute, lighting the streets and the water-filled fields in its glare. Right there, visible through the window, were the NVA — dozens and dozens of them, moving across the far side of the paddy field like ants, headed east toward the South China Sea. They were out of rifle range, but no artillery or mortar fire was called on them. Something about civilians or not hurting the buildings; Burghardt had heard something like that. And all it would have taken, he knew, were some artillery fire missions or one Spooky gunship with the Gatling guns that fired six thousand rounds a minute. The North Vietnamese moved — unharmed — throughout the night, carrying their dead and wounded out, and supplies in. It was stupid, Burghardt thought, absolutely pathetic.

Colonel Hughes was in the MACV compound that night, when another mortar raid hit. Later on, word came that the An Cuu Bridge over the Phu Cam Canal had finally been dropped by enemy sappers. In effect, the overland route between Phu Bai and Hue was cut. (There were other bridges toward the west, where the canal branched from the Perfume River, but they were in enemy hands). That was bad news, but unfortunately for the enemy, they had taken too long to do it. It had been a major flaw in their operation. The bridge had allowed A/1/1 and G/2/5 to get in on the first day, thus saving the compound and establishing a foothold for the U.S. counterattack. It had allowed more troops and supplies to get in; by the time the NVA blew the bridge up, there were five Marine infantry companies on the South Side. Considering the situation the North Vietnamese had allowed themselves to get into, Gravel finally had reason to smile.

The next morning, Monday, February 5, Alpha and Bravo Companies started moving to take the next houses along the paddy. Lance Corporal Neas ran across an alley with his machine gun team and opened up into the windows of the buildings in front of them. NVA fire poured back.

Sergeant Burghardt was still in the large building with Cpl. Norris Brennan, the machine gun squad leader, firing across the road. Burghardt got on the radio to Donnelly and said they needed some supporting fire. He told Brennan to stay away from the windows until they could get a tank or something up, then took off into the corridor.

He'd only gone a few steps when he heard Brennan start shooting again. Then there was the clatter of equipment hitting the floor. Burghardt sprinted back to the room. Brennan was a lump, his M-16 shot out of his hands, the charging handle of the rifle blown into his face, blood gushing out.

Neas was still firing from his window perch when he saw several Marines hustling by on the road below, carrying a body on a door. It was Brennan, his head wrapped in bloody bandages. Corporal Brennan had six weeks to go before he was due to rotate home. He bled to death.

That meant Lance Corporal Neas was now the squad leader.

In a few minutes, a tank came clanking up the street. It stopped, the turret turned slowly towards the house the NVA were in, and the tank blew hell out of it. The 90mm flash-boomed, the commander strafed the windows with the powerful fifty, and the plaster and brick flew, the smoke billowed. The enemy started bolting from the back door, wide-eyed with panic, not firing, just trying to escape across the courtyard. Burghardt ran to a second-floor window. The NVA were scrambling about seventy-five yards away. Some were jerking and falling in the fire. Others were getting away over the courtyard wall. He opened up from the window, but he couldn't tell if he was hitting a thing.

Finally he calmed down and swung his M-16 towards the back door where the NVA were running from. A North Vietnamese popped out. Burghardt fired. He went tumbling dead into the courtyard. Another NVA rushed out. Burghardt killed him. Then another. And another.

In a few moments, it was all over. The Marines peered down from the windows. They could see nine dead NVA lying so close their comrades couldn't drag the bodies away. Gravel was proud; the North Vietnamese soldiers were simply unable to match the teamwork and firepower of his young Marines. The battalion consolidated in the evening with another seventy-five yards regained.

Wounded Marines were constantly hobbling or being carried into the MACV aid station. During a lull, Dr. Hamilton went over to Colonel Hughes' CP. He was standing there when a message was handed to Hughes: some Marines had spotted a group of NVA in a pagoda and wanted permission to mortar it. Hughes followed the Rules of Engagement for Hue. His request was radioed to General LaHue's Task Force X-RAY in Phu Bai, relayed from there to General Robertson's 1st Marine Division staff at Da Nang, and then passed to General Cushman's nearby III MAF staff. Two hours later, Hughes received word that the pagoda could be attacked, but only by direct fire weapons so as to minimize damage to it and the surrounding structures. By the time the Marines got a recoilless rifle into position, the North Vietnamese were gone.

Daylight, February 6. Sergeant Burghardt was upstairs in the large building, when he heard shouts that there were NVA soldiers right out back. He ran to the window and looked down. There they were — one VC and two NVA crouched among the palm trees in a courtyard, silently sitting and watching the Marine positions. They didn't know they'd been spotted. Burghardt brought up his rifle but couldn't see through the palm leaves around them. He went downstairs, then jogged down a wing of the building and stopped at another window. He had a clear shot, they were just sitting there with their backs to him. He rested the M-16 butt against his shoulder, slowly and calmly aimed, and fired. One North Vietnamese spun against the trees. Another shot. The second NVA flopped back in turn.

The rest of the platoon opened up. The enemy and trees were shredded.

They must not have gotten all the NVA in the area, though. A little later, Burghardt was downstairs talking with Lieutenant Donnelly, when something came exploding through the wall behind them. The two Marines stood there, ears ringing, shaking the dust off and wiping the blood from the backs of their necks. The shrapnel had dug into the back of their flak jackets and helmets. Burghardt made a souvenir of an LAAW tail fin from the entrance blast; the NVA had used one of their own rockets on them.

It was the second Purple Heart for both men. Neither was evacuated.

During that first week of street fighting, 1/1 accomplished one of its happier assignments in the Hue battle. From the first day, Gravel had been in radio contact with a half-dozen U.S. Air Force pilots of the Cat Killer team, who were quartered near the MACV and surrounded by the North Vietnamese. They were holed up in their house, with claymores wired around them, waiting for rescue. Every time Alpha or Bravo closed in toward the building, heavy fire blocked them. The Cat Killer people had a map and they kept Gravel informed on the NVA around them. Whenever the North Vietnamese began to stir around them or fire on their house, they radioed Gravel and pinpointed the positions. Then 1/1 would lob in a few CS mortar shells to drive the NVA into the open, and pound in with HE. In a few days, the Air Force team's radio batteries began to run down, and Gravel told them only to call in every few hours to report their status. Another day went by and all they could hear from the team was a barely audible whisper; Gravel told them to keep in touch by clicking their radio handset. The USAF tried to parachute batteries to them, but missed the mark. Finally, 1/1 retook the house and the Air Force team was back in friendly hands. The experience formed a special bond between 1/1 and the Cat Killer team. After Hue, the pilots went out of their way to help Gravel's grunts.

MACV Compound, South Side. Courtesy of Terry Charbonneau

Hwy. 1 leading into South Side. Note destroyed command jeep. Courtesy of Jim Soukup

Main bridge connecting north and south Hue at Hwy. 1. Courtesy of Jim Soukup

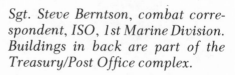

Sgt. Steve Berntson, combat correspondent, ISO, 1st Marine Division. Buildings in back are part of the Treasury/Post Office complex.

Inside MACV Compound, South Side, February 5, 1968. Marine Corps photo: courtesy of Richard Lyons

M–60 machine gunner from 1/1 goes for cover. Note tanks and trucks behind him, and UPI photographer. South Side, February 5, 1968. Photo: Bill Dickman; courtesy of Richard Lyons

Refugees. Marine Corps photo: S. Sgt. J. L. Harlan

Marine firing from window near the university, South Side. Marine
Corps photo: Bill Dickman

Gunnery Sgt. Thomas, H Company 2/5, finds humor in a toy car during Battle of Hue. Marine Corps photo: Sgt. Bill Dickman

Sgt. Dale Dye (far right) and USMC combat correspondent of ISO, 1st Marine Division, at Danang, celebrating being alive.

Marines of 1st Platoon, Hotel Company, 2/5, charging through garage gate toward province capitol, February 6, 1968. Photo: Bill Dickman

A 106mm recoilless rifle position, South Side, February 2, 1968. Marine Corps photo: Bill Dickman

Lt. Col. Marcus Gravel, CO of 1/1.
Courtesy of M. J. Gravel

Lt. Col. Marcus J. Gravel with nuns of Joan of Arc School in front of their chapel. Courtesy of M. J. Gravel

A priest and Gravel. Note 90mm shell holes and intact crucifix. Courtesy of M. J. Gravel

Joan of Arc Cathedral, after the battle. Courtesy of M. J. Gravel

Marines taking cover in courtyard of a home, South Side. Photo: Bill Dickman

Marine hit by sniper, being evacuated in a poncho. They are moving through a hole blasted in courtyard wall. South Side. Photo: Bill Dickman

A resupply convoy, led by an Ontos, under Gunnery Sergeant Thomas (fifth man from left). Marines are from Hotel Company 2/5. Courtesy of Bill Dickman

U.S. Army Huey evacuating wounded Marines from LZ on South Side. Note Perfume River in background. Courtesy of Terry Charbonneau

Lt. Ray L. Smith, CO of Alpha 1/1, after Joan of Arc fight. Courtesy of M. J. Gravel

Grunts of Hotel Company 2/5, moments after raising the Stars and Stripes over the province capitol, South Side, February 6, 1968.
Photo: Bill Dickman

Team led by Maj. Ralph Salvati, 2/5, setting up teargas launcher to support attack on the capitol, South Side. Photo: Bill Dickman

Marines of Delta Company, 1/5, along northeast wall of Citadel. Photo: Steve Berntson

Chapter 5

"Stars and Stripes" on the Capitol

The day after securing the treasury complex, 2/5 seized the Cercle Sportif, the Hue university library, and the city hospital. The records show thirty-eight Marines wounded, while sixty-six NVA were killed, and another thirty wounded Communists were captured in the hospital. The next major objective for the battalion was the Thua Thien Province capital. Captain Ron Christmas, whose Hotel Company had been assigned to take it, had some real tactical problems. The capitol building itself was a large, two-story construction of French design; the top floor was a good vantage point for the NVA to fire from into the street. The capitol compound was surrounded by an eight-foot high wall with firing slits at the top. Christmas had no idea what might be behind that wall.

But the young captain had one major advantage — his men wanted the building. On their first day in Hue, the enemy had raised a gold-starred communist banner on the flagpole in the capitol courtyard. It was constantly in sight over the roof tops, and the company gunny, Frank Thomas, echoed many grunts' thoughts when he said that they "were bound and determined to take down that North Vietnamese flag. . ." On Tuesday, February 6, they did.

They got going in the early afternoon on February 6th, accompanied by literally a squad of newsmen, including Don Webster of CBS-TV and his two-man Vietnamese film crew; and the team of Sergeants

73

Berntson and Dye, plus Sgt. Bill Dickman and Sgt. Paul Thompson. The grunts moved forward, winding past blown-down palm trees and a couple of burning hootches, until they got into a large, tree-dotted courtyard. Behind them was a large, one-story building. To their right was Le Loi Street and the Perfume River. At the end of the courtyard was a row of low garages, facing the next street. And right across that street was the capitol. The grunts moved across the grass, hunched low, toward the garages with the NVA fire filling the air.

When the shooting started, Major Salvati took his driver and the two young Marines with the 3.5-inch rocket launcher, and worked his way through the secured hospital complex. The place was deserted except for one long ward, filled with people lying in beds. They were very old and frozen motionless; Salvati figured they were dead. The Marines set up at the end of the ward, found a window facing the capitol, and sighted in with the 3.5. The gunner fired, and as the back blast roared down the corridor, the beds went skidding away, crashing into a corner. The Marines watched, astonished, as the old people in the beds suddenly came to life, slowly climbed out of the wreckage, and disappeared out the door.

They fired some more. Salvati contacted Cheatham, brought up some more E-8 launchers, and fired them toward the capitol. He was hoping for a repeat of the success they had had at the treasury. This time, the cold wind simply blew the tear gas away.

Captain Christmas stood on the lawn of the bullet-pocked house, his M-16 slung over his shoulder, talking calmly on the radio. He was a young man, but his face was haggard and stubbled, and when he talked, he sounded very tired. It was day five for him and his company in Hue. Around him were his two young radiomen and the reporters. Gunny Thomas stood nearby, his pump shotgun over his shoulder like a tramp's stick. He radioed Cheatham for something to soften up the target.

Soon a lieutenant drove up in an Ontos. He came up Le Loi on Hotel's right flank, and stopped along the courtyard wall. The capitol was on the left across the intersection, and to get a clear shot, they would be obliged to drive past the wall and partially into the open street. That's exactly what they did. The Ontos poked its nose beyond the wall and opened up with the 106s. Three rounds blew up in the capitol — then the North Vietnamese zeroed in.

Christmas's CP group was still standing in the courtyard when the shell whooshed from somewhere down the street. There was an explosion, a terrific clang of metal against metal. The radiomen and grunts crouched and grimaced, looking for a moment like frightened children beside the older Christmas and Thomas, who did not move at all. A flurry of M-16 fire broke out ahead. A few seconds later, a young voice boomed, "Corpsman!"

Gunny Thomas and several Marines jogged forward. The lieutenant and his three Ontos crewmen were behind the garage walls, all of them wounded or rattled by the concussion. Thomas dropped his shotgun and kneeled beside the man who'd been hit the worst, a young kid, his helmet gone, lying belly down in the grass. He rolled him onto his back. The man mumbled weakly and pointed to his eye. There was a sliver of shrapnel in it.

Thomas looked back toward the CP. "Medic, corpsman up here!"

They got the wounded man behind a bullet-scarred wall, out of the way of the shooting still cracking from the capitol. A corpsman worked his way to them. He gingerly wrapped a bandage around the kid's face, the white of the bandage startling against the dirt and grime. The bandage covered the man's eyes, and he started to whimper, "I'm hit, I'm hit."

Up ahead, the NVA were still spraying rounds over the garage rooftops. Christmas decided to give it a try, and ordered First Platoon to attack.

The First Platoon leader, Lt. Leo Myers, was a young man with glasses and a mustache. He and his grunts huddled outside the garage buildings, waiting for the word to go. They were to rush through a pair of iron gates into the street facing the capitol. The gate was in the open and Gunny Thomas was concerned that the men would get hit simply trying to open it up. He made his way to the corner behind the gates, found a red brick in the junk there, and tied it to the frayed end of a length of rope. A couple of throws with the brick over the gates and he got them pulled open and tied down.

Lieutenant Myers, holding an M-16, waved his men on and they went sprinting through the gates in single file, all of them wearing gas masks. Sergeants Berntson and Dye and Maj. Aloysius McGonigal, an Army chaplain, fell in with the assault platoon. Dye was terrified — the gas masks were hot, stifling, and he couldn't see a damn thing.

Firing began again. The Marines got across the street and tried to take cover against the capitol courtyard wall and the trees along the sidewalk. The NVA put fire over their heads; the grunts couldn't move. Christmas called up a tank for fire support. One came rumbling up, and he ran to it. He unhooked the radio on the back of the tank, crouched down for cover, and directed its 90mm firepower. Explosions tore through the capitol building. A B-40 suddenly blew up on the front of the tank, spraying shrapnel. Another rocket burst against it. Christmas was unscathed. The tank kept firing.

The 81mm mortars at the battalion CP began dropping rounds in. Major Salvati and his crew laid down another salvo from the E-8, and this time the tear gas landed on target. The NVA fire lessened, and Christmas was back on the radio to Myers — Go! The platoon blew a hole in the courtyard wall, and charged in, doubled up under their helmets, flak jackets, and gear. They crouched behind the trees and a low stone wall in the courtyard, then darted two or three at a time toward the main building. The front door was blown open, grenades tossed in, and the grunts went in firing. AK fire erupted from within and the first two Marines through the door were gunned down. Amid all the firing, Father McGonigal rushed forward and lay beside the dying men, giving them last rites. The rest of the Marines threw more grenades. The NVA began falling back. Fire poured after them.

Second Platoon, under Staff Sgt. John Miller, and Third Platoon, under Lt. Mike Lambert, moved across the street, along with Christmas, Thomas, and the CP group. The first thing Gunny Thomas and another grunt did was to run to the flagpole and tear down that North Vietnamese flag.

The compound was secured and the Marines stood there, exhausted, leaning against the buildings, talking in weary, clipped sentences. Gunny Thomas balanced his shotgun between his knees, unzipped his flak jacket, and pulled out — an American flag. To the grunts, it was a beautiful sight.

Before the attack had gotten under way, Cheatham and Christmas had discussed raising the colors. According to South Vietnamese law, no U.S. flag was allowed to be flown over RVN soil without an accompanying red and yellow government flag, since the Americans were considered guests in the country. But no one really wanted to put up the Vietnamese flag — it was the Marines, their buddies, who were getting killed in the streets, not the ARVN. The colonel and the captain were proud of their men, so the rules were not to be observed on this occasion.

"We're not authorized to fly the U.S. flag," Cheatham said, "but go ahead and run it up before anyone tells us not to. We're doing the fighting, we may as well have our flag get the credit. I want those NVA guys across the river to see this."

Gunny Thomas had been a recruiter before arriving in Vietnam, and had mentioned to Christmas how he used to raise the flag every morning at his home. When the skipper told Thomas they had permission, the gunny quickly sent some of his best scroungers out to find a flag. They came back empty-handed. He sent them out again, with instructions not to come back without one. They found one; someone said they'd stolen it off the flagpole in the MACV compound. Thomas didn't care where they got it. He folded the flag and went into the battle with the colors tucked inside his jacket.

Thomas, a family man from Camden, New Jersey, looked like a Marine gunny — lean and wiry, and stolid, he wore a crew cut, and had a dragon tattoo down one forearm and a huge bulldog on his biceps. But, in seventeen years in the Corps, he had never been in a war. Hue was his first battle, and the province capitol was his moment of glory.

Captain Christmas turned to Gunny Thomas and shouted, "Let's go!" It was a little past four in the afternoon. Thomas ran to the flagpole and grabbed the lanyards. Firing popped from outside the courtyard walls. Two of Lieutenant Myers' nineteen-year-old PFCs, Walter R. Kaczmarek and Alan V. McDonald, helped the gunny. The CBS crew and the USMC photographers knelt in the grass, filming the event. Thomas hoisted the Stars and Stripes amid spontaneous shouts and cheers from the Marines. Christmas was wiping away tears. They'd done it! Webster, the CBS reporter, described it on television: "There was no bugler and the other Marines were too busy to salute, but not often is a flag so proudly raised."

Back at the battalion CP, Cheatham got the word, then contacted Colonel Hughes' staff at the MACV compound. "Be advised," he said. "We have taken the province headquarters, and somehow or other, an American flag is flying above it."

Thomas and McDonald and Kaczmarek and Myers and a couple of other grunts lined up at the base of the flagpole, holding up their trophy — the NVA flag — for the photographers. The Marines were filthy and exhausted, unshaven, cold, laden with equipment — but for one of the first times since they got to Hue, they were laughing and smiling.

Gunny Thomas, with his shotgun back over his shoulder, yelled to the CBS crew as they panned over them. "We're hungry, hard Hotel Company!" Some laughs. "Keep it!"

One of the grunts shouted at the cameraman, "Are you finished? We want to get the hell out!" More laughs.

Thomas drifted away from the jostling crowd around the flagpole, and sighed in relief. He had felt "proud, happy, scared" raising the colors, and now his emotions welled up. Tears brimmed in his eyes. He walked alone to the courtyard wall to collect himself — then suddenly stopped dead in his tracks. There, not more than a yard away, crouching in a spider hole at the base of the wall, was a North Vietnamese soldier with an AK-47 between his knees. Their eyes met.

Thomas swung down his shotgun and pumped a round. The man sagged in his hole.

He hauled the body out, and shouted back at the Marines, "Check the holes! Check these holes over here!" There were a half-dozen other spider holes along the wall. PFC McDonald and his fireteam jogged up, then started walking down the line, putting quick, perfunctory bursts into each one. In a few minutes, it was done; the NVA hadn't fired one shot in defense. The Marines yanked six dead or dying NVA from the holes and threw their weapons next to their bodies.

One North Vietnamese survived. He was a young, barefoot soldier who had been quick enough to raise his hands out of his hole in surrender before the Marines had a chance to shoot him. Two radiomen, one black, one white, dragged him away by his wrists.

A short time after securing the capitol, Christmas was radioed by an Army colonel at MACV ordering him to conform to the law and lower the American flag. He didn't. A little later, two Army captains showed up and told him they were there to supervise the removal of the flag. Christmas said simply that if they really wanted it down that badly, they could do it themselves, but he could not guarantee what his grunts would do.

The grunts were standing back watching their skipper deal with the two captains. They were aghast that they had come to take down the flag. Their dead hadn't even been evacuated, they were still exchanging shots with the NVA across the courtyard wall, and here come these two bastards worried about protocol. Marines were mumbling, "I can't believe it," and cursing out the damn lifers and the damn Army fish. Gunny Thomas was trying to calm them down. But Pfc. Kaczmarek locked and loaded his M-60 and mumbled bitterly to Berntson, "If one of them doggie sons of bitches touches that flag, I'll blow 'em away."

The two captains departed empty-handed.

Finally, a Marine officer at MACV got on the horn, and Christmas agreed to take the flag down when they left the compound.

In the morning — after a nighttime mortar raid — they saddled up to move out. Several Marines lowered the flag, but they flew nothing in its place. Said one lieutenant to a civilian reporter, "If we can't fly the American flag, we aren't putting anyone's on that pole." With that, Gunny Thomas folded the flag, put it in his pack, and he and the rest of the grunts of Hotel Company pushed out into the next rubble-strewn row of houses.

As Don Webster of CBS reported: "Right now this province head-quarters is the front line, and they're holding an assault, much like those that made them famous in other wars; and to a great extent this assault is being won or lost on the basis of sheer courage. And there's no shortage of that in the Marines."

Chapter 6

From MACV to Phu Cam

Position South Side Consolidated

After Hotel Company 2/5 secured the province capitol on February 6, it was discovered to have been the North Vietnamese command post. Found were weapons, gear, maps, payroll receipts, and other such documents. Lieutenant Colonel Cheatham told reporters, "When we took the province headquarters, we broke their back. That was the tough one. We are meeting only scattered resistance now."

The colonel was being a bit too enthusiastic (not as enthusiastic as high command, however, which declared the South Side secured on February 10), but basically he was right. The first week had been it for the NVA/VC on the South Side. For 2/5, it had been the taking of the treasury and capitol buildings that firmed up their position. For 1/1, it had been the securing of MACV and the bloody two days of fighting around the Joan of Arc school. After that, the ball was rolling for the Marines. With 2/5 along the Perfume River and 1/1 farther south on the Phu Cam Canal, they pushed forward on line, driving continuously west toward where the canal swung north to meet the river. After that first week, the Marines never took another step backward. They pressed on, to the next house, the next block, consolidating at night, then up again at daylight and on to the next house. Enemy resistance weakened. They didn't fight for every room of every house as before, but turned more to sniper, mortar, and rocket attacks.

With the intensity of the battle waning, there was time to reflect. One of the major gripes among enlisted men in some units — and one of the sadder reflections on the officer corps — was that officers were leading from their armchairs. Often cited were company commanders issuing orders to their platoons from underground bunkers back at basecamp, and battalion commanders logging their combat time by swooping over firefights in helicopters thousands of feet above the shooting. There were no such discrepancies in Hue. The Marine officers were up front with their grunts throughout the fight, as the casualty rate among the captains and lieutenants would show. Even the battalion commanders who had seen little action because the short, sporadic firefights of the paddy war were almost always over by the time they arrived — were leading from the front. Both Cheatham and Gravel saw their share of action, and were noted for moving along with their troops during the heaviest fighting. Cheatham, in particular, won high praise. Reporters on the scene tended to gravitate to 2/5 and wrote highly of his bravery. His executive officer, Major Salvati, was later to say, "Of all the people I've known in my career in the Marine Corps, I would venture to say that Colonel Cheatham is probably the finest leader I've had the opportunity of serving with, and serving under. His leadership was dynamic. The first few days of the battle, he exposed himself to enemy fire on several occasions to point out targets which the troops could take under fire. He was leading his battalion in the best tradition of a Marine officer."

In Hue, there was a good deal of pride in the fact that despite all the hit-and-miss patrols, frustration, and stagnation of An Hoa, the Marines were winning in a real, brutal battle with North Vietnamese regulars. As Captain Christmas told a reporter, "It's a squad leader's war, this kind of fighting." And the young Marines were responding magnificently. Said Major Salvati, "The Marines that we had in Hue City had come, by and large, from having fought down at An Hoa. It was just a Marine combat base out in Indian Country; we were pretty much isolated. Most of our time was spent patrolling. More often than not, if you patrolled along the roads, you got ambushed, and if you patrolled off the roads, you got booby-trapped. These Marines were not used to any major confrontation with the NVA. Morale was difficult. But, in Hue, I observed some of the finest fighting men in the world. These youngsters knew how to fight. They learned; from each day you could tell how they improved in what they were doing. They learned how to fire and maneuver, how to cover each other, how to employ Willy Peter white phosphorous detonations. Individuals who were wounded refused evacuation, so many of them, because they felt they were accomplishing something. They had the opportunity of engaging the enemy in a nose-to-nose confrontation — and they were winning. It was a thrill to me, just to watch these young Marines perform as they could."

Still, the battle was far from over. While substantial gains had been made, and the enemy was putting up less of a fight, there were still enough NVA left to make "mop-up" the wrong term. The firefights were just as vicious when they happened, and just because resistance was weakening didn't mean men stopped being killed or maimed or wounded. It just happened less frequently. And for the individual grunt on the ground, the guy with only his M-16 and wits to keep him alive, the battle didn't seem to drop off. They were still out there every day in the streets. No slack.

Sergeant Burghardt was with his platoon in what looked to be a hospital. They were getting geared up to go across the open field in front of them to the next row of buildings. Two point men started across. They ran past a trench in the field — then there was the sudden clacking of AK-47s, and the two Marines fell wounded to the ground.

Burghardt saw it from the window, then shouted over to two corpsmen crouched inside with them. He told one of them to get out there and get them.

The corpsman he told to move was short — due to rotate home in a couple of weeks. He balked.

Burghardt got angry and snapped, "You damn coward!" Burghardt himself took off out the door. He sprinted across the grass, and went tumbling down into the ditch. Fire cracked over his head. He reached out, grabbed one of the wounded, and dragged him down in the ditch with him. By the time Burghardt was going for the second man, the enemy fire had died down. The platoon came across and got them.

Lieutenant Colonel Gravel was with Alpha Company as they moved down another street. The point reached an intersection near the Nationalist Chinese Consulate, and the NVA started dropping mortars on them. Shrapnel scudded into the brick walls, and everyone dove for cover, hugging curbs and anything else to escape the flying metal. Gravel glanced around, and there was Gunny Canley — just standing there amid the explosions. He leaned with his foot propped against a streetlight pole, his rifle looking like a baton in his hands, shouting orders in the din, completely oblivious to the danger. My God, Gravel marvelled, Gunny is waiting for a bus. He'd never see the equal of J. L. Canley.

In their retreat, the NVA had left one of their younger, chubbier comrades chained in a building with a rifle with which to delay the Marine advance. The soldier proved less than enthusiastic about his mission, and quickly surrendered to some 2/5 grunts sweeping through the area. They turned him over to a gunny sergeant in Intelligence. But the grunts were bitter over their casualties, and started seriously talking about beating or killing the prisoner who was tied up. The gunny stepped in, "Hey, this kid is terrified. He's more scared than you are. You think you're going to be a big man by hurting him?" The grunts sort of shuffled their feet and backed down mumbling, "Aw, shit, he ain't worth it." Sergeant Dickman, the Marine photographer, took a picture of the gunny sergeant holding the bound prisoner; he was mightily impressed by how the man had used simple psychology to avert a potentially murderous situation.

The refugees were streaming out of the houses, coming back towards the Marine lines. Corporal Soukup and the grunts his squad had attached themselves to were detaining the refugees, grabbing the old men and the mothers clutching their babies, checking IDs, looking for infiltrating VC, shaking them down for weapons. Everyone was checking out okay and being directed back to the MACV compound, where the advisors and ARVN were set up to handle the thousands of newly homeless.

An old papa-san and a young boy started edging away, going across a courtyard in front of the Marines. Soukup saw the two and shouted at them to come in. They started running.

Soukup snatched up his M-16 and loosed off a burst. The kid fell forward, then got back up, crawling on his hands and knees. The old man ran back toward the boy, the other Marines all opened up, and the papa-san fell too, riddled. Someone popped an M-79 grenade, it sprayed the kid, and he lay motionless. When they moved up to check the bodies, they couldn't find any ID cards. They rolled the man over and found an RPG round tucked under his shirt. The Marines weren't sure what the old man had been up to. He must have been a communist sympathizer and been trying to get ammunition to them. Maybe he'd brought the kid along to look innocent.

In the wake of the Marine push, there arose other problems besides combat that had to be dealt with: destroyed homes, refugees, and the dead. The American MACV advisors were delegated to handle the problem and, as it turned out, one of the major stumbling blocks came from the South Vietnamese themselves. Lt. Col. Pham Van Khoa — the Thua Thien Province chief, mayor of Hue, and ARVN overseer of the Hue district — should have been the candidate for leadership in the mop-up problems. Unfortunately, he was not.

For the first five days of the battle, Khoa was trapped behind enemy lines and forced to hide out with his bodyguard. Then, on February 5, Fox Company 2/5 found him. There was a brief firefight, several NVA were killed in a building, and when Captain Downs came in, he found one of his staff sergeants (the acting Second Platoon leader) with two Vietnamese spread-eagled against the wall. "Skipper," the sergeant said, "this silly son of a bitch is trying to tell me he's the mayor of Hue." Downs checked it out and the prisoner's assertion proved true. The Marines gave Khoa some candy and water and sent him back to battalion.

The events of the invasion appeared to have been too much for Khoa. He was meek, unable to cope, and overwrought with worry about his family, still hiding someplace in enemy-controlled Hue. When Golf Company 2/5 finally did uncover the family around the 10th of February, Khoa began to function, but he still didn't have it in him to assert the necessary control. There were numbers of ARVN soldiers milling around MACV — they had been on leave when Tet started and were thus cut off from their units — but when an Army advisor suggested they be put to use, Khoa balked, saying he had no authority over them.

Whether or not the mayor of Hue had the stamina to deal directly with the problems, they could not be ignored. To handle the refugee problem, Maj. Jack E. Walker, a U.S. Army CORDS officer from Baltimore, was selected. For support, a platoon from the 29th Civil Affairs Company, U.S. Army, was sent up from Da Nang. One of the more grisly tasks they had to perform was the removal of the dead. Many NVA killed by the Marines lay where they'd fallen. Civilian dead were sprawled in rubbled homes and courtyards. Bodies had begun to bloat, fester, and attract rats; the health problem was serious. With a detail provided by the Hue police chief, Walker had planned to dig mass graves, but the Vietnamese objected to such practice and refused to touch the bodies. So, with another detail of enemy prisoners manning the shovels, they started the back-breaking process of digging individual graves for each body they came across. The dead were buried where they were found.

Turning to the living, Major Walker made an inexact head-count and found there were five thousand refugees gathered at the Catholic Church (where the Vietnamese priests had them well organized), and another seventeen thousand swarming around the university. Walker and his team had twenty-two thousand people to care for, but there was a shortage of food and medical supplies, and neither utilities nor sanitation was available. He went to Khoa to get food for the civilians, and was told there was a two-month supply of rice stored in twenty-five warehouses in the city. Such a supply was provided by the RVN government, and was required to be in stock to feed the populace in case of emergency. When Walker tried to collect the rice, he couldn't find it. (He was never able to find out who had taken it, but he did notice that those refugees with money were always able to get their share of rice. One correspondent reported the black-market price for a kilo of rice soared from twenty cents to four dollars.) Walker sent an emergency request to I Corps headquarters in Da Nang for an issue of rice, and before long, they were supplying 380 bags per day. There were still a few problems: when twenty-one sides of pork arrived for the refugees, Walker received them through Khoa and his officials, and by then, six sides had disappeared. Despite such commandeering, no refugees went hungry.

At the Hue hospital, Walker was confronted with a more serious problem. Among the refugees, scores had been wounded, people were dying, and there was little medical care. Sanitation problems were severe, with people defecating where they slept and bodies rotting where they fell. With the help of U.S. civilians from the I Corps Public Health Office and an Australian MD, a Dr. Froweys, the dead were removed from the hospital grounds, burial details were organized, and the facility was cleaned up. Vietnamese doctors and nurses in the city arrived to help, a U.S. medical team from the Navy was sent in, and the refugees were innoculated and the hospital opened for patients.

Considering the battle environment and the pressures on everyone involved, things functioned as smoothly as could be expected. Still, ARVN leadership in Hue was lacking. Asked by an Army historian a week after the battle ended whether the South Vietnamese could have handled the situation alone, Major Walker said, "Not at all. They're too selfish, self-centered, afraid, and they lack administrative ability. The junior officers fear to make a decision; they absolutely refuse, and they have all kinds of faction problems. . . The Vietnamese weren't functioning, so we had to take over."

Another problem encountered behind the lines of the Marine advance was looting. Everyone was involved; a Marine officer would have to be very naive to think that his young troops were above liberating what booze or money they found in deserted homes. During the first few days of the fighting, the grunts made a souvenir bonanza of the micro-scopes in the university; and when 2/5 secured the treasury, a number of grunts pocketed gold bars. Many of the grunts, accustomed to the beggar-poor villages in the field, were amazed by the affluence of Hue, and there was some petty souvenir-taking. It was also common practice to commandeer civilian vehicles off the street, and use them for supply and evacuation of casualties until they ran out of gas.

However, looting by Marines was relatively minimal for several reasons. First, and most important, the battalion commanders did not tolerate any full-scale looting. Strict orders came down to respect property, and there were even shakedowns among platoons to look for signs of looting. Secondly, the individual grunt had little chance for looting. He was in combat, constantly on the move, and he just didn't have time for such activities, or the means to carry around anything big. Despite the actual minimal amount of looting by the grunts, there were press reports describing massive pilfering. For example, Welsh photographer Philip Jones Griffiths charged that the Marines "tore the city apart" in a looting binge. (Griffiths' reliability may be marred by the fact that he also wrote that the Marines in Hue were poor fighters.)

By and large, the looting in Hue was done by the South Vietnamese. Refugees were reported pilfering houses, but the biggest culprits were the ARVN. In their role of mopping up behind the Marines, they were seen moving from house to house in organized looting parties, taking beer, stereos, refrigerators, money, and other goods. In some instances, ARVN soldiers were searching refugees and taking what they wanted. Within the first week of the battle, ARVN soldiers' looting had reached such intolerable levels that the South Vietnamese leadership decreed that the most drastic measures be taken; looters were to be executed. Lieutenant Colonel Gravel, fearing headlines like "U.S. MARINES RAPE, PILLAGE, AND PLUNDER ANCIENT VIETNAMESE CAPITAL," passed word to the U.S. advisors: "After 1200 today, any ARVN seen looting will be killed on sight." He added, "I'll turn this attack around if I have to."

He didn't have to, nor did any Marine actually kill an ARVN looter. The advisors made it known to the South Vietnamese soldiers what could happen, and although the looting never stopped completely, it did lessen. But the whole experience left those involved with a bitter taste in the mouth. As Sergeant Dye noted, "The ARVN were an un-ruly lot and they made sure to stay far to the rear of the advancing Marines when we were fighting on the South Side. We'd see them after a pitched battle, driving up in trucks to loot the buildings we had just captured. There was a lot of bitching among the Marines about this and I think if the ARVN ever enjoyed any fighting reputation with the Marines, they lost it in Hue."

On the early morning of February 7, the second and last bridge over the Perfume River was destroyed by enemy sappers. However, that called for little tactical change because the Navy boat ramp was still open and functioning.

The next day, the ramp was where Dr. Hamilton and his four corpsmen waited for their ride home to Phu Bai. They had been in Hue for five days. The day after they'd set up shop in MACV, an ARVN lieutenant named Ba, who said he was a Saigon-trained doctor, pitched in to help. They called him Bac Si Ba (Dr. Ba) and he did a tremendous job helping with the casualties. What struck Hamilton the most greatly about Hue was that the morale of the Marines was "absolutely tremendous" — almost all of the wounded kids he treated wanted to get right back to their units. Finally, all the battalion surgeons were able to get into the city from their Da Nang conference, and Hamilton figured it was time to take his people and rejoin their company in Phu Bai.

A light rain was falling at the boat ramp, as Hamilton watched the crowd gather for the trip out. There were dozens of Vietnamese refugees, several reporters taking pictures and doing interviews, a few Marines, soldiers, and ARVNs; and about thirty wounded Marines, some hobbling around with bandages under their helmets and flak jackets, some on stretchers and covered with ponchos. Six more Marines were with them, zipped up in OD body bags. There were sporadic explosions nearby. Mortars and grenades. Hamilton barely noticed them; they weren't close, and something was always going off.

A Navy LCU churned up and docked. The people boarded, the body bags and wounded on stretchers were carried up the ramp. Marines and civilians crowded on the open deck. That worried Hamilton; a single mortar round on the exposed deck would kill and wound a lot of people. They pushed out into the current and slowly steamed north, through a channel near the Citadel wall. As soon as they got into the narrow strait, NVA fire started cracking from both shores. Hamilton ducked behind the rail of the deck, looking toward shore. It was thick with trees, shrubs, elephant grass — and muzzle flashes burst from the undergrowth.

The walking-wounded Marines opened up from the rail. Dr. Hamilton grabbed an M-16 and joined in. Nobody on the ship was hurt. They sailed on, out of sight on the Citadel wall, leaving the shooting behind. Then they were back in the Perfume River and headed for the open waters of the South China Sea.

Two days after Dr. Hamilton's departure from Hue, another batch of reinforcements moved in. They were the 4.2-inch Gun Platoon, Mortar Battery, 1st Battalion, 11th Marines, 1st Marine Division, under the 1st Field Artillery Group and Task Force X-RAY. There were twelve men and two four-deuce mortars, under the charge of a Sergeant Reliss, a stout career Marine, a good NCO by his troops. When Tet started, the platoon had been firing missions from the muddy fire-bases in the Phu Bai–Phu Loc area. They got word to pack it up and move back to the Phu Bai Combat Base. On February 10, after a few days of cleaning up, resupply, and getting organized, the platoon boarded a Sea Knight for Hue City.

The chopper roared in six feet off the deck, jinking and dodging in case of NVA fire; Reliss and his men sitting on their flak jackets so that the hundred-to-one shot wouldn't blow them away. The Sea Knight dropped into the LZ beside the Navy boat ramp, the Marines started out the back gate — and the North Vietnamese opened up. Snipers from across the Perfume, up on the Citadel wall, started cracking, and two light mortar rounds erupted in the river. A grunt machine gun team set up by the ramp returned the fire, shouting at the mortarmen to get moving. The platoon worked as fast as they could, lugging out their two 650-pound four-deuce mortars.

They got behind cover, the chopper bolted into the misty sky, and the shooting abruptly died away.

After a twenty-minute wait, a truck came for the platoon and took them a couple of hundred yards east of the ramp. They gathered in a hotel, across the street from a 1/1 position, with the Perfume River and the Citadel's southeast wall right to the front. There were Marines on guard at the 1/1 gate, but mostly only Vietnamese were around. The hotel was loaded with them; women, kids, even men of military age. That struck one of Sergeant Reliss' Marines, Pfc. Edward M. Landry, as strange — he was used to the bush of I Corps where all the young men were either ARVN or VC.

A Marine showed up with a load of one-hundred 4.2-inch mortar rounds. The man was obviously an older, career Marine, and Landry asked, "Hey, Gunny, who we shooting for?"

The man replied that he wasn't a gunny, he was a major with 1/1; he said the platoon would be shooting for his battalion and 2/5. Then the major got them moved into a nearby abandoned house and designated them WHISKEY X-RAY on the radio. They broke out the ammunition, built parapets around the two-tubes with dirt-filled ammo boxes, and readied themselves for their first fire mission.

There were to be many. For Pfc. Landry — a twenty-year-old from Lynn, Massachusetts who had joined the Marines because the Army sent him a draft notice, and who had six months in Vietnam — Hue was to become the worst experience of his tour. It was the highlight, he thought, if that was the right word. There were twelve of them there in Hue — he and Sergeant Reliss, Dave Raby, George Schamberger, Billy Barr, Ed Shaw, Powell, O'Neil, Edenfield, Miller, Torres, and Fuerst — and they took to calling themselves the Dirty Dozen because they were away from their outfit and stuck in the middle of all this crap. Landry didn't think he was going to make it. Sometimes he was so worn out and scared, he felt like crying. As a mortar gunner, he'd never been so close to the action before. The place stunk from rotting bodies in the rubble; the rain and low overcast just pressed the gloom right down on him.

They fired CS and the gas stayed in the air for days, making a clean breath impossible. Choppers came into the nearby LZ, but the only thing that came out was ammunition, and the only thing that went in were body bags and wounded. They had to drink the poor water out of the river, and fire constant fire missions. There were supposed to be seven men to each gun; with himself, Reliss, a radioman, and a frontal fire direction control man, there were only four. They worked most of the day and most of the night; getting behind the sandbag parapets they built, listening to the firefights around them, then getting the word on the radio and registering in and dropping the rounds down the tube. CS and High Explosive, and Illumination at night. A lot of times, the FO with the infantry calling in the fire would say, "Repeat," over and over after a salvo of 35-pound shells had pummelled the NVA position. "Repeat," meant to fire again on the same target. The NVA were dug in tight; Landry had never heard so many repeats. There was little sleep. Always tired, Landry slept through a rocket barrage once, curled up under a table in a room, too exhausted to care one way or the other. When the sun went down, there were only a few moments of darkness, and then the flareships and gunships came in, turning night into day. It was eerie, Landry thought; it just reinforced the unreality of everything. It was like looking into hell. And there was almost constant mortar and sniper fire peppering the area from across the river in the Citadel. One NVA gunner opened up on them when they were down by the river. Schamberger rolled to cover, then heard a round an inch from his head, and grabbed his M-16. He spun, saw the smoke from the rifle, and sprayed the window. The firing stopped. Days later,

Landry almost caught it — the sniper's round clipped the collar under his chin, then thudded into the arm of O'Neil, who was standing beside him.

There were some good moments, like when they took in lost or orphaned children. Once, Schamberger had to go to MACV, and a little girl named Lee warned him not to go down a certain street because there were "beaucoup VC" down there. Schamberger was sure that warning saved his life, and he was so impressed that years later, he named his daughter Sherri Lee.

Even their first night in Hue was bad. They'd turned in for some sleep inside the Navy compound. Landry had guard duty. He was patrolling on the road between the gun pits and the river bank, when the sudden shrill whistle of incoming fire split the air. He threw himself down, crab-walked to cover, and watched the fireworks — NVA mortars walking through the area, huge yellow tracers from a heavy machine gun stitching through the black. Finally it died down and the flareships came on station, bathing everything in a stadium glare.

The flares were dropped every night, and Landry would have bet you couldn't find three Marines in all of Hue who didn't have a piece of parachute nylon hanging off their gear, or tied around the head or neck.

At night, the Marines would hold up and consolidate their positions, making sure they had claymores wired in front of them and guards posted all night. Every night there was some shooting — an NVA sneaking up to fire a few quick bursts or throw a couple of grenades at the Marine lines; someone caught in the sudden glare of a tripflare and gunned down, like the Marine from 1/1 who was blown away by a nervous sentry. Sometimes the grunts could hear glass and rubble being crunched underfoot in the houses ahead and they'd open up with their M-16s and LAWs through the windows. One night, Corporal Soukup and what was left of his squad had dumped their 106 in the back of a house and holed up inside with some men from 2/5. To the front, across the courtyard, was a wall; the NVA held the next block, and if any of them slipped over that wall in the middle of the night, it would be bad news for everyone.

Soukup and a grunt he didn't know volunteered to man a listening post on the wall.

They passed the word through their building, then gathered their weapons and started crawling low across the grass. They pressed up against the wall, then poked their heads over the top. What a view! The moon was up and they could see straight down the roads of an intersection. The buildings looked gray, the windows black. Nothing moved. Just silence. They sat for a couple of hours, hands on their weapons, watching, waiting. Nothing happened. Then they started to worry — what if somebody hadn't received the word they were out there and accidentally wasted them? They decided to sit tight in position until daylight, taking turns sleeping and watching.

Soukup had nodded off beside the wall, when his partner suddenly shook him awake. He bent close, whispered that he heard something right across the street, thought he saw something. Soukup cautiously peeped over the wall.

Four NVA darted into the street.

The grunt beside him blasted off a round from his grenade launcher. There was a flash, a shower of hot metal in the street. Soukup let loose with his M-16. Then they threw themselves down as all hell broke loose. Red and green tracers flew back and forth over their heads, rounds thunking into the wall from across the street. Soukup crawled down the wall one way, his partner took off in the other direction, and they got to the back door of their building. They screamed the password and jumped in.

There was a quick head count — everyone was okay.

As soon as the sun came up, they charged across the street, but the houses were empty. The enemy had retreated during the night. The Marines found four North Vietnamese with packs and rifles, bunched up, dead in the street.

Lieutenant Colonel Gravel had set up his CP near Highway 1, in what had been a redevelopment office. It was near a school, the same school where they'd seen the NVA moving through on the fight to the MACV compound that first day. Gravel was grateful they'd been in too much of a hurry to fire on those NVA; the Roman Catholic priest in charge of the seminary told him that the classrooms had been packed with children from an orphanage. On February 10, some grunts from 2/5 escorted the liberated Archbishop of Hue back to his seminary near the 1/1 CP. Gravel paid him a visit, and the archbishop, a gray-haired Vietnamese wearing a large silver crucifix, invited the Marines to join him and the others of his community in a mass of thanksgiving for the continued success in recapturing Hue. In his halting French, Gravel accepted, then passed word that interested Marines should join him at 9:30 the next morning. Fittingly, the mass was to be on a Sunday, February 11. Gravel and some of his Marines visited the seminary chapel with the priests. Gravel was struck by one thing — there were four 90mm-shell holes blown through the tile of the front wall, but the wooden cross hanging there was untouched.

The night before the mass, the NVA struck.

Around midnight, Gravel was back in his CP when the North Vietnamese started dropping 120mm rockets in. There were no bunkers to run to. It was just drop down, hold onto your helmet and grit your teeth. It lasted five minutes; several quick explosions. The dust settled and the grunts poked their heads up and looked around. Their worst casualty was a blown-up truck. It soon became painfully clear why they had come through unscathed. Most of the rockets had fallen short, exploding in the archbishop's seminary. The children had been gathered there as an evacuation center; of those whom fate had spared on the first day, nearly twenty were killed, another forty seriously wounded. A priest ran to Gravel's CP. Gravel got on the radio to Colonel Hughes, and within minutes, trucks and corpsmen were mobilized. The most seriously wounded of the children were evacuated immediately to the hospital in the Phu Bai Combat Base.

The Marines were visibly shaken, and Gravel boiled with anger. Charlie didn't have any Rules of Engagement, he thought. They didn't care whom they killed.

By February 11, Fox Company 2/5 had secured a vacant apartment complex overlooking a bridge over the canal, a little south of where the Phu Cam branched from the Perfume. That was it — the battalion had driven all the way west from MACV to the eastern bank of the canal. The Marines set up, then rummaged through the buildings, looking through drawers and such, pocketing a few souvenirs. Lance Corporal Carter found a drawerful of letters, and photos of a white man and his wife. In some of them, the man was wearing the uniform of a World War II German army officer. Others in Third Platoon found some old K ration bacon, and decided to make a proper meal of it. Second Platoon across the street liberated a few chickens, and Third Platoon bought three eggs for four bucks. Carter almost got sick when they cracked the eggs — the yolks were a slimy green. He wouldn't touch them, but a few diehards cooked up the whole mess and ate it. Captain Downs was able to bring in some pipes from battalion and install a makeshift shower in a garage. The weather was chilly and the water was freezing, but nobody really cared much. The grunts were just glad to strip off their filthy clothes and try to wipe away some of the mud and sweat and dried blood.

While all the good stuff was happening, Third Platoon even got a number of replacements, a bunch of crew-cut, clean, and very green kids just flown in from the States. Lieutenant Hausrath had brought the replacements inside the apartments to give them a talk. First, though, he and his platoon sergeant had to call in mortars on some buildings across the canal where several snipers were thought to be hiding. The rounds exploded on the far bank, landing dead on target, and Hausrath got excited and edged too close to the window.

There was a sudden, ripping burst of AK-47 from the opposite shore.

Hausrath jerked upright, the rounds punching him in the chest. He came crashing down, as the replacements all jumped and scrambled and stared wide-eyed. He breathed a few times; his eyes rolled back. He was dead.

Corporal Allbritton came up the steps, and Corporal Burnham told him the news. Burnham muttered, "Hell, and I was just getting attached to him."

Carter was saddened by Lieutenant Hausrath's death. He wasn't too fond of officers with all their petty regulations and abuse of power, and Hausrath was only a new guy, fresh out of officers' school, but he seemed all right. He always looked out for his people, made sure to share the cakes and *Playboy* magazines his fiancée mailed him, and didn't pull that "You Do it Because I'm the Boss" routine with the platoon. He was respected. He was also liked. Once, back before Hue, when the lieutenant had just shipped in and was looking for combat, Carter was rigging a tripflare beside a claymore mine. He accidentally set the claymore off, blowing up a few bushes. Lieutenant Hausrath came charging down from the CP, holding his helmet down backwards with one hand, trying to jack a round into his M-16 with the other. When he saw what happened, he started shouting at Carter. But then, seeing Carter standing there looking sheepish, and realizing what he must have looked like himself, charging down like John Wayne, he started laughing.

When Captain Downs got the news he rushed to Third Platoon's position. The lieutenant's death was a real blow to him. Only four days before, the NVA had killed his favorite radioman, a handsome young kid nicknamed Red. They'd been pushing through the houses along the Perfume River when the firing started and the bullets and ricochets began flying among the CP group. Somehow, Downs wasn't hit; Red was blown away right beside him. Now a sniper had killed Hausrath too. It was hard. The captain called the men who'd been members of Third Platoon since the first day.

They gathered behind the apartment buildings, and Corporal

Allbritton looked around in horrified amazement — there were no more than maybe twelve guys standing there; out of his squad, only he and his radioman, a kid nicknamed Moses. Downs started talking to them. "You men have done fantastic," he said, "I just wish I could have been a better company commander." Then he choked and everyone could see the tears in his eyes. He's all right, Allbritton thought, the captain was good people.

———

Maj. O. K. Steele, USMC, had one hard time just getting into Hue. Steele was a tall and handsome thirty-five-year-old family man from Oakland, California, former Pfc., very quiet and very bright. Before Tet, he'd been counting off every day at an unexciting rear-area job as CO, Headquarters Company, Headquarters Battalion, 1st Marine Division, back on the Da Nang line. He had talked with Colonel Bohn and managed to wrangle a job with his regiment as the executive officer of 2/5. He was to flip-flop assignments with his old friend, Major Salvati, who was due to rotate home in a few months.

The transfer orders were effective February 1, 1968, and Steele found himself stuck in Da Nang during the sapper and artillery attacks on the perimeter, while Salvati fought his way into Hue.

Finally, after a few days, Steele was able to hitch a ride aboard a giant CH-53 helicopter. The pilot took the long route over the South China Sea instead of flying over the ground, and when they went inland to Phu Bai, he had the bird hugging the deck to avoid antiaircraft fire. At Phu Bai, Steele reported in with Colonel Bohn at the 5th Marines Regimental Command Post, then made visit after visit to the airfield. He couldn't get a ride; the weather was bad, and the few choppers flying to Hue were all crammed to capacity with ammunition. A few days later, he got word to report to the executive officer of the 1st Marines. He was given orders to go into Hue as a convoy commander; to take in replacements and equipment to repair the An Cuu Bridge, which, he was told, had some shell holes in it. Steele had a jackleg group: a lieutenant and a rifle squad from G/2/5, the Scout-Sniper Platoon of the 1st Marines, an artillery fire-support team, an engineer detachment with trucks full of lumber and a big Bay City Crane, replacements, and an assortment of R&R returnees, wounded men just out of the hospital, and such, returning to the line companies of 1/1 and 2/5.

Major Steele was in charge of some 120 men, none of whom he'd met before.

They pushed out on the morning of February 10, going full speed up Highway 1 because everyone expected an ambush. But the only people

they saw were Marines from CAP units guarding the bridges. Task
Force X-RAY radioed Steele and told him that 1/1 had not yet secured
the An Cuu–Phu Cam area, and he was directed to stop at a radio
tower one mile short of Hue. They pulled up, and formed a perimeter
with the trucks and escort Army Dusters. Steele stared up at the three
giant radio towers, wondering why the enemy hadn't demolished them.
They waited there all day. A few refugees passed by on bicycles. Some
questionable-looking ARVN soldiers with slung rifles walked past, jabbering and grinning like they were out for a stroll in the park. Everyone
was headed away from Hue.

By the time it got dark, X-RAY ordered Steele to return with the
convoy to Phu Bai.

The next morning, they mounted up again. Word came that a convoy was on its way from Phu Loc with reinforcements from the 1st
Battalion, 5th Marines. They waited all morning, but the trucks never
showed, and the G-3 of X-RAY directed that Steele's convoy start up
Highway 1 again. They clipped along past the three radio towers, and
Steele stood in the back of the truck carrying the command group,
watching the Bay City Crane swinging back and forth behind him. On
the outskirts of Hue, they stopped and Steele sent the trucks back to
Phu Bai with a handful of infantrymen aboard for security. Then he
ordered one of his composite platoons to scout ahead and secure the
bridge over the Phu Cam. There was no firing. In a few minutes, the
lieutenant leading the platoon radioed Steele and they walked up with
the Dusters and the Bay City Crane.

The An Cuu Bridge was about a hundred feet across, made of
concrete — and the center had been blown up. The two ends sagged
against the banks like big slides. The water flowed across the middle,
and twisted metal supporting-rods jutted from the smashed concrete
like spaghetti.

Steele and the engineer captain stood on the bank, surveying the
damage.

"Well," Steele said, "go ahead and fix it."

The captain said he couldn't, the damage was beyond his capabilities. He'd been told there were only some craters in the bridge, and
he'd brought along only some patching material.

Steele felt like booting the man into the canal. All this way for
nothing. He would learn later that the bridge had been down for a
week. Seven days, and Task Force X-RAY still thought it had a couple
of holes in it. Intelligence was just plain bad.

He got on the radio to Phu Bai, told them the bridge was beyond
repair, and recommended they delay any reinforcements from 1/5 until

it could be fixed. He then radioed Lieutenant Colonel Cheatham and was told to come across and report in with his new battalion.

The engineer captain said they could construct a hasty footbridge. Steele told him to get to work on it, then positioned his group in the houses along the bank. The opposite shore looked secure; the houses were undamaged except for a few shell holes, and he could see Marines inside them. Vietnamese civilians in conical straw hats walked along the banks. Steele and a lieutenant from 1/1, who was packing a shotgun and was very anxious to get back to his unit, found an old dugout near the bridge. They stripped down, threw their clothes and weapons into the canoe, and pushed out into the chilly water. They made sure to keep their heads low along the canoe, just in case of snipers.

On the other side, they got dressed and headed for the Marines in the houses. They were from Golf 2/5, and Steele found Captain Meadows. The captain, a thin fellow with glasses, now reminded Steele of a schoolmaster. Meadows was bundled up in his flak jacket, had an M-16 over his shoulder, and his face was gaunt and bearded, his eyes very tired. The grunts had several Scouts and commandeered trucks there, and Meadows offered Steele a ride to the battalion CP. He climbed into one of the bullet-riddled Scouts, hanging on tight as the Marine driver hauled down the streets, making sure to roar through the intersections at top speed.

They arrived at the CP in one piece. Steele knew many of the people there. Cheatham had been a company officer when he was a recruit at boot camp, Salvati had gone to officers' school with him, and he had served with Christmas and Downs before Vietnam. Steele officially took over as executive officer from Salvati, and Cheatham instructed him to go back and keep his force where they were for the night.

The colonel said that Christmas' Hotel Company would secure an intact bridge near the apartments, and they could come across in the morning. They didn't know it, but despite Major Steele's recommendation about the bridge, reinforcements from 1/5 were already on their way.

The grunts from the 1st Battalion, 5th Marines, 1st Marine Division were packed aboard eight trucks, slowly churning through the muddy, leaf-covered road, the sky dark and low. The Marines in the truck beds had their weapons and ammunition piled around them, uncomfortable in the brisk monsoon chill. There was a reporter crammed into one of the trucks with them, Michael Herr of *Esquire* magazine, a short, heavy fellow with glasses. He was lucky to be in the middle of the convoy; the front and rear usually got the most attention when a convoy was ambushed.

But the Marines and their reporter friend were relieved that there was no firing. As they rode along they saw hundreds of refugees heading south on the highway, leaving Hue. The children seemed excited and friendly while the old stared with their usual unemotional mask.

Everyone was talking and whistling and smoking cigarettes. As Herr noted, "it sounded like a locker room before a game that nobody wanted to play".*

Ahead of them, they could see the black smoke rising from Hue.

When they pulled up to the An Cuu Bridge, the Marines, Herr, and some other reporters climbed out of the trucks. They were met by Sergeant Dye, the combat correspondent from ISO, 1st Marine Division. Herr was struck by Dye; he wasn't an "average" Marine. He was twenty-three, from Cape Girardeau, Missouri, tall, thin, and handsome. He also had a sharp wit. On the back of his flak jacket, he'd drawn a portrait of Alfred E. Neuman with the slogan, What, Me Worry? And sticking out of his helmet cover, he had a tall yellow plastic flower. Dye had picked it up during the South Side fighting. He and his partner, Sergeant Berntson, had ducked into a Buddhist temple. Up front was the yellow flower in a long-necked vase. A Buddha statue sat behind it. Berntson relaxed and strolled up to check out the ornate decorations of the temple. Dye saw it then — movement behind the Buddha. He braced and blew off the clip in his souvenir ARVN Thompson. The statue and vase blew to pieces, Berntson almost jumped out of his skin — and a North Vietnamese soldier came flopping forward, shot full of holes. Berntson picked up the flower from the mess and stuck it in Dye's helmet cover, a present for saving his life, he said.

It made an outstanding sniper's target, but Dye grooved on it and left it there. He was kind of crazy that way.

Dye had already been through two weeks of it with his friend Berntson, so he stood there, talking with Herr and the others, rolling his eyes and grinning under his droopy mustache. "Oh yes, Charlie's got his shit together here, this will be oh so bad, indubitably."

Major Steele had just swum the canal back to his command, when he found the Marines from 1/5 already parked and disembarking. He started to get the new Marines tied in with the perimeter defense. When the reporters wanted to get across the canal into the main city,

*Michael Herr, *Dispatches,* N.Y.: Avon, 1978. Page 72.

Steele told them to keep it down and directed them into an abandoned house; they would have to wait until the next day, he said. He just wanted to get them out of his hair; he had to be set in by dark.

He climbed the stairs up to the third floor of a building so he could get the lay of the land, and just when he got to the roof, he saw two Huey gunships from the 1st Air Cavalry Division. They were flying low down the canal. And then he stared unbelieving: their machine guns were sputtering, and he could hear empty brass bouncing on the ground.

Dye, Herr, and some grunts were stretched out along the canal bank, eating a C ration dinner, when suddenly, red tracers were skipping towards them. Dye had always considered the Cav the trigger-happiest bunch of bandits ever to set foot in Nam. He and the rest made a mad scramble for cover, dropping food and helmets. In a few seconds, the choppers shot out of sight, and the grunts sood up, more surprised than scared. Incredibly, no one had been hit.

They spent the night in the deserted buildings along the canal, sleeping on their ponchos thrown over the shattered brick and glass. Down the canal to their left, up around the northwest, flares and firing went on all night.

There was a bridge (Ga-Hue) intact over the Phu Cam to the northwest of Steele's position, near the point where the canal flowed from the Perfume. The Marines held the east bank, the NVA the west, and to get the reinforcements across, the enemy side would have to be secured. Under a covering mortar barrage, Lieutenant Myers' First Platoon of Hotel Company charged across the bridge and captured a block around it. Their orders were to hold all night under continuous enemy attack. They did.

It was a tough fight — two popular squad leaders were killed. Lieutenant Myers was also in the thick of it, hurling grenades — but in the morning, February 12, the Hotel Marines were still in position. Down the canal, with Major Steele's group, the Scout-Sniper Platoon and the grunts from 1/1 were detached and moved across the engineers' footbridge to link up with their battalion. Steele took the remainder of his force and the 1/5 reinforcements and started sweeping up the canal bank. They were surprised that they didn't take even a single sniper round. Two hours up the canal, they found Hotel Company still holding at the bridge. The grunts were keyed up, anxious to get back across to the other side. They waved the newcomers to move it. The first group sprinted across the bridge. Sniper fire started cracking around them.

Major Steele crouched over and ran with the rest. The sniper fire whined off the mark. Then the Hotel grunts came running back, and they all secured in the apartment complex and power plant near the bridge. The Frenchman who owned the power plant, and his family, had been discovered unharmed in North Vietnamese territory and were back in friendly hands.

On Monday, February 12, the day after Lieutenant Hausrath was killed, Fox Company went across the canal hunting for the snipers. Carter, with his 3.5-inch rocket launcher, was assigned to Second Platoon, the point element, which made an amphibious landing north of the bridge in commandeered motor boats. Then they started moving back down, cleaning out the houses between them and the bridge. They fired, moved into a house, fired at the next, kept moving. They found several NVA bodies. The platoon got into the Hue railroad yard and a sergeant told Carter to blow a hole in one of the cars sitting on the tracks. He put two shells in it. They moved up and Carter looked inside. There were two dead enemy inside it, one with his head blown off. Carter ripped a green and red NVA scarf off one of the bodies, and the men kept moving.

Third Platoon, now led by the platoon sergeant, Staff Sgt. James H. McCoy, came across the bridge and started sweeping through the streets, popping cover smoke as they moved. Corporal Allbritton was up against a building when he looked back and saw Major Salvati and the battalion sergeant major strolling up the street — right in the middle of the road, like gentlemen out for their morning constitutional. The sergeant major was a veteran of the street-fighting in Seoul, Korea. Allbritton had seen the two in action and respected them, but he was bone weary and had seen too many dead Marines.

"Get your butts out of there!" he shouted at them. "I don't wanna get my men killed dragging your bodies out of the street!" Allbritton jumped behind cover so that the major and sergeant major wouldn't see it was just a corporal shouting at them, while the two men quickly moved to cover.

The shooting kept up sporadically. A sniper popped more rounds at 2d Platoon, and Carter moved to the front. He put a rocket in his launcher, and the shell simply slid down the tube and fell to the ground at his feet. He had fired the 3.5 so much during the battle, it was starting to malfunction. A few blocks farther on they came upon the house from where they thought the shot had come that killed the lieutenant. There was no hesitation; they just backed up, radioed the mortar and recoilless rifle teams, and blew the building down to its foundation.

By nightfall, the platoons had gone back across the canal.

Carter spent the night back with his 3d Platoon. He fell asleep, wrapped up in some curtains against the monsoon chill, watching the rats scurrying around on the floor. His rocket launcher lay beside his leg, a round in the tube, just in case.

Before saying good-bye to the battalion, Major Salvati went out with Major Steele to find a new command post for the colonel and the 2d Battalion. The two old friends walked along Le Loi Street on the Perfume River, and Steele was amazed at the destruction. When he'd reached the Phu Cam, the buildings had been relatively unscathed, nothing more than some bullet holes and a few shell holes here and there. But Le Loi was where the NVA had put up the toughest defense; it was where the battalion had fought and bled for the last two weeks. It reminded Steele of the old World War II newsreels about Monte Cassino — a crumbling wall standing amid piles of rubble.

They walked to the Cercle Sportif, the old French athletic and social club overlooking the river, with its beautiful green lawns sweeping down to the banks, with its terraces and tennis courts. From the outside, it looked in good condition, but when they started going door to door, they could see shell holes through the walls of each room. The insides were a complete shambles from the shrapnel whirlwinds. Bloody bandages were evidence that it had been used as an enemy hospital. The North Vietnamese and Viet Cong had no helicopters to evacuate their seriously wounded, no real hospitals, and only a few trained field doctors. The place had seen much suffering.

They finally moved on and set up the new command post in the apartment complex that Fox Company had secured. The first floor was given to the two battalion surgeons for the BAS, and the second floor was used by Cheatham and his command group. The third floor was left unoccupied, in case the NVA dropped mortars on the roof. (They did, almost every day.) The apartments were used as the 2/5 CP for the remainder of the battle.

Sergeant Dye was standing above a pit found in an area recaptured by 2/5. Other grunts stood nearby muttering, "Jesus Christ." An incredible stench rose from it, a stomach-turning putrid smell that seemed to press down on them all the more with the low clouds and drizzle. There, below their boots, were a hundred bodies. They were South

Vietnamese civilians, all tangled and twisted, as if they had clung to each other when the machine guns were turned on them. Dye had heard rumors of the Communists having massacred civilians in Hue — but he'd never expected to see anything like this. Relatives and friends of the dead picked their way through the jumble of rotting bodies, handkerchiefs tied to their noses and mouths against the stench, trying to dig out the dead.

It was a scene Dye never forgot, and he thought about it a year later when the My Lai killings hit the papers. It was incredible, he thought, that the press made such a fuss about My Lai, but never said much about the NVA massacre in Hue. He finally dismissed it as a sign of the times and the sentiments about the war.

———————

Tuesday, February 13. Lieutenant Colonel Cheatham wanted the west side of the Phu Cam finally cleared of the snipers, die-hards and stragglers, and sent Fox and Hotel across. Christmas was to sweep down south through the railroad station with his men, while Downs would move north and drive the NVA ahead of them in a pincer movement.

Carter and his new A-gunner, Lance Corporal Chek, a Chinese-American from New York, were up in front of their platoon. They blew down the doors of one building with the 3.5, and some grunts moved in. The place was deserted. Carter went inside and scared up as souvenirs a couple of track pennants out of a kid's room. They moved on; still, there was no firing. No one was around, not even civilians. Finally, they spotted something. A hundred yards ahead was an L-shaped building. The door was shut — a bad sign. Allbritton, up front with his squad, waved the rocket team forward and told them to put a few rounds inside, just in case. The only clear shot was through a window covered with steel mesh. Carter carefully sighted in from a second-floor terrace, and fired. The little window blew away, and smoke poured out.

The A-gunner jubilantly jammed in another round and Carter aimed again. Then Chek suddenly flipped the contact latch so the launcher wouldn't fire, and Carter could hear Allbritton shouting, "Cease fire!" Then he noticed the people coming around the building from an unseen side door. An old Vietnamese man stumbled out first, bald-headed and with a white beard down to his waist. His face and hands were covered with blood. Two crying children clung to his white robes. More people began coming out, some dragging others who were wounded, maybe dead. One of them told the Marines they were only civilians, that several North Vietnamese had been holding them hostage. The grunts had accidentally liberated them.

Captain Christmas left Gunny Thomas in charge of the rear of the company, then took his radiomen to accompany the point platoon of Hotel Company. He vaguely thought about it being the 13th; not a good-luck number, he mused.

They swept through the railroad station, and moved west into the outskirts of Hue, passing an ARVN compound, going through wood-lines and rolling hills, past old cemeteries and Buddhist shrines. Some of the Marines spotted several freshly-dug, shallow graves in one area and Christmas moved up with the grunts to take a look.

In a few moments, all hell broke loose. They all heard the deep thunk of mortar rounds popping from their tubes. Christmas and his command group were caught in a cluster in the open, as the shells began saturating the area with flying shrapnel. Everyone went dashing and rolling for cover, pressing themselves into the smallest fold in the ground, as the rounds kept walking through their position. Christmas happened to look over his shoulder just in time to see the little figure of an NVA soldier jump from behind a distant Buddhist shrine. The man let go with a B-40 rocket and all Christmas could think was, "But I'm not a tank," as the spray of razor sharp, red-hot shrapnel dug into his right leg. He went tumbling into an open grave, then recoiled — a North Vietnamese corpse was lying in the grave beside him. The mortars kept falling. Christmas pressed farther down in the grave; the dead man silently beside him.

Carter and a few grunts went through a small treeline and came upon a tiny pagoda in the middle of a field. They paused to look around inside. It was beautiful, with carvings and a tiled roof. Unlighted incense sat in a container. Carter saw a Buddha statue sitting there; he wanted so badly to take it — what a souvenir. But he knew he'd have to lug it around in his pack until he went home in nine months. And, besides, he thought, if he did steal it, it would probably get him on the wrong side of God.

They left the pagoda and began hiking up a little hill covered with barbed wire. Carter and Chek struggled through with their rocket launcher; a radioman and a few other Marines were up ahead. Suddenly, they heard the mortars starting to pop, then explosions maybe five hundred feet away. They looked around — wasn't that where Hotel Company was? Then the mortars started getting closer, walking towards them. They all took off back down the hill. Carter saw it then — a black ball suddenly shooting over the top of the treeline. He watched it arch down, hit, explode. There was another explosion maybe thirty feet away, and something whacked against his leg with a dull thud; it felt like someone had thrown a baseball hard at him. He fell forward, tripping into the wire, and found the crotch of his trousers hopelessly tangled in the barbs. He gingerly tried to get out. More mortars exploded. Clutching his vitals, he frantically tore his trousers off, and went rolling, stumbling, running down the hill.

He ran back to the pagoda and jumped inside. There were a couple of grunts crouched inside, another wounded man with shrapnel sticking out of his knee, and a Navy corpsman. The corpsman checked Carter's wound, said it looked pretty bad. The shrapnel had dug upward about a foot from the entry wound and was embedded in the bone. Blood poured out. The corpsman slapped a battle dressing on. Then the wounded were carried or helped back across the Phu Cam. A jeep from the Fox CP picked them up and drove them to the apartments where the BAS was. They pulled up and the battalion chaplain, built like a football player, rushed to them. He picked up one of the wounded Marines like a feather and quickly ran back inside with him. Carter gingerly climbed off the jeep and started limping towards the door.

Gunny Thomas had been with the rear platoon when the mortar rounds started exploding. A confused message came over the radio, and Thomas and several Marines started toward the sound of the shooting. They found several Marines coming back down the road. They were platoon leaders — Lieutenant Myers, Lieutenant Lambert, and a few staff sergeants — and all of them were ripped and bleeding and hastily bandaged. They said they'd been bracketed by the mortars, and pointed the Gunny's group in the right direction. Thomas saw Christmas lying flat against a small building. There was a corpsman beside him and the captain's leg was bandaged. He started jogging toward them.

Another mortar round exploded. Thomas went diving flat beside Christmas and the corpsman. More rounds whooshed in and Thomas climbed on top of Christmas, shielding his skipper with his own body. They got on the radio and somebody came hauling up in a commandeered pickup truck. They quickly piled in the wounded and got moving. Twenty-three men from the company had been hit; somehow, no one was dead. Thomas sat beside Christmas in the truck bed as they bounced along, talking to him, trying to keep his mind off the pain.

Behind them, Marine counter mortar-fire was dropping shells on the NVA.

They got back to the apartments by noon. Christmas lay on a stretcher across the back of a jeep, while a corpsman worked on his wounds. Cheatham, Steele, and the rest gathered around and Christmas propped himself up on his elbows, smoking a big cigar and talking about how soon he'd be back just as soon as the doctors patched him up. He seemed to ignore the fact that his leg was badly mangled and must have hurt like hell.

After the wounded were evacuated to MACV, Cheatham contacted 1st Lt. William L. Harvey, the battalion's assistant operations officer. He gave him his new orders in three words, "Pack your pack." Harvey was the new commander of Hotel Company. A twenty-four-year-old from the Vermont farmlands, Harvey was an experienced combat officer, having already served a year in the field as a platoon leader with Golf Company before extending his tour and being assigned to the 2/5 command group. In Hue, his closest call had come not from the NVA but from another Marine officer. A day or two before, he'd been sleeping in a bathtub in a bungalow used by the battalion officers. In the other room, Captain Fine was fiddling with a captured B–40 rocket launcher and it suddenly went off. The round blew through the wall, then exploded above Harvey's head. He woke up thinking he was dead.

The battalion ALO, Captain Pyle, took over Harvey's job as S-3A, so the lieutenant gathered his gear and went out, trying to find his new company. It took him an hour. He took over from Staff Sergeant Miller, the senior enlisted man there and the only officer of staff NCO, besides Gunny Thomas, who hadn't been hit by the mortars. Harvey looked at the grunts; they were sitting around disorganized, utterly dejected, sullen. Their morale was shot. Cheatham had them pull back to the Christian Brothers School to reorganize, but mostly, just to rest.

Later, when intelligence had pieced it together, it was discovered that the shallow graves were inside the retreating NVA's command post. Like good soldiers, the North Vietnamese had registered their mortars on top of their positions. And Hotel Company had accidentally walked right in the back door.

Carter was driven to the university soccer field with the rest of the WIAs. When he'd first landed there two weeks before, almost every chopper took fire and the only people out in the open were those who had to be there. By the 13th, however, helicopters were coming and going at will. There were reporters and photographers there. Refugees

collected in swarms, sitting around, waiting to go back to their homes
— or if they were privileged, to be evacuated.

Carter sat there, nursing his leg, looking around. There was a pile of
dead North Vietnamese lying stiff in one part of the field. An engineer
crane was there, and the operator dropped the bucket into the pile of
corpses. He scooped up three or four bodies, raised the crane as high as
it would go, then opened the bucket. The dead men came tumbling
back to the ground, and the South Vietnamese civilians started laughing and cheering. Carter thought it was hilarious.

And over in another part of the field he could see their own dead,
Marines piled like cordwood, white and black arms hanging out, all of
them wearing those jungle boots that on a corpse looked like they
weighed a hundred pounds apiece. The bodies were stacked in the back
of a truck. They don't even rate a ride in a chopper anymore, Carter
thought.

A little later, an Army gunship landed and they were carried aboard
for the ride to Phu Bai. The pilot skimmed and jinked sideways to
avoid NVA ground fire, and the wounded clung to each other. Captain
Christmas held on to Lance Corporal Carter to keep him from falling
out.

After the sweep on the 13th, the Marines of 2/5 began to encounter the
enemy with less and less frequency. There were sharp firefights every
day, but for all practical purposes, it was the end of the bitter street
fighting for them. Their patrols started pushing out across the canal,
out into the treelines and villages on the city's edge. But every night,
snipers continued to harass the command post in the apartments.
Finally, some Marines located the building where the NVA were
located — a little pink house — and Cheatham had the engineers wire it
with explosives. That night, they watched through the Starlite scopes
and saw several NVA sneak in. The engineer pushed the plunger and
the whole house blew to smithereens.

In a normal situation, awards for valor are recommended after the
fighting ends. But in Hue, the combat was so intense and the casualties
so many, a captain and several enlisted men flew in from the Awards &
Decorations Branch, 1st Marine Division. They set up shop inside the
apartments and began processing the medals right there in the middle
of the battle. It was quite an unusual situation. There was one story
about a dud mortar round landing outside the captain's window. He
watched a Marine run up to defuse it, and immediately started typing

up a Bronze Star citation. Major Steele heard another story about a young Navy corpsman in Fox Company who was up for several awards. As the story went, he had just arrived in Vietnam, spent his first couple of days in orientation courses, then was sent to the grunts. In a short time, he was slightly wounded while rescuing a wounded Marine, and was put in for a Silver Star. The next day, he was badly wounded going after another grunt, and got another recommendation and a ticket to be medevacked. While lying on a stretcher at the LZ, he was hit by mortar fragments. So the man was rotated home after a week in the war with the Silver Star, Bronze Star, and three Purple Hearts.

A day or two after getting Hotel Company, Lieutenant Harvey got a new platoon leader to take over for all the lieutenants and staff sergeants wounded on the 13th. He was an up-from-the-ranks second lieutenant transferred down from Division — and he couldn't read a map. He radioed the CP that he was in such-and-such a building, and Harvey took his radioman to go find them. They started up an alley, then Harvey looked up and — Jesus Christ! They were standing toe to toe with two North Vietnamese soldiers. All four of them stood there in shock for a second, just staring at each other. It seemed like forever to Harvey. Then they all bolted in different directions. Harvey saw one of the NVA swinging up his AK-47. He flattened himself against the wall. The rounds sprayed beside him, burning bullet splinters and cement into his nose and ear. The next second, and the NVA were gone. Harvey looked back at his radioman. The kid was shaking with fear and puking into the street.

By February 10, when the area from MACV to the Phu Cam was pretty much in 2/5's hands, Lieutenant Colonel Gravel was directed to turn around, go back over Highway 1, and start pushing east from MACV — up around the Hue stadium and the canals running on the eastern fringe of the South Side. At that time, he still had only a two-company battalion; Lieutenant Smith's Alpha, and Bravo Company under Capt. Robert A. Black, Jr. (the original Bravo CO, Lt. C. B. Matthews, was killed by mortar fire on February 7.) The sweep east was more of the same; not quite the same intensity as the first week in Hue, but still enough snipers, die-hards, and stragglers to keep everyone alert, scared, and tired. On it went — another house, another block, another house.

During the battle, Gravel headed for MACV to attend Colonel Hughes' morning staff command briefing. He went into the command center and, lo and behold, sitting on a canvas cot in the hallway, wearing a flak jacket and steel pot, was Walter Cronkite.

He walked past him, into Hughes' briefing, and joked, "Looks like you've got a live one out there!"

"Yeah," Hughes said, "and he's all yours."

He said that since Gravel was the first Marine commander into Hue, he could explain the battle to the TV people. Hughes introduced him to Cronkite. Gravel walked back to his CP, being interviewed by Cronkite, with a few grunts along and a gaggle of film crews, sound men, photographers, and reporters. Gravel, who took an instant liking to Cronkite, asked him to call his wife when he got back to New York and tell her he was doing fine.

At the battalion command post, Gravel wanted Cronkite to meet one of his officers, Capt. Jim Gallagher, the new operations officer. Gallagher had served with distinction as commander of Delta 1/1 and was due to rotate home around February 1, but when he heard about Hue and Walt Murphy's death, he quickly made his way to the fighting. The day before Cronkite's arrival, Gravel and Gallagher had been working on the night defense plans, and kibitzing about who their favorite Americans were and whom they would like to meet. Gallagher had settled on Walter Cronkite.

When Gravel and Cronkite reached the CP, Gallagher was bent over the map board. Gravel spoke. "Excuse me, Jim, there is someone here I want you to meet. Walter Cronkite, this is Jim Gallagher, one of the finest combat Marine officers you could hope to know."

Gallagher just managed to stammer out, "Nice to meet ya."

Later, Gravel found out that when the film of the roadside interview was shown on CBS News, gunfire had been dubbed in the background. Well, what the hell, he thought — that's show biz.

Lieutenant Smith's Alpha Company was sweeping near the Hue stadium when they ran into the worst firefight of the push east. They were moving down a dirt road, with one tank in front, an empty flame-tank behind, and the grunts along the flanks. Ahead was the front wall of an abandoned ARVN compound.

Lance Corporal Neas was with his machine gun squad off on the right side of the tanks. Up ahead, he could see a hole in the compound wall — and suddenly, a B-40 rocket came booming out of the hole. The lead tank shuddered under the impact and shrapnel glanced off the metal. AK-47 fire started raking them. One corporal nicknamed Chunky, who'd already been wounded twice, was hit by shrapnel, then took an AK burst and collapsed in the street. Some of the Marines started firing back, while others grabbed Chunky as the flame-tank hauled up behind the lead tank, which was sitting dead in its tracks and belching smoke. Neas and others piled the casualties aboard the tank, and the dying tank driver was pulled out of his hatch. The flame-tank drove away. Sergeant Burghardt watched the tank hauling back — only to run over a wounded corpsman lying near the intersection, breaking his arm. A couple of Marines pulled him behind a tree, and he lay there, stifling his cries for fear of drawing more fire.

Neas looked back at the lead tank. He could see the tank commander, a black sergeant, on his knees behind the smoking wreck. He was crying, and shouting that he wished he had another tank to go after the NVA who had destroyed his M-48.

Neas shouted for one of his gun teams, and they went low crawling off the street and jumped through a window. They set up their M-60 at a window facing the NVA wall, and Neas crouched behind the next window. There was a small building facing him, right behind the compound wall, and he knew sooner or later, the enemy would have to come out. He put his M-16 against his shoulder, wedged the magazine against the windowsill, and sighted in on the last door of the building. The mortar teams behind them started lobbing tear gas shells, and in an instant, three NVA jumped up from behind the wall and went scrambling into the little house. Neas looked away for a second, and glanced back to see a North Vietnamese coming out of the door. Marines were yelling to shoot. Neas squeezed the trigger once and the man hurtled to the ground. He started crawling away and Neas jumped to his feet, not believing that the man was still alive. The adrenaline was coursing through him and he sprayed his whole magazine at the NVA.

The firing continued with the Marines hammering away at the compound, and the enemy return-fire dying down. Neas' M-60 crew was running through ammo belts, when he saw some green-clad figures in helmets bolt across the open courtyard. He couldn't see their faces, but figured a squad was making its rush, and started shouting, "Cease-fire!" The M-60 gunner let off the trigger, and the men got into the main building. But there was no M-16 fire from within. Damn, Neas thought, some NVA must have been wearing U.S. uniforms. He cursed himself; it would have been an easy shot to blow them all away.

Mortars began crashing into the compound. The NVA fire petered out.

The Marines got up and rushed across the street into the compound; there was a little shooting, then not much more to do than make the body count. Sergeant Burghardt went into the small building where

Neas had shot the NVA. He called to Neas and pointed. The NVA was sprawled in the doorway, stone dead, clutching his hands to his belly, holding his guts which had spilled from the rifle wounds. There were two rifles lying beside him. Burghardt shouldered the AK, and Neas made a souvenir of the Russian-made submachine gun with a drum magazine. He was walking back down the street, when the company's Vietnamese Kit Carson scout saw the machine gun and started jumping up and down, smiling, shouting, "Number One!" Through the interpreter, the scout explained that those types of weapons only went to NVA officers.

Within another day or two, 1/1 had secured itself along the eastern canals. It was time to clean out the die-hards and the ones who hadn't got word it was time to retreat.

Lt. Allen W. Courtney, Jr., was the leader of Third Platoon of Alpha Company. He was a big blond Texan, an ex-enlisted man, well respected by the whole company. He'd already been put up for the Silver Star when the battalion was fighting at Con Thien, during December. Like all the lieutenants in Alpha, he'd been stranded when the battle for Hue started (in school at Da Nang in his case), and didn't beg there until the 11th. He lasted two days. He was up along the canal with his platoon, when one of his squads ran across a bridge to secure a building on the other side. They got inside, but a B-40 round exploded against a windowsill. Several Marines were wounded and more NVA fire started cracking around them. Courtney ran up, grabbed an M-60 from Neas' machine gun squad, and started hosing down the enemy positions. A bullet dug into his calf, but he kept firing until the squad was able to get back across the bridge. A corpsman tied a bandage around Courtney's leg, and he ignored it until Lieutenant Smith noticed it and ordered him out. It was a bad wound, but Courtney balked; he wanted to stay with his platoon. Finally, Lieutenant Colonel Gravel had to order him to the safety of the Phu Bai hospital, in the style he thought the Texan would understand, "Be out of town before dark." Gravel heard another story this way: One of his young Marines was on a stretcher at MACV waiting to be medevacked, when a reporter asked, "How many times have you been wounded?" The kid looked up and said, "Today?"

Alpha Company was patrolling along the outskirts of the city, mopping up, when Sergeant Burghardt was directed to take three Marines and check out a treeline in front of them. They went through it, came out — and there was a NVA soldier standing a hundred feet away, just standing there and looking as surprised as the Marines. Then he dropped to his knee, fired off a B-40 rocket, and everyone went for cover. The round hit a tree in front of them and exploded harmlessly. Burghardt came up first, firing his .45 pistol. The North Vietnamese took off running. Burghardt dropped his pistol, shouldered his M-16, and shot the man dead into the dirt.

Sunday, February 18. Corporal Soukup and his squad were with some 1/1 grunts, setting up in a house for the evening. They were all turning toward the walls to shed their packs and gear, and suddenly, a B-40 came flying out of nowhere. It shrieked through the window, blew up in the ceiling, and hot metal and plaster shot down, digging into the back of flak jackets and helmets. Shrapnel ripped Soukup's thigh, hand, and scalp. Two other Marines were wounded.

A second after the explosion, everyone was shouting and moving. Soukup and another grunt opened up with their M-16s out the window. Another Marine started chucking grenades. In a few seconds, somebody shouted, "They got him!"

Soukup and the rest ambled out. The NVA was lying in the grass, wounded by shrapnel, a loaded B-40 next to him. He was young, kind of chubby, wearing shorts. The Marines stood around him, as he looked up at them, not knowing what to expect.

Major Steele was outside at the 2/5 command post, when a group of North Vietnamese were spotted across the Perfume River. They were running away from the Citadel wall, making the most basic kind of retreat: a mad running dash for their lives. Everybody nearby was firing furiously at them. All except one, that is. Standing near Steele was an old, fat Army master sergeant from MACV. He shouted, "Why don't they let 'em get away, so we can get the hell outta here!"

The Marines ignored him and kept shooting. The guys in the Citadel needed all the help they could get.

Marines of 1/5 near the Citadel, February 1968. Courtesy of R. H. Thompson

ARVN troops in the Citadel. Courtesy of Col. R. H. Thompson

Inside the HQ of the 1st ARVN Division, Citadel. The aluminum buildings were used as an aid station. Photo: Steve Berntson

Maj. R. H. Thompson, CO 1/5, directs advance on Citadel from jeep-mounted radio. Courtesy of R. H. Thompson

Civilian television crew films a Mechanical Mule. Courtesy of R. H. Thompson

Cpl. Stephen Wilson and Lance Cpl. Thomas Mitchell carrying the flag down a street in Hue before it was placed on the wall of the Citadel. Courtesy of Southeast Asian Institute, U.C. Berkeley

Pfc. Eric Henshall, wearing neither helmet nor flak jacket, raising the American flag on the northeast wall of the Citadel, February 19, 1968. Photo: Steve Berntson

Charles Johnson of the New York Times *and other Marines in 1/5, the Citadel.* Photo: Steve Berntson

Marine grunt from 1/5 and tank commander of an M–48 from Alpha Company peer down northeast wall of the Citadel, February 12, 1968. Marine Corps photo: J. L. Harlan; courtesy of Richard Lyons

Inside the Citadel wall, after a firefight. Courtesy of Southeast Asian Institute, U.C. Berkeley.

Loading casualties up on the back ramp of a CH–46 Sea Knight helicopter, February 14, 1968. Marine Corps photo: N. F. Schrider; courtesy of Richard Lyons

Grunt from 1/5 fires M–79 grenade launcher, February 22, 1968. Marine Corps photo: N. F. Schrider; courtesy of Richard Lyons

Marines of 1/5 and 3/5 secure the last NVA position, the Imperial Palace. Courtesy of R. H. Thompson

Capt. M. C. Harrington being presented with Navy Commendation Medal by Lt. Col. R. H. Thompson, Bn. Cmdn., in the field near Phu Bai, April 1968. Courtesy of M. C. Harrington

Lance Cpl. Richard W. Carter, USMC, on right, at Danang medical station, October 1968. Courtesy of R. W. Carter

Wounded marine of 2/5, being treated by corpsman, February 6, 1968. Photo: Bill Dickman, courtesy of Richard Lyons

Capt. Ron Christmas, CO Hotel Company, 2/5, with toy M–16 on his lap. Behind him is one of his radiomen. Photo: Bill Dickman

Phu Bai, March 1968. Memorial services for men of Hue. Courtesy of M. J. Gravel

Hue City, rebuilt after the war. Courtesy of Southeast Asian Institute, U.C. Berkeley.

Chapter 7

The Citadel, Part One

The Tower

Just as Hue was actually two cities, the battle to retake it turned into two distinct fights. For the Marines, the first phase had been to get the South Side under control; phase two was the retaking of the north side — the Citadel. The South Side had been tough, but the Citadel became something worse. It was almost incongruous, modern Marine infantrymen pulling out of the rice paddies to storm an eighteenth-century wall, moat and all. The casualties were terrrible, the progress measured in meters, and with the rubble growing with each day, it brought back chilling memories of Monte Cassino in '44. Michael Herr, one of the many correspondents who accompanied the Marines in the Citadel, tried to explain what it meant: "On the worst days, no one expected to get through it alive. . . . They all knew how bad it was, the novelty of fighting in a city had become a nasty joke, everyone wanted to get wounded."*

Pfc. Lewis C. Lawhorn was a fireteam leader in First Platoon, Delta Company, 1st Battalion, 5th Marines, 1st Marine Division. He was black, a bright twenty-year-old high school jock from the steel town of Vandergrift, Pennsylvania. He'd been sent to Vietnam back in November 1967, over two months before, and in that time, he'd learned what

*Michael Herr, *Dispatches,* N.Y.: Avon, 1978.

it meant to be an infantryman. He lived hard, like the Marine grunts always did; there were the rice paddies he sloshed through, the sand fleas, mosquitoes, the bone-chilling monsoon rains. There were no showers, no clean beds, no cold beer; only the broiling sun, that damned fifty-pound pack on his back, and another mile of sweltering jungle to hack through on patrol. Then, little sleep that night because he had to pull radio watch or night ambush or listening post. And, of course, there was the enemy.

Lawhorn didn't put much thought into exactly why he was fighting in Vietnam, but he had a gut belief in his country and in the cause, and that was enough. What Lewis Lawhorn was really fighting for was the Marine Corps. That's where his trust was. The company commander, Capt. Myron Harrington, was brand-new; Lawhorn would have to wait and see how he did in combat. But the First Platoon leader, Lt. Maurice "Mo" Green, was pretty good. And the Pfc.'s and corporals and sergeants he was serving beside were just great. Lawhorn's line company was about the only place where his being black made no difference. As he said, "I know that there was problems in the rear, racial incidents back in the rear. But we didn't have time for stuff like that. We were too busy ducking and dodging and trying to stay alive. The North Vietnamese didn't care what color you was when he shot. My outfit — we had people from down south, deep south, we had people from New York, we had people from Massachusetts, different places, different accents — but we all was together as a team. We had blacks, Puerto Ricans, Indians, whites. We had no problems. The white brothers, the blue-eyed brothers we called them. We got along great because, for one thing, we were Marines; we were all there to do our tour and go home. Another thing, we had to depend on each other. That's one thing about being in the infantry, when you're a grunt. You live with each other, you sleep with each other, you cry with each other, you pray with each other. We depended on each other to do a lot of things. I was friends with everybody in the platoon; we were all friends. My unit — good leadership, good ability, and we had a good reputation. Our motto over there for Delta Company was 'We'll-Do-It Delta.' Any nasty job, we had to take it. But any job we did, we did it well, with pride."

Pfc. Lawhorn and the rest of the grunts would need all the pride, comradeship, and courage they could muster to make it through the Citadel.

The commander of Delta Company, Capt. Myron C. Harrington, had more than a few worries. He was a twenty-seven-year-old family man from Georgia, who'd already spent six months in Vietnam. But he'd been with a Da Nang supply unit, had only taken over Delta on January 23, and had no combat experience. He and his company were manning the firebase perimeter bunkers of Hill 147, north of the Hai Van Pass, when the Tet Offensive broke, and the radio reports he received were far from hopeful. The battalion basecamp at Phu Loc, more than ten miles south of Phu Bai on Highway 1, started taking constant mortar fire, and nearby CAP units came under ground attack. Units from 1/5 were being dispatched like fire brigades to help hold the villages, and on February 1, when CAP H5 was being overrun by the NVA, the battalion commander, Lt. Col. Robert P. Whalen, personally led the relief force. The convoy got mortared, Whalen was seriously wounded, and the reaction platoon that moved up was ambushed before it could reach CAP H5. A third force was also halted. It took the fourth attack to secure the ville. The colonel had been hit two hundred yards outside the Phu Loc wire. Things were that bad.

Finally, on February 3, Captain Harrington got word that he was to enter the fray. He was directed to walk the twelve kilometers down Highway 1 from Hill 147 to Phu Loc, and come in to reinforce. No one at battalion had any real intelligence on the enemy; they told him there was no one between him and them. Harrington had to leave one platoon atop the hill to protect the artillery, and in the morning, he was on the road with his other two platoons, marching for Phu Loc.

On their route was the hamlet of Thua Luu, nestled between two rolling hills, with the South China Sea about a kilometer away on their right flank. Lawhorn and the other young grunts had a certain affection for Thua Luu; the people there treated them well, and they'd never even drawn a sniper round during patrols around the ville. Sometimes, when they were sent out on ambush on a dark, miserable monsoon-drenched night, they would sneak into Thua Luu and spend the night in someone's hootch, radioing in fake location reports, and maybe getting some boom-boom or smoking a little grass. But that was all before Tet.

They were on the outskirts of the ville when a burst of AK–47 suddenly went off from somewhere ahead. Lawhorn and the rest went flat, but Captain Harrington got on the radio, said it was probably only a couple of snipers, and to keep moving. The grunts swept into the ville, everyone getting more and more spooked — all the houses they passed were empty. The place was deserted. Lawhorn gripped his M–16 and glanced from hootch to hootch. Something bad was going to come down. Halfway inside Thua Luu, it happened.

Lawhorn watched the shacks ahead of him suddenly erupt in a flurry of tracers. A couple of Marines on the road collapsed, the rest scattered, more fire started cracking from the jungled slopes around the ville. Then the NVA started lobbing in mortar shells. Lawhorn was scrambling for cover when he heard the shot crack past his ear, felt the heat, and stumbled off the road, thinking his ear was shot off. The platoon sergeant ran back, rolled beside him, and grabbed for his head. But he was okay, it had only been a close call. Up ahead, they could see shadowy figures flitting between the hootches. The Marines were belly-down, firing furiously. The NVA fire kept raking them from three sides.

Back down the road, Harrington crouched down with his radiomen, scared, concerned, and wondering what was happening. There was enough fire coming in for a battalion of North Vietnamese soldiers; his first action and he walked into a battalion ambush with two platoons. Harrington quickly got on his radio, calling for artillery and directing the support fire of a Navy destroyer firing from the nearby ocean.

Up front, the firing grew withering and Lawhorn and his platoon bolted back, running like hell, and scurried over the earthen road berm, down into a field flooded from the monsoon rains. Pinned down, they were waist-deep in muck. Lieutenant Green wanted to charge the ville — he couldn't stand to sit in the mud and slowly see his platoon blown away — and he started shouting, directing fire, trying to get the grunts back over the berm. He started to move, and an AK-burst blew up mud and water around him. He went down with a bullet in his ankle, and another Marine, a black grunt who'd started over the berm, flopped back with a bullet in his head. Everyone else just hunkered down in the field, confused and scared.

Back down the road, they could see the medevac choppers coming in through the wall of fire. The black Marine who'd been hit in the head was still breathing shallowly. Lawhorn, two other grunts, and a walking-wounded with a shoulder injury rolled him onto a poncho. The field was too full to struggle through, so the four of them climbed onto the road with their buddy and began hustling back as fast as they could to where the helicopters were landing. They got maybe fifteen yards, and then Lawhorn could hear the zing-zing-zing of AK rounds going past his head, could see the chips flying up in the road. They dropped the wounded man, and then Lawhorn heard the pop of flesh being hit, heard the Marine with the shoulder-injury scream, "Mother-fucker!" as another bullet tore through his wrist. They piled back over the berm and hugged mud.

Lawhorn and one of the Marines grabbed the man with the head wound by his ankles, and dragged him out of the fire. Then they started again toward the landing zone with their loads of wounded, heads ducked low, forcing themselves through the mire. Another helicopter, a big locust-shaped Sea Knight, swooped in, fire pouring at it, and landed with its back ramp already down. The grunts made a rush for it, carrying the wounded on ponchos or with arms over shoulders. Lawhorn threw in the black grunt, and abruptly the chopper lurched up. Lawhorn hung on for dear life, his legs dangling, gritting his teeth as AK rounds burst through the aluminum floor of the bird. The corpsman inside screamed at the pilot not to raise the ramp, then reached for Lawhorn, grabbed his arms and shoulders and hauled him aboard. He stood up in the chopper, breathing hard, his flak jacket and trousers soaked with sweat and mud and other people's blood. The door gunners looked at him like they'd never seen a grunt before.

The Sea Knight touched down in Da Nang and more corpsmen rushed to the back ramp to off-load the casualties. The pilot, a major, apologized to Lawhorn about their hasty departure. He asked if there were any more casualties back at Thua Luu. Lawhorn said yes, and as soon as they refueled, they were airborne again. The chopper skimmed in over the paddies outside the ville, and Lawhorn ran out the back at a crouch. Fire still cracked ahead and Marines were running back down the road. The wounded were carried on (the official record was that Delta had ten seriously wounded that day while killing twelve NVA) and the chopper departed again. By the time Lawhorn found his squad, the whole company had backtracked down the road. They said they'd been fighting hard and steady, but they simply couldn't get in, so finally Captain Harrington radioed battalion for permission to pull back.

They walked two or three kilometers back to their firebase and spent the night there, watching the glow of artillery around Thua Luu. In the morning, February 4, they went back down the road — and it started all over again. NVA fire rattled from the village and the high ground, mortar shells popped in their tubes, and the Marines got down in the outlying paddies and opened up. They could hear whistles off their flanks, as if more North Vietnamese units were maneuvering to encircle the company, and Harrington ordered them back once again. They called in mortars, artillery, and offshore U.S. Navy gunfire on the village, and got a chopper in for the casualties. This time, the records reflect seven Marines wounded and eleven NVA killed. The grunts again spent the night back at the firebase, knowing they'd have to go back to Thua Luu in the morning. Most of them choked back their fear and started getting their gear ready; but one Marine, a black guy named Campbell who was new to Vietnam, started talking to Lawhorn, saying over and over how he wasn't scared.

They went back toward the village at night, quietly sweeping through until they realized the NVA were gone. The enemy had simply picked up and moved on, leaving only a bombed village to show they'd been there. Delta Company crossed a river during the night over the damaged bridge, then joined up with the rest of the battalion which had moved south to support them.

By noon, they were back to patrolling the road. Lawhorn's squad was in the bushes off to the side, walking flank security, when there was a sudden terrific explosion down the highway. Everyone hit the deck, but there was no firing, so Lawhorn hiked up to the road berm and looked down the street. There was smoke in the air, Marines and corpsmen running around, and he could see some grunts down on the dirt, wounded. There was another Marine down, spread all over the road — lumpy, blood-soaked rags, an arm here, a leg there. He'd stepped on an antitank mine — fifty pounds of TNT. It had been the new man, Campbell.

From that fight, Delta Company joined the rest of the battalion in the patrols around Phu Loc, encountering snipers, mortars, and quick firefights in the rainy, paddy-hedgerow country.

Rumors started circulating that 1/5 was going to be sent up north to help recapture Hue City. Pfc. "Lawman" Lawhorn hoped that wasn't true. He'd seen enough combat to last a lifetime.

On February 10, 1968, the decision was made to commit 1/5 to the Hue Citadel. Up until then, the Citadel had been a South Vietnamese fight. While 1/1 and 2/5 had been fighting for the South Side, Brigadier General Truong had led his 1st ARVN Division in taking back the old imperial city. On the morning of January 31, while the Marines were fighting to secure the MACV compound, Truong and his garrison troops were making a valiant stand of their own. The Black Panther Company, led by a fine captain named Tran Ngoc Hue, held positions at the Citadel airfield when the invading North Vietnamese swept in. The South Vietnamese soldiers let go with a fusillade of LAW rockets, buckling the initial attack. Another NVA battalion attacked General Truong's ARVN HQ and broke through into the medical area. A staff officer, Lieutenant Nguyen Ai, although shot in the shoulder, led a counterattack of ARVN clerks and repulsed the initial NVA thrust. Truong ordered the Black Panthers to move in, and together with the two hundred-man division staff, they secured and held the headquarters.

Truong's foresight in ordering his staff into the HQ had saved the command-structure of the division. From his HQ enclave, he ordered his infantry, paratrooper, and armor units — positioned outside Hue — to move in and reinforce. Encountering tough resistance, and inflicting and suffering heavy casualties, the ARVN units fought their way one by one into the HQ. By the time the battle ended, General Truong's task force consisted of the following combat units: 1st and 2d Companies, 1st Regiment; 4th Battalion, 2d Regiment; 3d Regiment; Division Black Panther and Reconnaissance Companies; 1st, 2d, and 3d Troops, 7th Armored Cavalry Regiment; 2d, 7th, and 9th Battalions, 1st Airborne Task Force; 1st, 4th, and 5th Battalions, Task Force A, Vietnamese Marine Corps; and the 21st and 39th Battalions, 1st Ranger Group. From the HQ, they began the brutal attempt to recapture the Citadel. For the South Vietnamese soldiers fighting in the streets, there was one ugly twist which did not confront the Marines — many of them had family in Hue and they had to fight on, not knowing how their loved ones were faring. In some cases, they had to destroy their own homes to drive the NVA out.

It was a grueling episode. Buildings were secured, only to be lost in NVA night attacks with grappling hooks thrown over walls. Whole ARVN battalions found themselves cut off and had to fight for days to get back to the HQ. The Vietnamese Air Force received permission from General Lam to bomb inside the Citadel, but still the North Vietnamese hung on tenaciously. As one example of the brutal combat, on February 5, the 4th Battalion, 3d ARVN Regiment crossed the Perfume River and made seven unsuccessful attacks against the Citadel wall. One ARVN cavalry unit came into Hue with twelve APCs; in short order, eight were destroyed. Finally the South Vietnamese soldiers began to lose their fighting spirit, and within the first week, they had, in effect, circled their wagons and sat back to wait.

General Truong was no slacker. He was a short, wiry man and quite capable. He had assumed command of the division in 1966, when it was in a demoralized state following the Buddhist revolt, and had shaped it into a top-notch fighting force. General Westmoreland himself had high regard for Truong; there were several U.S. Army officers who told Westmoreland that they'd trust Truong to command an American unit. Nevertheless, the Citadel had taken the starch out of the division. Fighting an enemy that was constantly resupplied and reinforced with fresh troops, faced with bad weather that minimized air support, suffering heavy casualties, lacking most of the street-proven weapons like the 106mm recoillesss rifle, and — worst of all — not having the vigor that had carried the U.S. Marines on the South Side, the ARVN went from the offense to the defense.

Major Swenson, the Marine liaison officer who had fought at the

MACV compound and then helicoptered to his post inside the ARVN HQ, explained it this way: "I retain the utmost respect for General Truong and the majority of the officers he had on his staff. The ARVN Division had excellent regimental commanders and the regiments could fight well, but not on all occasions. Truong himself was demanding, tough on his staff and division, honest and cooperative. But, I can assure you, the Marines and only the Marines won the battle of Hue. Although many South Vietnamese were killed and others fought extemely well, beyond day four of the offensive, their casualties were low and their tempo of operations can be characterized as 'remain in place, don't take more casualties'."

As a point of pride the South Vietnamese had hoped to retake the Citadel with only ARVN troops. But, on February 9, Truong was compelled to request U.S. assistance. The message followed the chain of command until reaching General LaHue at Phu Bai with the decision to commit 1/5.

The Citadel was about to become a Marine show.

Maj. Robert H. Thompson was the commanding officer of 1st Battalion, 5th Marines. He was thirty-seven years old, married with children, and from Corinth, Mississippi. A tall, rawboned man, he had a stern, stolid character. He had taken over the battalion on February 2, more by default than anything else. When Lieutenant Colonel Whalen, an old friend of his, was wounded on the 1st, the regimental commander, Colonel Bohn (who knew Thompson), directed him to assume command from the battalion executive officer, Maj. P. A. Wilson, who was acting CO. At that time, Major Thompson had already been in Vietnam for six months, serving on the III MAF staff in Da Nang — complete with cold beer and barbecued steaks every night, and an easy Bronze Star. Thompson's first day in the field with 1/5 provided a dramatic contrast to life in the Da Nang rear. As soon as he stepped off the resupply chopper at Phu Loc, NVA mortars began whistling in, and Thompson spent the first five minutes of his new command at the bottom of a muddy hole with his luggage and several grunts piled on top of him.

Thompson had only one week to get to know his unit before the order to the Citadel came. A battalion from the 101st Airborne Division moved into their Phu Loc basecamp, and the Marines began leapfrogging north to Phu Bai during the 10th and 11th of February, the companies breaking down into platoons and squads as they hitched rides on choppers and trucks. Once they were at Phu Bai, the move to Hue was almost immediate. Two platoons from Bravo Company, under

Capt. Fern Jennings, were loaded aboard helicopters and dropped inside the compound walls of the ARVN HQ. But the Sea Knight carrying Third Platoon took fire and came limping back to Phu Bai with a wounded pilot.

Major Thompson got to Phu Bai aboard a convoy on the 11th, and reported to General LaHue's Task Force X-RAY command post for his orders. LaHue said that 1/1 and 2/5, under Colonel Hughes, had pretty much taken care of the South Side, but the ARVN in the Citadel were moving slowly. There was little reliable, up-to-date intelligence from the South Vietnamese, he said, and Thompson was to move 1/5 into the Citadel and attack under Hughes' direction. LaHue stressed to Thompson that he was to take orders only from Hughes, not Truong. Afraid that he might be overly influenced by the ARVN general, LaHue considered making Thompson a brevet colonel. No, Thompson declined, that wouldn't be necessary; he didn't wear rank insignia. If LaHue preferred, he could introduce himself to Truong as a colonel. With that, General LaHue wished Thompson luck and said it shouldn't take more than a few days to clean up the Citadel problem.

Alpha, Charlie, and Delta Companies began convoying north to Hue. Thompson left his XO, Major Wilson, in charge of the battalion rear at Phu Bai, then followed the infantry companies with his small command-group and the stranded Bravo platoon. The trucks dropped them off at the MACV command post on the South Side, and Thompson reported in to Colonel Hughes. Hughes filled him in on what was going on across the Perfume River and they drew up a brief plan of action: Thompson was to take Alpha and Charlie Companies, link up with Bravo in the HQ, and start driving south, forcing the NVA in the Citadel back toward the Perfume. For the time being, Delta Company was to be attached opcon to 2/5.

They set up for the evening in several abandoned bullet-pocked buildings around the MACV compound. Thompson was turning in when an Army major appeared. The man had a helmet, flak jacket, and a .45 on his hip, and he introduced himself as Father McGonigal. He was, more fully, Maj. Aloysius P. McGonigal, U.S. Army Catholic chaplain, forty-six years old, from Philadelphia; a bespectacled, gregarious fellow who had volunteered for Vietnam and was assigned to the MACV staff.

Father McGonigal said he had heard 1/5 didn't have a chaplain with them, and that he had MACV permission to go with the Marines into the Citadel. Thompson didn't check if he really did have permission, but simply welcomed him aboard. It was peaceful that night around MACV.

The sun never really came up in the morning; it was hazy gray, misty, and cold. Major Thompson was down at the Navy boat ramp with his command group, trying to get his people organized for the move into the Citadel. They waited for hours for the U.S. Navy LCUs that were supposed to ferry them across, but every time they churned up the river, NVA fire from the Citadel wall drove them back. One ventured too close to the ramp. Something exploded against it, probably a B-40, and it sank.

Finally, by late afternoon, the shooting slacked off and the LCUs pulled up to the ramp. Thompson, the command group, the Bravo platoon, and Alpha and Charlie Companies crammed aboard, and the boats started off. They steamed to the right down the Perfume, along where the river looped up to touch the northern corner of the Citadel, and the NVA opened up from the brush-choked banks. Rounds whined, criss-crossing around the LCUs from both shores, and rockets exploded in white shadows in the river. Marines on the boat railings shot back at the muzzle flashes. Fortunately, no one aboard was hit.

They docked at a ramshackle ferry landing north of the Citadel at the Bao Vinh Quay, and disembarked without drawing a shot. They organized, crossed the moat running along the northwest wall, and began marching through the brush and houses towards the ARVN HQ with Thompson in the lead. They were coming down a road when several Vietnamese civilians approached Thompson. They waved their arms and spoke in broken English, but they got their point across — a group of NVA were lying in ambush farther down the road. Thompson wasn't sure what other route to take, but the civilians led the Marine column down a different road right up to the back gate of the HQ. They were met there by Captain Jennings, the Bravo Company commander, and several South Vietnamese officers.

Thompson said he wanted to get his people inside the compound to set up. The ARVN officers said no, they couldn't let the Marines in. They said it might draw mortar fire. Thompson stayed calm. Either the gates were opened, he said, or his men would assault the walls. The gates swung open, and the grunts filed in.

Thompson checked in with General Truong and Colonel Adkisson, the senior U.S. Army advisor to the ARVN, to hear what exactly the situation was. Truong and Adkisson explained that the ARVN held the HQ and the northwest wall, through which 1/5 had just passed. South Vietnamese soldiers and marines were fighting along the southwest wall. The NVA still had a firm grip on the northeast wall and the southeast wall, where the old Imperial Palace was. Flying above the palace was the VC flag. Intelligence placed two North Vietnamese battalions inside the Citadel and a third to the west, keeping the enemy resupply lines open to the wall. The U.S. Marines were to be responsible for securing the northeast wall; like the others, it was approximately twenty-five hundred yards long, twenty feet high, and varied in width from fifty to two-hundred feet.

According to the maps, the 1st ARVN Airborne Task Force was operating halfway down the northeast wall, between the HQ and the palace, near a prominent wall tower. With that information, Thompson laid out his plans. He would take his three companies, make contact with the ARVN airborne, and from that line of departure, launch the attack straight down the wall. Alpha would be on the left flank, right along the wall, Bravo would be in the buildings to their right, and Charlie would be in reserve. In conjunction, what was left of the 3d ARVN Regiment was to attack on their right flank, on the southwest wall. General Truong and Colonel Adkisson readily agreed to the plan.

The Marines spent the night in the HQ compound. Again, it was quiet. In the morning, Tuesday, February 13, 1968, they were to begin the drive to recapture the Citadel.

At eight in the morning, Capt. J. J. Bowe and his Alpha Company were out in front of the battalion, going down the streets beneath the northeast wall, headed towards the position the ARVN Airborne was holding.

By 8:15 A.M., all hell broke loose.

Thompson was with his CP group, behind Alpha, when the firing broke out. It was absolutely withering, a shattering cacophony of AK-47 automatic rifles, B-40 rockets, and mortars coming from the houses and from that large tower on the wall. The NVA were dug in the tower, and it gave them a commanding view of Alpha's advance. One thing shot through Thompson's mind — where was the ARVN Airborne that was supposed to have secured the area? They were gone (pulled back, it was later learned, because the Vietnamese Joint General Staff considered the Airborne relieved of the fighting with the arrival of the Marines and had them shifted to Saigon. It was an utter failure of communications). The NVA fire kept raking Alpha Company, and Thompson ordered them back. A recoilless rifle team moved up, fired down the street and at the tower, and Alpha came straggling back down the road. The whole fight lasted only ten minutes. Captain Bowe was hit badly and had to be evacuated; most of the lieutenants were wounded; thirty grunts had been hit. And two dead Marines had been left lying in the street. That was it for Alpha Company; they spent the rest of the day just running their casualties back to the battalion aid station inside the HQ.

Thompson got on the radio to 1st Lt. Scott A. Nelson, who was commanding Charlie Company, and ordered him up on the right flank of Captain Jennings' Bravo Company. At a little after noon, they tried to move forward again. The NVA positions erupted with fire once more, the two Marine tanks up front supporting the attack took rockets in their turrets, and no one could advance a foot.

Before anyone else was hit, Thompson ordered them back to the starting point. The Marines fell back, and the NVA followed them into the vacated areas. The firing kept up, and at 2:55 P.M., Thompson received a message from Colonel Hughes, who had been monitoring the radios: "With situation as exists at present, hold positions, reorganize, and prepare plans for continuing attack utilizing maximum fire support. Submit plans for continuing attack indicating type fire deemed necessary and desirable."

Unlike the situation in the South Side, where South Vietnamese pressures had restricted the use of supporting arms, the Marines in the Citadel were going to get the support they needed. There was no other way. Five minutes after getting the okay on the firepower, Major Thompson radioed back: "Present plans are to continue to attack upon completion of prep fires, walking artillery in front of advancing troops. Fire support element necessary and desirable; artillery 8-inch and 155mm, fixed wing with zunie rockets to be used on the wall. Utilization CS on Citadel area."

Within a half hour, after Bravo Company had a man killed along the wall, artillery fire started crashing in ahead of the battalion. The day ended with three Marines reported killed and thirty-four wounded. There was no report of any enemy casualties. The grunts spent the night in the houses seventy-five yards short of where the ARVN airborne troops were supposed to have been.

On the evening of the 13th, Captain Harrington got word to bring Delta up into the ARVN HQ. He didn't have his whole company with him — Third Platoon was detached as convoy security on the trucks making the Phu Bai–Hue runs — so he went down to the Navy boat ramp with only First and Second Platoons. There were two LCUs there, but they were so jammed with trucks and supplies, Harrington could only find room for himself, his CP group, and one squad. Going up the moat along the northeast wall, they took fire from shore. The LCUs dropped the Marines off at the ramp north of the Citadel, then started back down the moat.

The grunts sat down to wait among the houses around the dock, and Harrington got on the radio for his two platoons to catch the next boats up.

The Marines waited around the boat ramp, and Pfc. Landry and some of the other WHISKEY 1/11 mortarmen took a break from their gun pits to talk with them. Two more LCUs docked at the ramp, some of the grunts boarded, and they churned towards the mouth of the moat. North Vietnamese fire started rattling from the wall, and the gunners quickly got back on their mortar tubes and pumped HE and CS shells toward the Citadel. Halfway across the river, the LCUs suddenly veered off and started back toward the ramp. The boat ramps went down and the grunts piled out, choking, puking, some crying hysterically, in an absolute panic. The tear gas from the CS shells they'd fired must have floated back over the boats, catching the grunts unaware and without gas masks, he realized. Landry and some buddies ran down to the bank and grabbed them by their arms, leading them back to a small building, fanning them along the way, giving them their gas masks so they could get a little unpolluted air. One of the mortarmen, Corporal Raby, grabbed a screaming grunt lieutenant and slapped him, shouting at him to get his shit together, to get his platoon organized.

More fire cracked in from the Citadel, and several of the grunts sprawled in the street, pinned-down — coughing, panicking, and firing blindly into an abandoned building. Landry shouted at the lieutenant to get his people out of the street, and they started bolting back. One of them was limping on a wounded leg. As Landry helped him inside the building, he muttered, "Can you believe this shit? I got five days left."

The sailors on the LCUs were reluctant to run the gauntlet again. Delta was stuck. Up the moat, Harrington still sat, waiting, cursing himself for letting himself get cut off from his men.

By the time Delta Company was fumbling at the boat ramp on their second day, Sergeant Berntson had been in Hue for fourteen days, and in Vietnam for ten months. He was twenty-two, a sharp young man from Idaho, with that cryptic, honest, rural American way of talking. He'd come to Vietnam in a roundabout way, dropping out of college when the Marines landed at Da Nang in 1965. He saw his duty, and he picked the Marine Corps because a favorite uncle had fought with the Corps at Guadalcanal, Saipan, and Tinian. His uncle had never talked about the war, never bragged, but Berntson knew he'd been a Marine and that was all that mattered. After boot camp, he spent a year volunteering for Vietnam. He finally gave up, got married, and then just after he and his wife had decided to start a family, he found himself on the plane to Vietnam as a lance corporal. He was finally going to be a part of it.

He was assigned as a combat correspondent with the Information Services Office, 1st Marine Division. The Marines there were an independent lot, somewhat rebellious, who saw themselves as combinations of Ernest Hemingway and John Wayne. Six days in-country, Berntson was teamed with a young buck sergeant to cover the 5th Marines in Operation Union II. They flew right into a hot LZ, tumbling out with a firefight rattling on the perimeter. Berntson stumbled around, new-guy dumb, standing straight up in the fire, until the sergeant grabbed him and dragged him behind a paddy dike. He lay there, suddenly scared to death and shaking, and the sergeant said to him, "This is it. This is Vietnam." Six days later, the battle was over and Berntson flew back to Da Nang, having vomited twice; feeling a numbness that never left him. That was just the first fight; the Marines wanted publicity about their units, and Berntson and the rest of the USMC correspondents spent twenty-seven days a month in the field. They roamed from battle to battle with blanket travel-orders, writing stories on the back of C ration cartons or on rickety field typewriters, sending copy back stuffed in door gunners' pockets, on convoys, or whatever was available. They didn't write the big war stories; that was for the civilian news people — the guys, as Berntson described them, who fly in, take ten minutes of hot film, then bug out on the next chopper. Berntson wrote about the combat Marines and he knew their axiom: If you ain't a grunt, you ain't shit. The only way to write about them was to become one of them. So Berntson trudged with them through paddies, helped haul ammunition, dragged the WIAs and KIAs in ponchos to the medevacs, and stood up and shot when the time came. He survived the siege of Con Thien, an uncountable number of firefights, and it made him hard. He was tough and numb beyond the thousand-yard-stare, hard to the point that despite grenade scars from a night ambush gone wrong, despite his wife and baby daughter, he'd already started the paperwork for a six-month extension in Vietnam. He also developed a tremendous sense of comradeship, a bond with his fellow Marines that at times seemed even stronger than the one with his family. There were so many good guys — like Tom Young, whose body he had pulled out of a ditch near the burned AFRTVS building, and Dale Dye.

He'd gone into Hue with Sergeant Dye, hitching a ride with the 1/1 reaction force, not knowing what they were getting into. They'd tried to stick together the rest of the battle, fighting with Hotel 2/5 through the treasury, the province capital, and the barrage that wounded Captain Christmas. But, by the 13th, things were getting quiet, Hotel Company was dug in along the Phu Cam Canal, and Berntson decided to see what was going on elsewhere in Hue.

Around dusk, he started wandering back toward the MACV compound, walking down Le Loi Street past the gutted buildings, too worn
out to worry about snipers. Around the compound were some grunts
from 1/5. He couldn't believe the scene that greeted him: there was
Walter Cronkite, surrounded by a battery of reporters and cameramen,
and Colonel Hughes with a microphone in his face. The colonel was
denying reports of Marine looting, and saying they were doing everything possible to protect the civilians, etc., etc. Berntson knew he was
right; Jesus, he thought, after what the Communists did, the Marines
were like saints. After Marine mortar fire set a house on fire, he'd seen
a grunt run in and carry out an old lady. He'd seen a corpsman deliver
a baby in the middle of a firefight near the province capital. But, he'd
also seen Marines helping themselves to booze, food, and occasionally
to recorders and cameras. But with all the dead people lying around, it
seemed strange that anyone was concerned about such trivial things.

Finally he left the colonel and the reporters and found some C
rations and a corpsman he knew from 2/5. They found a place away
from the jostling people at the interview. They sat in the corner of the
room, listening to the rain tap on the roof, talking quietly, sharing a
couple of dry cigarettes the corpsman had managed to scrounge. They
made plans to lay claim to a pair of cots the corpsman had found in
one of the rooms, and sack out for the night; and if anybody tried to
roust them out, they'd tell him to screw off. Berntson would have given
anything for a couple of hours of sleep in a dry place. But then again,
the cots were next door to where the dead Marines were stacked up in
body bags. There was a bad smell, and even worse imagery.

They were still talking when a grunt from Delta 1/5 came in. Berntson had met him the day before, when Delta had been temporarily attached to 2/5. He was a big black dude, a former Philadelphia gang
lord nicknamed Philly Dog, who carried an M-79 grenade launcher,
that the Marines called a blooper. Philly Dog walked in, obviously
excited about something.

He called to Berntson, "Hey, Storyteller, you gonna go with us up
the river?"

"What the hell you talking about?"

"We got a Swift out there and we're gonna tow up a bunch of gook
junks. Me and the whole company. We're gonna go up the river and
land up back there somewhere and kick the shit outta the gooks up
there."

"Who's going?" Berntson asked.

"We got Delta Company, and we got a bunch of guys from Alpha
Company. We're just gonna haul up there. There's a bunch of ARVN
up there and they ain't doing diddly shit, and they're getting overrun

all the time, and we're going to go up there and take over their building for 'em."

Berntson mulled it over; he could either spend the night with the dead Marines or link up with Delta 1/5 for their attack into the Citadel. He opted for the latter. He pulled out his prized possession, a Hue City tourist map he'd found in the rubble of the CORDS building, and stared at the Citadel. It seemed like suicide to storm across the Perfume River against the wall, but then he traced the route up the moat and realized they could bypass the NVA positions and move down on them from above. He knew it was going to be tough, but he'd been staring at that damned VC flag over the Imperial Palace for two weeks now, and he relished the thought of seeing it go down. And besides, Philly Dog seemed pretty excited about it all.

"Hey," Philly Dog called again, "You wanna come along and be a blooper?"

"Nah."

"I'm looking for another blooper man. I'm going to be on one side of the boat, why don't you be on the other side? You can fire a blooper?"

"Oh sure, I can fire a blooper." He'd fired an M-79 exactly two times.

With that, Philly Dog scrounged up another grenade launcher and an ammo vest, and they moved out. It was dark, around midnight, by the time the Delta Marines organized again at the ramp. In a few minutes, a Swift (a Navy PT-type gunboat with .50-caliber machine gun mounts) came sloshing up to the dock, lights out, towing a string of three Vietnamese junk boats. The sails and riggings had been knocked off the junks so the grunts could pile aboard. They started up the moat with another Swift following them as escort. Berntson and Philly Dog walked up to the front of the lead Swift, where one sailor was hunkered down behind a twin-fifty mount piled with sandbags. He gestured to them to crouch down with him behind the sandbags, and Berntson climbed to the left, Philly Dog to his right. They sailed up the moat, lights off, no one talking, afraid the low rumble of the engine would draw fire. The channel narrowed to fifty yards, shore to shore. To the right Berntson could see the bank crowded with buildings, trees, floating sampans; then giving way to a flat, open cemetery. Up on the left was the Citadel wall, a low, black silhouette. Berntson stared at it, just knowing the bastards were going to unload on them any second, hoping they wouldn't because he hardly remembered how to use the M-79 grenade launcher he was gripping.

When it started it came from the right, from the cemetery. An NVA mortar tube, set up someplace in the flat field, popped and two rounds sprayed up in the moat. Then a machine gun started stitching red tracers through the black. Philly Dog screamed, "Get 'em!" and the sailor swung his twin-fifties around and started pounding. The skipper hit full throttle, and they went roaring ahead, the three junk boats snapping in line behind them, the grunts ducking and hanging tight. Philly Dog started pumping grenades, and Berntson joined in, not aiming, just breaking the shotgunlike launcher open, shoving a round in, firing from the hip, firing again — until he'd popped ten grenades at the enemy. The escort Swift screamed up alongside, between them and the right bank, and started hosing down the cemetery with its fifties.

In a few minutes, the shooting was all over. No casualties.

Within twenty minutes of leaving the South Side, the tiny flotilla came to the small wharf where Captain Harrington was waiting. It didn't look like much of a dock, Berntson thought, just a bunch of stilts the Viets used to dry their fishing nets. The Swift pulled as close as it could to the shore, then cut loose the wooden junks, and the grunts paddled for land. They off-loaded, rowed back, and Berntson, Philly Dog, and the other Marines on the Swift deck piled in and sloshed toward shore. By the time they met up with Harrington and got organized in a little street-plaza, the sun was just starting the glow on the horizon. They started toward the ARVN HQ gate, filing down a battered street, expecting to get hit again.

Up ahead, Berntson could see a black mass piled to one side of the street. When he got a little closer, and the sun was up a bit more, he saw the mass was a burned out truck, the front blown off. Closer still and the stench became almost unbearable — there were five or six dead ARVNs around the truck, a couple of them lying where they'd fallen beside the wreck, the rest burned to death inside the cab, roasted into charred, black lumps. Berntson thought that they must really be in bad shape, since they hadn't even had time to clean up their dead.

A few minutes later, shots rang out from ahead. Everyone went flat. Someone shouted that the shots had come from an ARVN sentry at the HQ gate. He'd opened fire on the Marine point team. An interpreter team with Delta Company started shouting in Vietnamese at the nervous sentry, and Berntson lay there wondering: who the hell coordinated this gang-bang? A pair of ARVN officers appeared at the wire and they and the interpreters shouted back and forth. One of the interpreters, a Marine lieutenant, got up and walked slowly towards the gate, his rifle slung, his hands out. There was a brief exchange of words at the wire, then finally, the gates were opened and the Marines moved in.

Berntson followed the grunts in and looked around the HQ. It had a football field–size parade deck; pretty, ornate French-style buildings; rows of palm trees; a clear, reflective moat. Then he walked off to the left, where the northeast wall touched the HQ. The backs of the buildings were blown away, everything was riddled by bullets and shrapnel, and smashed vehicles were strewn about the courtyard.

Inside the compound, Harrington ran into Captain Jennings, the Bravo CO. Jennings told him how Alpha had gotten chewed up going against the wall tower, how his company had been hit too, moving forward on the second attack. "I'm sure," he said, "tomorrow, you're going to have to do it."

Harrington felt anything but honored.

Delta Company spent the remainder of the day inside the HQ, getting some rest and getting organized, while Bravo and Charlie attacked down the street again. Lieutenant Nelson's Charlie Company captured one NVA who was strolling down a street. Then, with tanks and mortars, they destroyed an NVA rocket position, killing six. A sniper with Captain Jennings' Bravo Company gunned down two North Vietnamese, but then the company itself came under sniper fire, losing one man dead and four wounded. During the day's fighting, the two companies managed to press forward a hundred yards, but heavy fire poured from the tower on the left, and Thompson ordered them back. More artillery pounded in, then there was a break in the overcast and rain, and jets from the 1st Marine Air Wing came on station, sending rockets, napalm, and CS into the wall. All ordnance was on target, but only slight damage to the NVA positions was evidenced.

After the second day of fighting, 1/5 had made no progress. That evening, Harrington visited the battalion command post, set up in a tile-roofed villa outside the HQ walls. In the morning, Major Thompson told him, it would be Delta Company's turn to attack the tower.

———————

The air roared all morning with the freight-train sound of artillery shells coming in overhead, with the explosions of mortars and five- and six-inch gunfire from a U.S. Navy cruiser rumbling in shells from the South China Sea. The tower shuddered under the barrage, parts of it crumbling into a huge rubble heap, with only some of the curved archways and walls still standing in the destruction. Avalanches of masonry and brick spilled into the street below; the houses near it were flattened or gutted. The rain kept drizzling from the gray sky, keeping the jets away. Harrington saw only one air strike in Hue, back when his company was on the South Side, on the sweeping-operation in which Captain Christmas was wounded. Delta had just swept and cleared an area, when two F-4s suddenly flashed in and bombed the place, less than five hundred yards from the company. No coordination at all. But the tower was a little worse.

The wind and rain blew cold, the Marines waited nervously around the CP, and then, finally, the prep fires were lifted. Harrington gave the word to go. The two Delta platoons pushed out, filing down along the sides of the streets, hunched over, stepping through the plaster and bricks and smashed wood piled everywhere. The distinctive clacking sound of AK-47 automatic rifles began coming from the tower. Sergeant Berntson and his partner, Sergeant Dye, hooked up with one of the squads moving along a pocked wall. Fire suddenly erupted from the front and sides, toppling the lead Marines. Berntson and Dye threw themselves against the brick wall with the grunts. Rounds thudded into the cement around them, B-40s exploded, their shrapnel quadrupled by all the flying rubble. Grunts up front were screaming for the corpsman. Dye poked his head over the wall and could see little figures hunkered in the rubble of the tower. There was an enemy soldier on top, firing down machine gun bursts, and a couple more popped up on either side, zinging down rockets. The Marines were pinned down.

A tank came up from the CP and rumbled beside them. The 90mm cannon roared out shells, the NVA fire slacked off for a moment, and Dye and Berntson and the rest rushed forward. They grabbed the wounded Marines, latching onto flak jackets and collars and boots and wrists, and went stumbling back to the nearest doorways. The tank kept thundering out shot and they managed to drag the dead and wounded behind the wall. A young corpsman with a rubber tarantula hanging in his helmet band hustled from one Marine to the next, hastily tying bandages.

The tank pulled up closer, the man in the turret firing his fifty, and the Marines hustled the wounded to it. The corpsman jumped on board and the tank hauled back down the street toward the aid station.

The squad kept moving. The machine gun atop the tower started raking again, and they went flat in rubble-piles and doorways. Dye glanced down the street and saw two Marines come charging toward them with a 3.5-inch rocket launcher. The fire spattered around them and they jumped to the right side of the street. They loaded the 3.5, but the gunner couldn't sight in on the tower from there. They started to get up to rush to the left side of the street, but Dye and others started hollering at them to stay put for all the fire. They ran into the street. The machine gun kicked rounds around them. They made it. The gunner shouldered the 3.5, sighted in, blasted off three shells. They all exploded, dead on top of the machine gun. It ceased firing.

Lawhorn was with his squad as they inched forward. He bolted from his cover and the NVA fire grew louder in his ears. He got down again. Other Marines were scrambling behind the brick walls and shattered houses, firing quick bursts at the tower to cover their rushes. Lawhorn got back to his feet, ran and stumbled, rushing to the next little brick wall. He fell against it, sweating hard, gulping air. He was consumed with fear. Bullets and shrapnel kept crashing everywhere. Men were shouting, firing furiously. He had no idea what was ahead of him, behind him, who was hit, or who was still with him. He poked his head up and looked past the debris and slanted rooftops. He could see enemy soldiers moving in the high rubble of the tower, popping up to empty AK magazines down at them, dropping back to reload. He'd never seen anything like it. God, those bastards were tough. The tower was maybe a hundred yards away; it looked like a hundred miles to Lawhorn. He brought up his M-16 and started firing madly at the little figures.

Captain Harrington scurried through the rubble with First Platoon. In the first minutes of the attack, B-40 rocket fragments had wounded the Second Platoon leader, the platoon sergeant, and the radiomen, leaving the platoon disorganized. All he had left was First Platoon. The grunts kept crawling closer to the tower, and finally Harrington was able to get inside a bombed out house at the street corner right below the tower. He got on the radio, calling off the mortars because his men were too close to the target. Rounds sprayed the house, kicking up plaster and wood. The Marines inside kept shooting. Harrington got on the radio for tank support and one rumbled up beside his hasty CP, contacted him via the radio, and boomed out shells at his direction.

The Marine fire saturated the tower. The NVA fire grew less intense.

The leaderless Second Platoon, now reorganized under their wounded platoon sergeant, a very brave staff sergeant named Robert L. Thoms, moved up to support First Platoon. Harrington got on the radio to 2d Lt. Jack S. Imlah, told him to take a group up on the wall and come in behind the tower, while he and the whole of First and Second Platoons occupied the NVA from the front. Imlah got a squad up on the northeast wall and they worked their way down through the rubble and shorn trees, dropping grenades on stunned North Vietnamese still crouched in spider holes. Crawling and ducking, they made it to the rear of the tower. Down in the street, Sergeant Dye suddenly heard someone shouting, "They got someone inside!" Then came a tremendous volume of M-16 fire echoing from within the tower. Then silence.

Harrington and his Marines moved toward the tower, ducking low through the haze of gunpowder and brick-dust. There were dead enemy soldiers in the junk, some of them killed a day or two before, stiff and bloated and putting out a terrible stench. Nearly three hours since the attack started, the position was now secured. Harrington ordered his men off the rubble heap and they began setting up for the night in the shells of houses below it.

The tower was a good observation point — the outer wall of the Imperial Palace could be seen from its top — so Pfc. Dennis S. Michels, a twenty-year-old First Platoon grunt, was directed to take a five-man team up. They picked their way near the top by dark, found a crater among the heaps of brick and cement, and set in for the evening.

It was pitch black — around two in the morning — when four Chicom grenades suddenly came bouncing into the observation pit. NVA infiltraters! One thudded against Michels' back, another grenade rolled under his leg. He froze, staring at them, choking a prayer. They didn't go off. Another grunt instantly snatched up the other two grenades and flung them out of the pit. Another grenade, a boom, and two Marines were hit. They all scrambled to the rim and opened fire on the enemy slipping through the rubble.

Down below in the houses, Captain Harrington was shocked suddenly to see silhouettes flitting up one side of the tower. The North Vietnamese, less than a platoon of men, opened up with their AKs, pouring rounds up at Michels's group and down at Harrington's. Green and red tracers ricocheted in the dark, the Marines managing to pin the NVA between their two groups. But the enemy kept fighting. An NVA recoilless rifle down the street went off, and Michels and his grunts dove to the bottom of their pit, hunching up against the explosions. There was a sudden scurry in the bricks and Michels looked up to see a black figure stand up at the rim of the crater, drop two more grenades on them, and disappear. They were duds. Michels just sat there, thanking the Lord.

The firing went back and forth for a while, but by morning it was over, and Michels's group climbed out of their hole. There were fifteen dead North Vietnamese soldiers sprawled in the rubble between them and Harrington's position. There was little time to rejoice at the body count. The artillery started up again, crashing in farther down the wall along the long boulevard and shredded palm trees and abandoned cars. The grunts hunkered down around the tower, finding spots in the loose rubble and sitting quietly in their helmets and flak jackets, smoking cigarettes and spooning out tasteless meals of C rations. The artillery fire lifted and they kept pushing.

The first thing Major Thompson noticed on the morning of Friday, February 16, was the weather. It was a good day, not sunny, but clear enough for the jets to come on station. They made their sorties, bombing and banking around, chewing up the wall, dropping napalm. The Naval gunfire came in too. Then the companies pressed forward and were able to secure another 150 yards.

It was the fourth day of straight dawn-to-dusk fighting.

In the late afternoon, Thompson was in his CP monitoring the radio transmissions from Alpha Company. They were in deep trouble again. They had never really recovered from the disaster on the 13th. With Captain Bowe hit and medevacked, and so many others killed or wounded, they had lost their confidence, and Thompson tried to keep them in reserve, back behind the main fighting. But, somehow, a team of Alpha Marines had gotten near the front wall of the Imperial Palace and were cut off and pinned down. Several were wounded, and no one in Alpha — including the young lieutenant who was acting commander — was really taking charge to get those Marines back to friendly lines.

Thompson was trying to plan a way to pull them out, when 1st Lt. Patrick D. Polk showed up at the CP. Lieutenant Polk was a thin, blond, outgoing twenty-three-year-old ex-lance corporal from Oshkosh, Nebraska. He was an extremely patriotic young man whose father had been a Marine in World War II, and two of his brothers had already served in Vietnam. He was also an exceptionally fine combat officer who had been twice wounded and credited with several personal enemy-kills during stints as a platoon leader with Charlie 1/5 and as the battalion liaison officer to the "Blue Dragon" 2d Korean Marine Corps Brigade. But he was due to rotate home, and had been moved to the rear as the assistant operations officer of 1/5. Polk had been at Phu Bai when he was asked to take a group up to Hue, with the understanding that he could decline since he was so close to going home. He agreed, wrote his parents to pray for him, and convoyed up with a motley collection that included walking wounded out of the hospital, Marines just back from R&R, and a motor transport detachment. Knowing what they were getting into, and being the only officer with the group, Polk made sure that several cases of hand grenades they found were passed out. They worked their way to the Citadel, Polk swimming the moat with a case of grenades (thus garnering the nickname "Handgrenade Polk"). Some of the other Marines followed, and taking a bit of fire, they began hiking towards 1/5.

For Major Thompson, seeing Lieutenant Polk suddenly appear in his CP was like manna from heaven. Thompson immediately briefed him on the Alpha Company situation. The lieutenant in charge was in no way lacking in courage, but the situation was simply over his head. Polk was to relieve the lieutenant, assume command of Alpha, and rescue those trapped Marines. Polk hitched a ride to his new company from a wild, black Marine named Howard who drove a Mechanical Mule — and found himself in the middle of a firefight. The Alpha grunts were hunkered in their positions, no one really doing anything.

Thompson had already radioed the CO about Polk taking command. Polk was a brand-new first lieutenant; the man he was relieving had about a month's seniority on him, and he seemed a little disturbed about being relieved. Nevertheless, Polk quickly got his people together and tried to instill some spark in them, telling them not to moan about how bad it was, but to take the attitude that "Damn it, we gotta get those people outta there!" Some of the grunts looked willing to go, others looked reluctant, but finally about eight men volunteered: a staff sergeant, a mortar FO corporal and his radioman, a squad leader and one of his fireteams.

Polk and his team moved out, firing and maneuvering, the remainder of Alpha Company also laying down a base of cover fire. They worked their way into a concrete house. Twenty yards away were the trapped Marines, huddled down with their backs to them along a decorative brick wall. There were five of them, four wounded, and the NVA fire slashed over their heads from three sides. Polk called in 81mm mortars, the NVA fire dropped off — and Polk and his volunteers rushed out to the wall and tugged and dragged the stranded Marines back to the house. By dusk, they had all safely made it back to the Alpha lines.

They had pulled off the rescue without any additional casualties, and after that, Major Thompson could see a change in the outfit. They had their confidence back, and they had a fine leader in Lieutenant Polk. Within a week or so, Polk was to take mortar fragments in his neck and shoulder. He stayed with Alpha Company.

Delta Company began the day swinging right to help Bravo Company. There were North Vietnamese dug in spider holes along the buildings and courtyard walls, and in a bedlam of shooting, the grunts scrambled from hole to hole, firing and dropping grenades into each one. They yanked the dead NVA from the holes, threw their AK-47s next to the bodies, and kept moving forward along the wall, past the rubbled tower.

They were ducking from house to house when NVA fire raked the front of the company, wounding a few Marines and sending the rest scrambling for cover. Sergeant Dye was crouched in a house on the left side of the street, when someone started shouting for a corpsman — and then he saw Doc Rhino, the big, quiet, redhead kid simply bolt from a door and start sprinting through the fire towards the wounded. Dye watched horrified as he was nailed in mid-stride, and Doc Rhino lurched forward into the street. He started getting up on his hands and knees, when a second burst drove him dead to the pavement.

Lawhorn heard the cries that Doc Rhino was dead, and shock and disbelief washed over him. Doc Rhino meant a lot to them all; he never let them down. And he was killed. One of the grunts who'd known him well suddenly stood up, just stood bolt straight in the fire, screaming. Lawhorn stared stunned as the man emptied his rifle over a brick wall at the enemy, hollering and shaking until two Marines grabbed him and held him down. Lawhorn never saw the man again.

Minutes later, two grunts made a break through the fire, and dragged Rhino's body back to the platoon command post. There was no way they could have left him out there. Captain Harrington put him in for a Navy Cross; he didn't get it.

Before setting in for the night, Dye went out with a three-man fireteam from Delta to scout the blasted houses west of the wall. They started picking their way around three large mounds of dirt, when Dye happened to glance to his right — and to his surprise saw an enemy soldier there. The North Vietnamese soldier was lying behind a pile of up-turned earth, one hand resting on his AK-47, just staring dreamily into space. Dye snapped his M-16 to his shoulder and started pumping rounds into the man. The other grunts spun around, opened up, and the NVA writhed and sagged.

They approached the body, muttering how lucky they were. He should have had the drop on them.

Then they kicked the body over and stared at it curiously. "Jesus, what was with him? What the hell was wrong with this guy?"

In a few minutes they found their answer. There were spider holes dotting the area, some containing the bodies of NVA killed by the Marine fire. When they started looking through the holes and packs, they found packets of what looked like white sugar. It was heroin. They found syringes, matches, bent spoons with scorch marks on the bottom; like a bunch of urban junkies. The NVA always fought professionally, and Dye couldn't figure why some of them would go into combat too stoned to know they were about to get blown away. He finally came up with an answer: they knew they didn't have a chance in the long run. They knew they were going to die.

Sergeant Dye's theory was probably correct. At 9:50 P.M., on the night of the 16th, Major Thompson received a message from Colonel Hughes's command post. It read: "Message intercepted from enemy radio message stating the commander of the enemy force inside Hue to his superior states that original commander of the force inside Hue had been killed and that many others had either been killed or wounded. He recommended to withdraw. Senior officer ordered new commander of the force in Hue to remain in position and fight."

Chapter 8

The Citadel, Part Two

Imperial Palace

The battalion command post, set up in the villa outside the ARVN HQ, presented a scene reminiscent of a Norman farmhouse a quarter of a century before. There were candles glowing on the tables, joss sticks on the family altar, bottles of red wine stacked along dusty, damaged shelves, French classics on a book shelf. A heavy, ornate cross decorated one wall. Major Thompson would sit there, vaguely aware of the chill in the room or the firing just outside, staring and staring at the Citadel maps, he and his staff trying to work out an impossible mission — how to dig out a firmly entrenched force without getting a lot of Marines killed. There was no way. It was a mess, Thompson thought, just a bloody, grinding mess.

Everything seemed to be in favor of the North Vietnamese. The Citadel itself was an almost perfect place to defend. There was row after row of one-story, thick-walled, masonry houses jammed together, with only narrow streets and alleys, too narrow for a tank or Ontos to maneuver in effectively. There were courtyard walls around most of the houses, big mature trees and hedgerows; it was hard to see anything clearly past twenty five yards. The northeast wall on their left flank was made of brick and filled with earth, rising up in terraces and parapets, dotted with trees and brush. The NVA had had two weeks to prepare before the Marines arrived, and the Citadel environment suited them well. They dug their spider holes along the walls and hedge-rows, put snipers in the lofts and windows, dug in tight atop the wall; they had literally hundreds of naturally camouflaged, mutually supporting, fortified positions. A small number of well-placed soldiers with automatic weapons could tie up an entire company.

Across the moat of the northeast wall, the North Vietnamese held several four- and five-story buildings, allowing them to cover the top of the wall by fire. Ahead of the Marines and to their right was the NVA-held Imperial Palace with its VC flag hoisted high. Enemy mortars were set up inside the palace, NVA riflemen could fire down on the Marines from the top of the walls, and the Marines could do little about it — the Rules of Engagement for Hue prohibited U.S. firepower from being placed in the historically and spiritually important Palace. The ARVN, however, were permitted to fire mortars into it, but the South Vietnamese allies proved less than totally reliable in that mission.

The weather was also an unfortunate factor. The constant cold, misty drizzle, and the low cloud-ceiling hampered air support, kept the jets from pounding the NVA and kept the helicopters away from the ARVN HQ — the only place with a suitable LZ, so supplies ran out and casualties backed up. The only other means of transportation to and from the Citadel was by boat, but the NVA held positions along the moats and along much of the Perfume River and were able to force back many of the supply-laden Navy craft. So the dead Marines stayed stacked up around the HQ, the seriously wounded sat and waited, and those with relatively minor wounds were patched up and sent back to the fighting. Everyone did without needed supplies.

Thompson and Hughes had been successful, however, in getting many of the firepower restrictions lifted. General Westmoreland's deputy commander, Gen. Creighton W. Abrams, came up to establish the MACV Forward Command Post at Phu Bai on February 13. He was responsible for having III MAF move an 8-inch howitzer battery from southern I Corps to Phu Bai to fire into Hue. Brig. Gen. Oscar E. Davis, an assistant division commander of the 1st Air Cav, personally set up shop in the ARVN HQ near the end of the battle, to coordinate support fire among the USMC, U.S. Army, ARVN, and Vietnamese Marines in action. Still, there were many problems. The offshore 7th Fleet gunfire (firing from twenty-six thousand yards) was accurate, but its flat trajectory sent most of the shells either thudding harmlessly into the outside of the northeast wall or shrieking over it and landing several hundred yards away. The only artillery came from the 8-inch and 155mm guns at Phu Bai, most of them from 1/11 and 2/11, and they were forced to fire at ranges of eight miles. The 8-inch howitzers were accurate (Captain Harrington directed them to within twenty-five meters of his position to hit snipers in a high-rise building along his flank), but the location of the artillery also put 1/5 on the gun target line. Since the two forces were often within yards of each other, forward observers became leery of calling it in. The density of the built-up areas also forced the FOs to adjust their fire by sound, not sight, an unreliable method. The battalion's own 81mm mortars were accurate, but unless the crews made a rare direct hit, the low caliber of the weapon did little but make the NVA duck their heads. The two 4.2-inch mortar crews from WHISKEY 1/11, set up across the river by MACV, did place accurate HE and CS fire inside the Citadel, but they too were having resupply problems.

On the ground, Thompson's Marines had some effective firepower. The four Ontos and the battalion's 106mm recoilless rifle crews were up front the whole time, supporting the grunts. Also, the Third Platoon, Alpha Company, 1st Tank Battalion, under the courageous leadership of Lt. Ronald Morrison and his platoon sergeant, did a great job with their five M-48 tanks, going wherever Thompson directed, all day, every day. Lieutenant Morrison (who was to win the Silver Star for his personal valor) developed a tactic of pairing one tank and one Ontos when fire support was requested by the line companies. The vehicle commanders would be briefed by the infantry commanders on the location of the NVA. Then the tank would roar up front, with the grunts pouring down cover fire, put a few 90mm rounds into the target, then haul back, as the Ontos followed and unleashed all six recoilless rifles. It was deadly effective. However, the tanks had problems getting around in the narrow streets. Crewmen were killed and wounded. Every tank had at least a dozen B-40s slam into it during the course of the battle. But, every night, they would pull back to the ARVN HQ, repair, and be back on the streets in the morning.

Besides the terrain and weather and all the other problems, what really made the Citadel tough was the North Vietnamese soldiers themselves. They were well equipped and supplied, and they were brave. There were reports of the ARVN finding three dead NVA chained to their machine guns. Dragging one of the few North Vietnamese prisoners to the CP, some grunts told Thompson they'd found him half-conscious, crouched in a spider hole. He'd been wounded several times, stank from gangrene infection, and would have died in place in his position had the Marines not uncovered him. The NVA had come to do a job, Thompson mused, and they didn't seem to mind paying the price. That's why the Citadel was such a bloody encounter. For the grunts, it was nothing but a war of attrition, moving from house to house through the rubble, counting their progress in yards. Major Thompson was frustrated and scared. Everybody was.

Supporting 1/5 in the Citadel, and the other two Marine battalions on the South Side, was an air, land, and sea supply-chain extending to Phu Bai, Da Nang, and even Saigon — controlled by the 1st Marine Division staff, Force Logistic Command, Force Logistic Support Group Alpha, and the Naval Support Activity headquarters in Da Nang. Whether by truck, helicopter, or boat, the first priority for supplies going to the Marines in Hue was ammunition.* During the battle, 104 convoys made the circuit between Hue and Phu Bai, many of them running ambushes over the Phu Cam Canal. Despite enemy fire on the LZs, Marine and Army helicopters brought in 525 tons of supplies, and made 270 medevac sorties to take out 1,000 casualties. Most of the support effort going to the Citadel Marines was made by a group of Navy LCU craft, with 106mm recoilless rifles mounted on their decks, and Swift gunboats providing escort. Despite sniper fire and ambushes along the banks, which halted many boats, the sailors brought in 400 tons of supplies.

A price was paid getting the needed supplies to Hue. Sixty helicopters were hit or shot down over the city; many came back to base with dead or wounded crewmen. The worst hit were the Navy boats plying the Perfume. NVA attacks in the form of rockets, mines, and ambushes to and from Hue, reached such intensity that, at the beginning of the third week of the battle, General Abrams requested the organization of a Naval group to coordinate the protection of the watercraft. Thus, under III MAF control, was born Task Force CLEARWATER. Commanded by Captain Gerald W. Smith, USN, it included river patrol boats of Task Force 116, helicopter gunships, aircraft, artillery, and ground security troops. But the NVA ambushes were never entirely thwarted; bringing supplies to the Marines in Hue, one ammunition-filled LCU, and two LCUs carrying fuel bladders, were blown up.

---

*When the final tabulations were made, the tally of ammo going to augment what the Marines already went into battle with was as follows: 1,000,000 5.56mm rounds; 550,000 7.62mm rounds; 19,000 60mm rounds; 30,000 81mm rounds; 4,200 90mm rounds; 6,000 106mm rounds; 12,300 fragmentation grenades; 4,700 CS grenades; 4,000 LAAW rockets; 350 E-8 gas launchers; 1,600 pounds of C-4 explosives; and 46,000 blasting caps. Add to that, 4,780 rounds of Naval gunfire and 9,059 rounds of artillery fired in support of the Marines in Hue.

The biggest thing Thompson had going for him were his Marines. The NVA were good, but individually the Marine grunt was better. The house-to-house battle was a Pfc.'s and corporal's war; young men took charge, struggling forward in the mad rushes on the houses, dragging the wounded and dead out of heavy fire, going at it day after day. There was little order in the battle, only confusion — and incredible bravery. Captain Harrington was impressed in particular by the esprit de corps of two of his young lance corporals, one of whom won the Silver Star, the other a Bronze Star. After their squad leader had become a casualty, Harrington had to break up a fight between the two men — they had both wanted to shoulder the responsibility of running the squad.

Said battalion commander Thompson, "I'll never forget how courageous those youngsters were. The Marines were magnificent, not so much for their skills, but their raw courage in overcoming unbelievable obstacles in accomplishing their mission. Everyone was frightened stiff; however, I saw no evidence of cowardice or Marines breaking under stress. Captain Harrington and his magnificent Delta Company carried the brunt of the attack most of the way. Everyone did the best they could, while some performed with extraordinary courage."

There was one grunt in Hue whom Thompson thought to be the embodiment of the term "combat Marine." He was a young black kid named Howard, a crazy sort of dude who used to wear his helmet backward and who inscribed on the back of his flak jacket, Howard Is My Name, Trouble Is My Game. He'd even made the papers. A reporter in Hue was talking with some grunts, and he piped up, "Put me in your paper."

"What can I say about you?"

"You can say Lance Cpl. Raymond Howard, eighteen, better known as "Trouble," from Bay Minette, Alabama; squad leader, Second Platoon, Delta Company, 1st Battalion, 5th Marine Regiment, is going 'cross the river to kick him a few behinds."

In Hue, Howard ended up driving a Mechanical Mule. He worked out of the 1/5 CP, and Thompson would give him the word on who needed more ammo or where there were wounded who had to be evacuated. He would just nod his head — and then off he would go, driving his Mule, dragging hurt grunts on it, or throwing off supplies to the men. And if that meant driving right up to a firefight or ducking a sniper, so be it.

One of Howard's partners on the Mechanical Mules was Lance Cpl. Brian S. Mayer, of the recoilless rifle squad, H&S Company 1/5. He was eighteen years old, a quiet, short kid who'd joined up right after high school in New York City. He went not because he cared much about Vietnam, but because his grades in school were bad. He'd never been on the football team or anything, and he wanted to prove himself. The Marine Corps seemed like the place to do it.

Mayer never did become a movie Marine; mostly he felt like a little kid struggling to keep up with the men around him. During high school, he'd been a busboy at a restaurant and several Marines had come in. They looked so strong and sure of themselves, and Mayer wanted to be just like them. But even after surviving boot camp himself, he couldn't believe he was actually a Marine. He still felt like a little twerp. Much to the derisive laughter of his drill instructors at the end of boot camp, he was made a laundry machine operator. Then he was retrained in an infantry MOS and given orders for Vietnam. It scared him to the bone and he wrote his mother and congressman trying to get out of it, until finally he dropped that, afraid that he would make a fool out of himself and embarrass his family.

So Mayer went to Nam, just trying to hang in there day by day, following orders without question, doing his best because he couldn't live with letting someone else down. He was in the field a lot; in the two months he'd been in Vietnam, he'd won two Purple Hearts. But, Mayer thought, he'd never seen anything as bad as Hue City. It was the worst. What am I doing here, he would wonder. The sergeant at the CP would order him somewhere, and he'd take off on the Mule. It was all catch-as-catch-can. You did what you could, where you could, because you were all Marines. But that didn't mean it wasn't frightening. Something bad always seemed to be happening. Snipers in the streets, B-40 rockets, firing everywhere. Grunts and sniper teams were always on the alert on the wall, and every now and then, there would be shouts of, "Movement!" and more exchanges of fire. There was never any rest during the day, little sleep at night. One time, Mayer pulled up with some grunts along the side of a road to get some C rations down, to relax awhile — then the mortar exploded down the street, and everything started up all over again. There were a lot of reporters with them and once, when there was heavy firing ahead, they said they wanted to get into it. The Marines told them to shut up and sit down. It blew Mayer's mind — it was like they were making a movie or something.

He never saw one NVA in combat, but there were so many of his friends getting hit — the Marine who came piling out of his smoking tank clutching his face, the black grunt with a bullet in his back he helped aboard his Mule. He kept hearing about buddies who got hit.

One evening, one of the Mule drivers, a studious looking kid with glasses and a sparse mustache who had been an H&S clerk before Hue, was sent to pick up some wounded at Charlie Company. On the way back, he got lost in the maze of streets, made a wrong turn, and the NVA blew him away in his seat; KIA. Mayer heard that the kid had died propped in his seat and the Marine's body had been used for target practice. And there was the day Mayer saw two friends die. There was a tank pulled up inside an abandoned ARVN compound, and about eight grunts were there, milling around the tank, talking and smoking. Everyone started to wander off and Mayer crossed the courtyard, rooting through some old C ration cartons, looking for something to eat. He heard it then — the shrill whistle of a mortar arching down. Then the explosion, closeby. It hit the two Marines still standing beside the tank. One of them, a guy who joked a lot, was down with a single piece of shrapnel in his throat. He'd been killed instantly. His eyes were half open, his mouth was parted in a sick grin, and Mayer choked — it was like he'd died laughing. The other man, a quiet guy, was moaning on the ground, peppered with shrapnel. They hustled him inside and called for a corpsman. The Marine was dead in a few minutes. It was hard for Mayer to believe — just one stinking round out of nowhere. Mayer kept waiting for his turn. It had to be coming.

It was the same for everybody. The battle fell into little bits and pieces, one coming right after the other, no one conscious of which came first.

Major Swenson was back at the ARVN HQ when one of the Marine tanks lurched inside with shell holes and casualties. He had to order the crew to scrub out the blood and guts of their dead tank commander. It was not the kind of thing you liked to talk about.

Berntson was wandering down the street one day, when he saw Father McGonigal, the MACV chaplain, walking towards him, headed for the front lines. McGonigal was always headed for the front lines; he was always up front with the grunts. "Good morning, Father." "Good morning, take care, my son." Berntson joked that the snipers were very good in the neighborhood and to be careful, and McGonigal laughed and kept moving toward the shooting. That was one good guy, Berntson thought.

Six mortar shells walked through the rubble and Mike Herr, the reporter, threw himself down. When the noise faded, he heard something incongrous behind him and looked to see three Marines huddled together, holding their helmets, singing, "We gotta get out of this place, if it's the last thing we ever do-woo!"

They were moving forward again below the wall, crouching and scrambling through a place blown flat by artillery, all cluttered with corrugated tin roofs, smashed wood, and junk. Lawhorn was down, holding his M-16. Another black grunt, a helmetless corporal, stood up ahead of him and hurled a grenade as if he were a javelin thrower, his ammo bandoliers bouncing on his chest. Suddenly, something exploded back at them and the corporal went down in a heap. A corpsman and a couple of Marines dragged him back, and Lawhorn looked at the man. His hand was mangled, it looked like a couple of fingers were blown off. He was clutching his arm, crying, looking at the smashed, bleeding lump. Another black grunt crouched beside him, staring with something akin to envy. "You're Stateside," he said. "You've got no problems. Stateside."

Saturday, February 17. It dawned overcast and gray again over the city. No air power could get in to support the grunts. There was no more ammunition for the tanks' 90mm cannons. There was no more ammunition for the 106mm recoilless rifles. The grunts were almost out of grenades. No food had come in for a day.

Major Thompson brought the battalion to a halt; there were to be no Marine attacks that day. The grunts spent the day resting, some of them being sent on probing patrols of the NVA lines. The fighting did not stop.

With the lull in the advance, Sergeant Berntson wandered off from Delta Company to see what was going on with the rest of the battalion. He was walking through some of the wreckage on the right flank when he heard firing up ahead, not wild shooting, but crisp, measured bursts of M-16 and M-60. Curious, he headed in that direction, rounded a corner, and saw a blue bus sitting in the middle of a long boulevard. There were two grunts lying on the roof, manning an M-60 machine gun, and two more crouched on either side, leaning comfortably against the fenders. Berntson bent down, ran to the bus, and crouched behind a fender with one of the Marines.

"What the hell's going on?"

"Hey, man," the grunt grinned at him, "welcome to the First Annual Hue City Turkey Shoot."

"What are you talking about?"

"Aw shit, we gotta bunch of NVA down there. Crazy bastards keep trying to get back from one side of the street to the other. Every now and then, a couple two or three of 'em will take off running. And that's when we get 'em!"

Berntson mumbled, unbelieving, "You gotta be shitting me," and the grunt just pointed down the street. About three blocks away, maybe a 150 feet, he could see four or five bodies lumped in the center of the road.

"Just watch," the grunt said, "Pretty soon, one of 'em will go running across the street." And just as he said that, Berntson saw a little figure sprint past the pile of bodies. Midway across, the four Marines all started popping, but the man made it. Berntson couldn't believe what he was seeing, so he hunkered next to the fender and waited. A couple of minutes later, another soldier ran from the building on one side of the street, got in the middle — then changed his mind, and started running back to where he'd started. The Marines were all firing and the man went down, crumpling to the pavement. Two more NVA rushed from the other side of the street to drag their comrade to cover. The M-60 gunner blew one of them away. The other scrambled back.

It was wild. "How long you guys been doing this," Berntson asked.

"Oh, we've been sitting here for about the last forty-five minutes. It's great. They just keep running back and forth. They don't fire at us. Hey, you want to take a shot at it?"

"Why not," Berntson said, and he brought up his M-16.

"We got it counted up here. I got two. He's got two. And the guns up there've got three of 'em. See how many you can get."

Berntson leaned up against the fender, got a good tight sling-grip, and stared down the barrel of his rifle, thinking it was just like the shooting range at boot camp. He sighted in over the pile of bodies in the street, staring and staring until his eyes started to water. Then he saw the little figure run across, and he squeezed back, spraying the whole magazine. The man made it without a scratch. The M-60 gunner grimaced down at him. "Aw shit, I should've got him. If I'd known you were that bad a shot, I would've dropped him."

The gunner asked if he wanted to give it another shot, but Berntson said no, he'd only miss again. He took a photo of the First Annual Hue City Turkey Shoot, then started to leave. The grunts started laughing and said to send everyone down for the free pickings, and Berntson walked away shaking his head. He'd never seen the enemy acting so stupid. They hadn't even fired one shot.

Berntson kept roaming around until he came to a hole in a house facing the street. The grunts learned quickly that when moving through an opening, you run like hell. And that's exactly what Berntson did, charging through the hole, then jumping into a ditch on the other side of the street. A couple of grunts from Bravo Company were already huddled in it, a sergeant and a corpsman. The sergeant said he had two wounded men up ahead and needed some help to drag them back. He pointed toward them. Down the street, in the middle of an intersection, Berntson could see two figures lying, big enough and green enough to be Marines.

"When were they wounded," he asked.

"Just a few minutes ago," the sergeant said. "I gotta get 'em back. C'mon!"

The corpsman suddenly spoke, slow and firm. "Bob, they're dead."

"No there're not, man. They're wounded. I seen 'em move out there. I know they're wounded. I gotta go get 'em, now let's go get 'em!"

"Bob, they're dead."

"Damn it, if you won't go, I'll go myself."

"Bob, they are dead. They were killed last night."

Berntson suddenly realized that the sergeant was over the line. The sergeant's squad had been ambushed the night before, the corpsman told Berntson. Four of the Marines were killed, and only the sergeant came through alive, dragging back two of the bodies. The enemy knew the Marines would try to recover their dead, and snipers had the intersection zeroed in.

"Damn it!" the sergeant cut in. "You know better than that. They're both alive out there. You're just chickenshit, you won't go get them!"

"Bob, they're dead and there's no sense in us going out there to get them right now."

"Well, I'm going," the sergeant said. He lunged out of the ditch and started sprinting down the street. When he was halfway to the bodies, the sniper started shooting. Two more Marines dropped into the ditch with Berntson and the corpsman, and they all opened up, trying to cover the sergeant. The corpsman muttered, "That damn fool's going to get killed," and he was up too, zigzagging down the street. Berntson and the two grunts followed after him, firing from the hip. They all made it to the bodies, and Berntson and the corpsman grabbed one of the dead by his ankles and ran madly back down the street, the body dragging roughly behind them, face down. The sergeant and one of the Marines followed with the other body, and the fifth grunt came in last, firing magazine after magazine into the windows. Berntson and the corpsman piled back into the ditch, going flat against the dirt, breathing hard. The other three jumped in after them, and the sergeant looked at the bloated body Berntson and the corpsman had dragged back. He started crying, "Jesus, did you guys have to drag him back on his face?"

The dead man's face was all bruised and cut from the mad dash down the street.

The sergeant slumped in the ditch, suddenly shuddering and sobbing. "You guys didn't have to drag him back on his face . . . his mother's never going to know him . . . you ruined his fucking face!" The corpsman went over to him, put his arm around him. "Bob, we got all your squad back now. They're all safe. Let's go back to the aid station."

They all started walking slowly towards the ARVN HQ, the sergeant crying and the corpsman holding him, leading him away from the front lines. Berntson and one of the grunts followed, carrying the boy with the smashed face. Inside the compound, the sergeant was taken to the chief corpsman and they sat him down in a corner. Somebody laid the body near him, and when Berntson turned to walk out of the building, he saw the sergeant sitting there beside his dead friend, crying into his hands.

The next day, February 18, the resupply problem which had halted the advance the day before was still unresolved and the battalion again operated at half-step. Sergeant Dye holed up in a house with some Delta grunts, hoping to get a little rest, but there was an NVA sniper somewhere ahead of them. He had a heavy machine gun and kept laying bursts across the house, blowing away chunks of the wall and scaring everybody. Dye had one other problem; his stomach felt like it was eating itself. Two days without food is a long time. There was a supply point being set up down the block. Maybe they had some C rations. But the sniper had the road covered.

Finally, Dye's belly got the better of his common sense. "The hell with this," he said. "That bastard is either going to kill me or wound me, but he ain't going to starve me to death!"

He ducked out of the building as everyone watched, and ran behind a stone wall. Then the sniper cranked off a round and Dye heard it come over his head, buzzing like a huge yellow jacket, and smash into the opposite wall with a thunderous crash. Mortar dust showered him and he lunged forward even faster. He made it to the supply point, loaded up with C ration cans, and ran back to the house. Then they all sat in the rubble, chowing down.

It wasn't until later that he looked at his helmet. The big yellow flower that Berntson had stuck in the cover back at the Buddhist temple was clipped off about an inch above his head. Then it hit him —

when he'd run down the wall, the flower had been sticking up like a periscope, marking his progress, and the sniper had shot right at it. Later, he'd start to have bad dreams about what his head would have looked like if the sniper had aimed an inch lower. But in Hue, the decapitated flower was good for a joke.

Bravo Company was moving house to house, the platoons on line, through an affluent part of town, complete with cars in garages. Berntson hooked up with one of the squads. They moved into the next courtyard, crawled past a stone fountain to the back door of the home, then tossed in a barrage of grenades, and charged. They kicked through the back door — and suddenly realized there were three North Vietnamese crouched inside. They saw the NVA and the enemy saw them; there was a second of wide-eyed panic, then everyone scrambled. A line of AK rounds ripped past Berntson, stitching the wall behind him and covering him with plaster, and he cut loose with his M-16. One of the NVA tumbled out the door, the other two bounced dead against the floor in the roar of rifles. The Marines were standing there shaking. It had lasted about three seconds.

They quickly checked each other, expecting to find holes and blood, but there were none, and they broke into hysterical laughter. They sat down for a smoke and the squad leader said they would hold up until the rest of the company moved forward on the flanks. One of the grunts tugged the field pack from a dead NVA, dumped its contents on the floor, and out rolled three neatly-bound, one-pound caches of shiny gold metal. The kid picked up the package. "Hey, what's this? Man, it's heavy. What is this stuff?" He tossed it to Berntson. They were thin gold wafers, like bookmarks, and he turned them around, examining them; each one was neatly stamped *Or Pur Saigon Da Nang Hong Kong Bangkok*. "My God," Berntson exclaimed, "it's gold! This stuff is gold!" The kid who'd found it quickly snatched up one of the satchels, and another grunt grabbed the third. Berntson counted about twenty leaves in his package, then took one out and stuck it in his pocket diary.

They started to look through the other packs — when suddenly, two B-40s crashed through the window above them. Fire erupted from ahead and they scrambled out the back door, just as bursts of AK splintered around the front door. A mortar went off in the courtyard and Berntson tripped on the cement plaza, dropping his M-16. He bent down to pick it up, his packet of gold fell from his pocket — two more mortar shells exploded, and he took off, looking back forlornly at the package sitting there. After he got back to cover, he remembered the one gold leaf stuck in his diary and he felt a little better.

After saying good-bye to the Bravo grunts, Berntson started making his way back to his old friends in Delta Company. He was passing an aid station when some of the guys asked him to help carry back several dead Marines. The body detail made its way into a riddled house and Berntson saw three dead grunts lying in the smashed interior. Someone said they'd been on a night LP in the house when the enemy threw in a bunch of B-40s and blew them away. Berntson bent down to pick up one young kid and noticed something strange — he was wearing all-black leather boots, had brand-new unscratched PFC chevrons pinned to his collar, and was wearing a Stateside-issue uniform. He could even see the starch creases in the dead man's trousers. They dragged the three bodies back to the aid station, and Berntson sat down for a quick smoke. The corpsman went through the pockets of the dead kid with the Stateside utilities and pulled out a scrap of paper. He read it, then started mumbling, "Look at this . . ." He handed it to Berntson. It was the kid's PFC warrant — signed at Camp Pendelton, California on January 29, 1968. Berntson remembered he'd heard a rumor that a shipment of replacements had been loaded on the planes in California, flown straight into Da Nang, packed on choppers, and spit out into Hue City. And this was the end result. Berntson just sat there staring at the body. He felt the old numbness creeping back through him. He stared and stared, until he finally had to get up and walk out.

Monday, February 19. Three 82mm mortar shells from the NVA positions in the Imperial Palace arched over the Marine lines and exploded at the battalion's forward supply point. Two Marines were killed. The rules of engagement prohibited the Marines from firing back at the palace.

It was cold in the morning, the fog and mist blowing off the moat below the wall, and the Marines sat among the rubble, warming themselves in little huddles around cooking fires. In a couple of hours, the sun was up high, burning away the overcast and fog, and the Delta Company grunts began to stir. There were two scout-snipers with the company of the 5th Marine Regiment, Lance Cpl. David Morales and Pfc. Eric Henshall, both of whom were up for Bronze Stars for killing six North Vietnamese several days back. They were sitting up against the wall, when Henshall dug into his pack and pulled out a little American flag. He'd bought it at Phu Bai about a week before Tet broke and had planned to have all the regimental snipers sign it, and take it home as a souvenir. But he finally decided there was a better use for it. Henshall and some grunts scrounged around for a bamboo pole and tied the flag to it. Then, Henshall, who was wearing neither helmet nor flak jacket, stuck the pole through a chair they found in a bombed-out house and lifted it up on the wall. Berntson and a UPI photographer started clicking shots.

Berntson walked over to Henshall with his USMC reporter's notebook and called out, "Hey, Eric, how in the hell did you get the flag. Let me write a story about this."

Henshall grinned, visibly proud about the flag up there, and told him about it. "Damn it," he said as Berntson jotted in his book, "they've got their flag out there. It occured to me why in the hell haven't we got ours. So, we just stuck it on a chair and put it up there, and let 'em shoot at it."

The little flag flapped in the cold breeze and the grunts stood leaning against the wall, shouting insults at the enemy farther down.

A couple of NVA snipers down at the end of the wall started cracking single shots and the Marines ducked back down behind the wall. The shots passed overhead and Berntson felt a particular animosity at the men doing the shooting. The day before, he'd been helping a corpsman drag a wounded man away from the wall, when one of the snipers put two rounds past his head, so close he could feel the heat. All he could do then was exclaim, "Oh my God," and throw himself behind a pile of rubble, afraid to move for ten minutes. The snipers cracked off a couple more rounds, then an AK-50 machine gun opened up from somewhere ahead, stitching bursts along the wall. The firing finally died down. The chair and the flag were still standing.

The Delta gunnery sergeant was in a burned-out house across the street from the wall. He shouted to the squad leaders, "Who ya got?" and counted the names on his fingers. Berntson hunkered down while the gunny called the roll, watching some kid who was fumbling with a .45 pistol. The kid jammed a cleaning rod down the barrel, and it suddenly went off. No one was hurt, but the gunny stormed over livid, kicked the kid and yanked the pistol away from him. Then the gunny looked down at Berntson.

"You the guy who writes stories?"

"Yeah."

"You with us today, sergeant?"

"Yeah."

"Well, that's twenty-six." The gunny was almost finished with his count. There weren't many left after nine days in Hue.

The grunts were still sitting along the wall, waiting, when some reinforcements came walking up toward them. They were all clean-shaven and Berntson thought that looked incongruous — all the other grunts sitting there were hollow-eyed, bearded, grimy, covered with red brick-dust. A couple of them were toting cases of C rations, and everyone roused themselves to get a little breakfast. Captain Harrington walked over to the new men; they were his Third Platoon, which had been detached on convoy security and only now was able to make it to the Citadel. With them was Lt. Dean Williams, the Delta Company executive officer. He'd been a hard-charging platoon leader for over six months, but had been wounded and given a rear job. With Hue, Williams had volunteered to return to the field. Harrington told him to take over First Platoon. The company had been resupplied, and they were going to resume the attack along the wall.

Some time after 1:00 P.M., Harrington gave the word.

The wall narrowed at that point, the packed earth stretching only forty feet across, and Lieutenant Williams climbed atop it with only a squad. They started forward through the rubble on top, crouched low, moving quickly. Captain Harrington took the rest of the company and started to push through the houses at the bottom of the wall. A tank clanked up through the street, and Berntson stared at it happily. At least they were going to get some fire support. It fired one 90mm round, then, suddenly, took a B-40 in the driver's port, blowing off a headlight. The tank roared back down the street. Berntson grimaced.

The company got forward about half a block, then all hell broke loose. Withering fire raked across the Marines, everyone went diving for cover, and two Marines atop the wall were shot dead in their tracks. They never had a chance. AK-47s and B-40s sprayed the narrow pathway, and Harrington, crouched down seventy-five feet away, looked up at the Marines on the wall. Lieutenant Williams, out in front of his platoon, suddenly jerked upright as dust kicked up all around him, then flopped like a rag doll. He had a bullet in his neck, two in his chest, one in each leg. Oh God, Harrington thought, feeling sick in the pit of his stomach, he must be dead. He felt absolutely helpless.

Berntson saw the lieutenant go down too. He was crawling through a bamboo grove in one of the courtyards, sliding belly down with one of the squads. The fire from up ahead continued in an incessant roar; it was almost impossible to move. The squads kept inching forward. The place was a junk pile of shattered houses, hedgerows, trees, courtyard walls, and more rubble. Berntson crawled through it on his elbows, wanting to get away from an M-60 team laying down cover fire from behind. He knew they'd draw even more fire. He held his M-16 over his head, afraid to raise himself up for all the things snapping by and ricocheting, and fired blindly towards the NVA positions on the wall.

He scurried up over a wooden fence into the next courtyard, and quickly crab-walked to a stone wall, wanting only to get inside the next
house and hide behind a safe wall. Two grunts, one holding an M-16,
the other an M-79 grenade launcher, crawled up beside him. Someone
on the other side of the wall was shouting, "Corpsman! Corpsman up!"
and Berntson glanced around — he couldn't see a doc anywhere. The
grunts opened up over the stone wall at the NVA soldiers ahead.
"Corpsman up!" Berntson stuck his head over the wall. Thirty feet
away, huddled against the wall of the next house, were two guys in helmets and flak jackets, bent over a thrashing, kicking figure.

Without really thinking, Berntson suddenly found himself jumping
over the wall. He threw down his M-16 and sprinted towards the
group. He crouched down with them as more NVA fire started blowing
through the courtyard. One of the men with the casualty was David
Greenway of *Time* magazine, and the wounded man was Pfc. Michels.
Oh God, not Michels, Berntson thought; to survive that grenade barrage at the tower, only to be hit later on. And Michels was hit bad, shot
in the neck; the blood gurgled in his throat, his eyes rolled back, and
he gasped for air, flailing his arms and legs. Berntson shouted, "Corpsman up!" and reached to grab Michels' arm to drag him back. Just
then, a corpsman trundled up, helped Berntson pick up Michels, and
they ran towards the stone wall, screaming, "Cover fire! Give us some
goddamned cover fire!" The Marines back behind the walls opened up
with a fury. NVA fire whined around them. Berntson and the corpsman rushed to the wall, realized they couldn't get over it with Michels,
and scrambled with him into the street, running like hell down the
gutter. Berntson could hear more rounds popping and cracking in
the air.

They ran maybe thirty yards, then ducked through the nearest
courtyard gate on their left. Berntson tripped, cut his leg on a tangle of
barbed wire. He was scrambling back to his feet when he saw Al Webb,
a UPI correspondent, crouched inside the wall. "God, Al, give us a
hand! This guy's in bad shape!" Berntson, Webb, Greenway, and the
corpsman picked Michels up again and ran down a side street. There
was a battered French truck parked sideways in the street and they got
behind it, laying Michels down behind the tire. Charles Mohr, a *New
York Times* correspondent, ran up with several grunts to help. The
corpsman started to wrap a bandage around Michels throat, but the
kid was drowning in his own blood, so he ripped open his aid bag and
prepared to do a tracheotomy. Everyone was pressed down under the
truck, watching as the corpsman slid a plastic tube into his windpipe.
Berntson saw a big green window shutter lying in the street. It would
make a good stretcher.

He stood up. The NVA B-40 rocket exploded four feet away.

When Berntson came to, he found himself lying flat on his stomach, twelve feet from where he'd been standing. He couldn't hear, there was a ringing in his ears. The metallic taste of gunpowder was in his mouth, then he could taste the blood oozing down from his forehead. He tried to get up; he couldn't move. His arm began to hurt, to ache terribly and he looked down to see a big fragment sticking out of it just below the shoulder. His hand was numb. His legs were numb. His whole body was ragged with shrapnel. The pain was red hot. His eyes began to focus, and there was Michels lying beside him in the street, hurled there by the blast. He rolled his head and could see Greenway, Webb, Mohr, the corpsman, and some grunts flat under the truck. Webb and Greenway were hit, too. An AK suddenly clacked from down the street and a line of splatters raked past. Michels jerked, hit again. Berntson stared again at the faces under the truck. "For Christ's sake," he screeched, "somebody come and get me! Please!"

The corpsman and Greenway hurried out and dragged him back to the truck.

Two grunts ran back with Michels, and Berntson started mumbling to the corpsman, "Treat him first, I'm okay . . . treat him first."

Webb was lying there, clutching the shrapnel wound in his ankle and leg, and Berntson said, "Take care of Webb, I'm okay." Then, he suddenly realized he was passing out. The corpsman gave him a shot of morphine. Several Marines ran over, grabbed his arm, and the pain shot through him. God, it hurt. They carried him to a courtyard behind the shooting, and Berntson drifted back to reality, remembering, strangely, that Marines don't abandon their equipment. He pressed his camera and .45 on Greenway, telling him he had to make sure they got back to the ISO office of the 1st Marine Division.

A Mechanical Mule pulled up. A grunt with a shoulder wound climbed aboard, sitting up, and they put Berntson and Michels across the back. The corpsman jumped beside them, still trying to do the impossible for Michels. The Mule hauled down the street to the aid station inside the ARVN HQ. They were rushed inside some aluminum barracks-style buildings and placed on the cement deck with the other wounded. Some doctors and corpsmen ran to Michels and ripped his shirt off. "He's dead, he's going," one of the doctors said and they covered him back up, left him in a corner, and disappeared towards the other wounded. There was the smallest chance that Michels could have lived but, in Hue, there were too few doctors and too many casualties and often, the seriously wounded were shoved to one side so those who had a good chance could be worked on. The doctors didn't like it, found it hard to live with, but there was no alternative.

Berntson lay there, staring at the ceiling, thinking of Dennis Michels, and the tears started rolling down his face. A few minutes later, he started passing out again, everything getting foggier and foggier. Somebody crouched over him and suddenly jerked up, shouting, "My God, quick, get over here! He's bleeding bad!" A piece of shrapnel, the size of a silver dollar, had slashed through an artery in his leg, and his blood was slopping the floor around him. A bandage was slapped on, another shot of morphine, a corpsman inserted an IV needle and held the plasma above him.

A Sea Knight came into the HQ landing zone. They put Berntson on a stretcher with a poncho and hustled him outside with the rest of the casualties. The helicopter prop wash blew the poncho over his face. He couldn't move to pull it away, and he suddenly broke into a panic — oh God, take it off, please, I'm not dead, don't let them put me with the dead! Someone pulled the poncho off his face. The chopper took off without him, but a few seconds later, another one settled in on the pad and they carried him inside. It lifted off and Berntson stared out the open back ramp, only to see the first chopper trailing smoke and slowly spiralling back down to the LZ.

He woke up in the Phu Bai aid station, on the floor with the other WIAs. A corpsman bent over him, cutting away his frayed shirt. The corpsman went through his pockets, collecting his personal effects, and Berntson saw him taking the map he'd carried the whole battle. "Give me my map of Hue," he cried. "That's mine!" The corpsman said he couldn't, said they weren't allowed to leave anything of possible intelligence value. They carried him to the X-ray room and gingerly laid him out on the table. He was miserable in his pain, freezing cold in his nakedness. He kept fading in and out. Everytime he regained consciousness, a young Marine would come up, give him a cigarette, and start talking with him, trying to keep his mind off the pain. Berntson finally asked the kid what unit he was with, and the Marine said he was a clerk. What do you know, he thought, a clerk, a damned Remington Raider. But he was really doing his best to help out, and Berntson truly appreciated that.

While the first batch of wounded were being evacuated, Delta Company kept pressing through the houses. A tank came up, started putting cannon fire down the street, and within ten minutes, it had three B-40s explode against it. The tank retreated. Mortar fire from the palace started hitting the Marines, bringing them to a halt, and Harrington got on the radio, ordering a pull back to the jump-off position. Harrington looked ahead of him and his radioman — his third one since the battle started — suddenly came sprawling back in the debris. He was hit in the arm, and blood gushed with each heartbeat. Harrington and a corpsman quickly ran up and got the wound tied off. The grunts started putting down cover fire, and some men dragged back the dead and wounded off the wall. Someone carried back Lieutenant Williams, who was still conscious with five bullet wounds, and they evacuated him to the HQ LZ.

The company set up for the night back by the flag on the chair. In the morning, February 20, they fought again from daylight to dark. They consolidated for the night in some more rubbled houses along the wall, and Lawhorn and some buddies sat, talking wearily among themselves. Nobody wanted anything more to do with Hue, they were just plain tired of the fight. The NVA were tough, and it had been bad. Lawhorn was glad about one thing — Captain Harrington had his shit together. He was always right up front during the battle, taking his chances along with the grunts, and although he was a quiet man, he really seemed to care about them. But God, he was the only officer left in the company. The enemy had shot Lieutenant Green back at Thua Luu. The Second Platoon lieutenant had been hit back at the tower. A spray of shrapnel during a tough firefight after the tower had sent Lieutenant Imlah out in a medevac. Lieutenant Williams had lasted one day. The platoon sergeant who took First Platoon had gotten wounded somewhere in the streets, and the squad leader who took his place was WIA in turn. Doc Rhino was dead. Lawhorn was only a PFC, but they made him the squad leader, and he only had six men left. He hated the responsibility. There was hardly any ammunition or chow, and everyone was worn out, miserable, hungry. It had taken so much just to get the few hundred yards they had, it seemed so useless to go on. For all the artillery and jets and crap they'd thrown at the NVA they still weren't giving up. There seemed no end to it.

And some of the grunts were talking about it, wondering what they should do when the orders came to move out in the morning, some of them saying they might say no.

They were only a couple of hundred yards from the end of the wall, and that VC flag was still hanging on the flagpole in the Imperial Palace. Few of the Marines had the fighting spirit left to go get that flag.

Major Thompson could see the change in his battalion; they had run out of steam. It was frustrating, but he could dredge up little anger at his men. The casualty figures explained most of it. They had already been fighting for weeks without letup before Hue, and in eight days of straight combat in the Citadel, February 13-20, the battalion had 47 Marines killed, 240 seriously wounded, and another 60 wounded but still on the line. Even the chaplain, Father McGonigal, was dead. From day one, he'd been up with the grunt squads, even when Thompson tried to get him to lie back a bit for his own safety. Then, on February 17, Thompson noticed he was missing from the nightly briefing. They found his body the next day in a house, with a bullet in his forehead. It could have been a sniper, but the rumor was that McGonigal had wandered past the lines and the NVA had executed him.

The Marines had killed four times their number of dead (219 by confirmed body count), but still, all four line companies were attritted to half strength. There were only three platoon-leader lieutenants left, and the gunnies and sergeants were taking over. All four platoon commanders in Bravo Company were corporals.

Pressing on in this state of morale would just get a lot of people killed, Thompson knew, so he tried to come up with something to energize his people and keep them going. His solution: a night raid. On the evening of the 20th, Thompson called his company commanders to the CP and discussed the plan with them. Three hundred yards to the front was a large, two-story administration building surrounded by a large courtyard; it was occupied by the NVA and it gave them a clear field of fire on the Marine advance. One company was to seize the administration building in a night raid, secure it, and with first light, the battalion would attack across the line with the building as their beachhead. He laid out the plan and Harrington, Jennings, and Nelson said yes, they could give it a try — but Thompson could see their hearts weren't in it.

Lieutenant Polk spoke up. He said Alpha Company was ready to go. At the time, there were only eighty-one men still in the outfit.

In the predawn blackness of the 21st, they moved out; the Second Platoon, under Staff Sgt. James Munroe, a forward observer, and a sniper team. They split up and crawled into the administration building and two adjacent houses, without a shot being fired — the NVA were gone. A cough in the darkness sent fear through the Marines until they turned on a pencil flashlight and discovered a trembling old man and three children. The civilians were terrified, but the grunts couldn't afford to let them go and had to force them to stay. The Marines set up and waited for the sun.

At the CP, Thompson told his other company commanders to monitor Polk's radio so, he said, they could respond quickly in case of trouble. But his real reason was that he hoped hearing the young lieutenant's confidence would bolster them for the coming fight.

It was just before dawn when Staff Sergeant Munroe's Marines saw them coming — a group of North Vietnamese soldiers walking unaware across the courtyard towards the building. Everyone opened up, and the enemy were running, falling, rushing for cover, shooting back. The FO got on his radio to WHISKEY 1/11 across the Perfume, talking in an urgent, excited, almost panicky voice, ". . . We got 'em now, they're in the open . . . Danger close, fifty meters. . . Hurry up for Christ's sake, hurry, hurry, please. . ." The gun crews started moving on their four-deuces, pounding out twenty rounds of Variable Time shells — airbursts. They ran out of VT, but kept pumping with HE and CS. The searing gas burst in the NVA positions and some ran panicked back into the open. The Marine snipers squeezed off single shots from their Model 700 Remington hunting rifles. The shooting rattled on an hour. Nineteen NVA sprawled dead in the grass.

With that, Major Thompson gave the word and the grunts — for all their bitching and fear and hesitation of the night before — attacked. PFC Lawhorn was later to reflect that they got up and went because they trusted their leadership. It was also because the young grunts, although frustrated by the Citadel action, never became completely demoralized: when one of the Marines in Alpha Company was hit by mortars during the renewed push and Lieutenant Polk radioed as to whether he needed evacuation, the reply came back, "Nah, we're tough down here."

The FO with Polk's platoon finally got off the horn, and PFC Landry, back in the WHISKEY gun pits, relaxed a bit, stretching tired muscles. They'd already fired three missions that morning — one for Bravo 1/1, 800 meters south (NVA in the open, nine confirmed kills); one for a 1st Reconnaissance Battalion patrol operating 2000 meters down the Perfume River; and then the Alpha 1/5 call. There was never any letup; Landry and the rest just leaned against the sandbags, talking tiredly, smoking, waiting for the next mission. Around seven in the morning, it came — a few rounds on an NVA-held building in front of a 1/1 position. Then an FO from 2/5 called; he spotted some NVA in a building putting fire on the battalion command post. They dropped three HE rounds down the tube.

Landry heard the 2/5 FO's voice come back on the radio: Direct hit.

Another request from 1/5 to put CS on a city block. Then a few HE shells to catch the choking enemy.

They'd just put out those rounds, when some NVA mortars began exploding around the boat ramp — and them. A couple of AK-47s started clacking. Landry could see a houseboat moored in the Perfume, eight hundred yards to the right on the opposite bank; they all figured that to be the NVA's position, and Sergeant Reliss got on the horn to their 155mm howitzer section on the Gia Le Firebase, six miles south. His request for fire was denied; infantry had priority and all tubes were in operation. The NVA fire kept up sporadically, shrapnel and rounds sometimes thudding against the sandbag circles around the mortars. The natural instinct was to duck, to hunker behind the parapets, but Landry knew they couldn't — it was part of the job as a mortarman. They ignored the whizzing things in the air and kept shooting.

Another call from 1/5; the FO said he could see rockets being launched. They lobbed ten shells across the river and over the wall. And then, suddenly, four explosions frothed up in the river a hundred yards down from them. Word came on the radio that they were short rounds from the howitzers at Gia Le, and Reliss radioed back, "Check fire" (cease firing). But the artillery people radioed back that they hadn't fired; the NVA must have been firing rockets at the mortars. They kept working. Bravo 1/1 got back on the horn, requesting a spotter round on a suspected mortar sight; then the call of fire mission, danger close — one hundred yards — NVA mortar confirmed on roof.

The NVA mortar and sniper fire suddenly picked up again. A round burst ten yards from Landry's pit, and someone started screaming. Two Marines from 1st Tanks had been trying to repair their damaged machine stuck nearby, and the round had hit right behind them; one guy only had a piece of shrapnel, but the other kid had been raked and hurled off the turret. No choppers were available, but within ten minutes, a truck hauled up and ferried the casualty back to the MACV aid station.

The firing kept up from that NVA houseboat floating in the river, and some resupply Navy LCUs churning slowly up the river were forced to retreat. A few minutes later, two Navy gunboats appeared. Landry watched from his panoramic position as the crafts chugged slowly forward, NVA fire splashing around them, then opened up with their 20mm cannons, pounding shells into the Citadel wall and river bank and houses, some of the shells ricocheting off the concrete with a terrific waa-aaanng! Sergeant Reliss got on the radio to MACV for them to contact the gunboats and get them to fire into the houseboat. No results. North Vietnamese snipers kept cracking. Finally, the mortarmen just started screaming, leaned elbows down on the sandbags, and fired at the houseboat with M-16 tracers. The sailors on the boats quickly swung their 20mms and twin-fifties around and hosed down the shoreline and houseboat.

And then, abruptly, it was all quiet again. The Marines returned to their mortars.

Ten minutes later, they could see movement on the bridge crossing the moat of the northeast Citadel wall. Little figures were moving across it; they were too far away for the Marines to see anything but the white conical hats they were wearing. They were probably NVA infiltrators, Landry thought, but there were refugees everywhere and there was no way to tell. The Marines held their fire.

A torrent of requests for fire came in from 1/5, so many that Sergeant Reliss had to relay them back to the artillery outside Hue. Soon, the thunder of howitzer started crashing in, adding to the deep thunks of their mortars. Landry could hear M-16s and AK-47s dueling in all directions. Finally, at half past eight, there was a break in the firing. A small column of trucks came up with more ammunition. At the same time, a group of civilians appeared in the street behind the gun pits. The civilians amazed Landry every time; the firing could be tremendous, but as soon as it died away, they would be swarming back in the streets like nothing had happened. The Marines had heard enough stories about NVA in civilian dress, so they shook their rifles at the Vietnamese and screamed at them. The refugees flitted away. A Marine from 1/1 standing near the gun pits — he wasn't wearing rank insignia, but Landry could tell he was an officer — called to them. He said to shoot the refugees if they ventured too close again. He was absolutely serious; no one could afford to take a chance.

Back to the fire missions. A salvo for MACV on a suspected NVA rocket site; for 1/5 to cover troops moving across a street; for a 5th Marines outfit outside the city; a call from 1/5 to lay CS on an NVA machine gun — denied, friendlies too close to impact area. Another call from 1/5; NVA gun position, danger close, fifty meters.

Finally, they broke for a nine o'clock breakfast of C rations. They sat, spooning out the bland food, watching another series of LCUs head for the boat ramp. The boats slowly churned in and docked in spite of sniper fire. Then two NVA rockets sprayed up shrapnel and mud on the riverbank, and the LCUs started backing away, the sailors firing their 20mm cannons and twin-fifties. The NVA fire followed after them as they disappeared around a bend in the river. A half hour later, word came to secure the mortars because an air strike was coming in. The Phantoms shrieked in from behind the mortar pits, three stories off the deck, and snapped over the Marines' heads with a din that drowned out even the shouting. They shot over the Perfume River, the 500-pound bombs suddenly disengaged and hurled down, and the jets flashed out of sight. Several hundred yards from the mortars (Landry and the rest again watching from their front-row seats) parts of the Citadel wall suddenly shuddered and exploded. The concussion was tremendous, rushing back over them like wind whipping through a car window on the highway.

The Phantoms banked around, zoomed in again, spraying CS out of tanks like crop dusters. The NVA fire died away, and the LCUs returned to the boat ramp. Almost an hour later, a U.S. Army LST supply boat, stacked full of mortar rounds, came in. Everyone was getting tired of drinking the river water, so Sergeant Reliss told Landry and his buddy, Raby, to go see if they could scrounge up some fresh water and maybe some C rations from the Army doggies. They gathered the platoon's canteens and walked into the LST's forecastle, just in time to see two soldiers standing around, drinking beers. Landry was just about to ask for some beer too when — BAM! NVA mortar round. He was thrown to the deck, hard. The sides of the ship were punctured with shrapnel holes, the ship's water can was blown away, the two beer-drinking soldiers were running for their battle stations.

Raby was down, grabbing at his back, shouting, "Jesus, I'm hit!" Then Landry noticed his own legs were bleeding — light shrapnel, some scorch marks from the blast, nothing too serious. He helped Raby up and they stumbled to the top deck where several soldiers were sprawled out, also wounded. The boat lurched out into the river to get out of the NVA's range. Landry didn't want to be near all the ammo stacked in the ship as they might be hit again, and he didn't even have his rifle with him, so he shouted to Raby to get moving. But Raby said he was hurting bad and was going to stay on to be evacuated. Landry grabbed the canteens, then jumped overboard, splashing chest-deep into the Perfume River. He quickly sloshed ashore, then took off running, sprinting past the abandoned gun pits and diving into the house where the rest of the platoon was holed up.

"Man, you're lucky," one of the Marines exclaimed.

"Huh?"

"You just ran through a mortar barrage." Landry couldn't believe it; he hadn't heard a thing. He'd just been running on instinct and fear.

A bit later, the LST docked again — having simply sat out of range until the firing stopped — and dumped the wounded Raby back to shore. The fire missions started again; to the west to cover a convoy taking fire on the approach to Hue, to the east at NVA seen on an island in Perfume. More artillery and Phantoms pummelled the Citadel. LCUs moved back and forth at the boat ramp. Six trucks pulled up with more ammunition. A sudden firefight erupted back near the hotel where the refugees were. Muzzle flashes were visible from the top floor, above the civilians, and Marine grunts raked the building with fire. More NVA shooting snapped in from the Citadel. The truckers who came in with the supplies got behind their .50-caliber mounts and started stitching bursts across the river. Landry and the rest grabbed their M–16s and joined in.

By that evening — Wednesday, February 21 — the northeast wall of the Citadel was in Marine hands. They had accomplished their mission, but the fight was not over for them. While they had been battling to secure the wall, the ARVN had, in effect, been sitting and watching. Reinforcements of Vietnamese Marines had tried to take their last objective — the southeast wall and the Imperial Palace — but made little progress. Major Thompson was thus obliged to wheel his battalion to the right and do the ARVN's job for them. He did have one advantage, reinforcements in the form of Capt. John D. Niotis and his Lima Company, 3d Battalion, 5th Marines, 1st Marine Division.

Staff Sgt. Joseph L. McLaughlin, a twenty-four-year-old family man from Braddock, Pennsylvania, was the platoon sergeant of Lima's First Platoon. When he first heard that they were moving into Hue, he thought they were getting a company R&R. That would have suited him fine; Lima Company had already spent weeks patrolling the Rocket Belt around Da Nang, and some of his men who had been to Hue on liberty spoke about what a beautiful town it was. McLaughlin himself had seen heavy action and was in for the Bronze Star for leading a two-squad outpost in the thick weeds of Go Noi Island. They were surrounded, under heavy fire, and an Army Huey gunship flying support was shot down. McLaughlin took a couple of men, crawled to the wreck, stripped off the weapons, and dragged the terrified crewmen back. They spent the night in the weeds, four gunships strafing around their tiny perimeter, halting NVA attacks by shooting the enemy at three feet.

The company secured at Phu Bai on the evening of the 20th, spent the night in troop tents, and were on the road in a truck convoy the next morning. All hope of a respite from combat vanished then — they were going in full combat gear, and two U.S. Army Dusters pulled up for escort. They got set up around the MACV compound on the south side, and McLaughlin was taken aback by what he saw; everything was shot full of holes, the streets strewn with rubble, and there was still shooting in the streets. He saw a friend of his from their time as DIs at Parris Island, coming by with five or six grunts from 1/1, and joked, "Hey, what ya got there, a water detail?"

"No," his friend said, "this is all I got left." And McLaughlin knew it was going to be bad. By three that afternoon, Lima 3/5 had been air-lifted across the Perfume River and was holding positions adjacent to 1/5 on the northeast wall.

Thursday, February 22. Captain Niotis's orders were to lead the attack on the southeast wall, and after sunup (it was, finally, a clear, sunny day) his Marines were moving down the inside of the northeast wall toward their objective. Staff Sergeant McLaughlin, his lieutenant, and several grunts started down a street leading to their target. Up ahead, Marines were strung out along both sides of the road, cautiously filing past the bullet-pocked houses. They made it to the corner and bunched up, getting organized. The road ended up in a "T." Straight ahead was the southeast wall, to their right, a few hundred yards up the road paralleling the wall, was the Imperial Palace.

The lieutenant took the handset from his radioman and called back to Captain Niotis, while McLaughlin stood alongside, waiting to hear what he should tell his people to do. Everything was quiet. But, abruptly, AKs were roaring and all McLaughlin could see were white streaks flying by and Marines falling and diving. He went down, and just as quickly as it had started, it was over. Two magazines of AK and everything was still again. The platoon radioman lay dead in the rubble, shot through his flak jacket. A couple of other grunts lay beside him, wounded. McLaughlin and a few Marines got up, and crawled toward the casualties. There was no firing. They quickly dragged them back behind the houses, and shouted for the corpsman.

They started creeping forward, then someone shouted, "They're in there!" and McLaughlin saw some of his men putting rounds into a Buddhist temple off to their right, a few houses back from the street. The doors were shut and the only opening was a window on the side, about nine feet up. A few Marines ran forward, pressed against the wall, and hoisted one man up. He shoved ten grenades through the window, they boomed in an explosive chain. McLaughlin and several grunts rushed up, kicked through the front door, and sprayed the smoking interior with their M-16s.

Two dead NVA lay behind the altar, blown apart by the grenades.

They organized around the temple and prepared to push to the right, up the street along the southeast wall that led to the palace. McLaughlin was back behind a house when an NBC reporter strolled up wearing a weird contraption — a chest pack with wires and batteries and a minicam hanging from it. The reporter said he was going to move out between the houses and get some footage of the Imperial Palace.

"No you ain't," McLaughlin said. "I don't even know what the hell you got on. You jump out there with that thing, the gooks'll think it's some kind of new weapon. And they'll throw everything they got at us." The reporter looked unconvinced. McLaughlin was hyped up, scared, bitter over the casualties. He pulled out his .45 and turned angrily on the reporter. "You even step out in front of me and you're dead." The man with the camera disappeared.

Fire started pouring overhead from the palace, the platoon moved back, and McLaughlin led a group up on the wall. It was terraced, rising up in sections of brick, dotted with trees and shrubs, and spider holes and dead North Vietnamese. The grunts started fanning out. McLaughlin stood up and saw Captain Niotis, the lieutenants, and the radiomen talking in a huddle down below by the shot-up temple. He turned his head away and noticed it then — a camouflaged spider hole right at his feet. And then he saw the muzzle of an AK-47 move in the hole. He froze, afraid to move. Oh God, Jesus, shit, I'm dead. The AK barrel slowly slid out farther from the hole and sighted in down the street at the CP group. McLaughlin quickly flipped his M-16 on automatic, dropped his arm, emptied the rifle into the hole, then jumped back, trembling and sweating. The North Vietnamese crouched in the hole was killed.

Three tanks rumbled up through the streets and began shelling the palace. The NVA kept up their fire, and within five minutes, all three tanks had been hit by rockets and pulled back. A hundred yards up the road to the palace was the archway gate of the southeast wall. Lima Company made its move to get through it. McLaughlin lay hunkered down behind a tree up on the wall with some of his platoon grunts, afraid to even lift a finger for all the bullets and shrapnel whizzing through the air. Down below, he could see two- and three-man groups rushing from the buildings on the right, across the street, and through the gate on the left. Fire from the palace raked the street, and men kept tumbling down. By the time two platoons were through the wall, a dozen Marines were dead or wounded.

An Ontos pulled up to give cover fire for the wounded. The gunner roared off all six recoilless rifles, the driver jammed his vehicle in reverse and it stalled. The hatches flew open, the crew dove out, headed for cover, and then a round exploded against it. The wounded grunts managed to crawl into a slight depression between the road and the wall, but it provided little cover, and the fire kept pouring down.

McLaughlin was still crouched behind the tree when he looked down and saw one of his squad leaders, a Puerto Rican corporal named Giullemo Collins, crawling down the little depression where the wounded were huddled. He bellied up to them and pulled the men to better cover, patching up those he could. But he couldn't drag anybody back; to do so would have meant rising up a few extra inches. And that meant certain death. Corporal Collins had to crawl back empty-handed. As McLaughlin watched he wondered how in the hell they were going to get those people.

Brian Mayer, the 1/5 Mule driver, happened to be driving down the street, when he swung a corner right into Lima Company's firefight. Marines were firing furiously and running around — he had no idea what was going on. Then he saw wounded men huddled in a ditch. He hardly even thought about it; after all the months of training and the comradeship, he did what came naturally — he drove his Mule straight towards them. For the moment, his fear just slipped to the back of his mind. Fire exploded from the Palace wall, Marines among the houses poured rounds back. Mayer was vaguely aware of bullets smacking nearby. The Mule bounced crazily across the road, then he stopped it, jumped out, and ran towards the wounded. He helped a few of them aboard, then took off, the fire following him the whole time. He looked back to see a wounded grunt kneeling on the Mule deck, barely on board, and he shouted at the others to get the man aboard. Then he disappeared toward the aid station. Up on the wall, McLaughlin watched astonished. There was no way anybody could have survived that fire, he thought. It was impossible. While he shook his head in amazement and still worried how to get the rest of the wounded evacuated, he saw the Mule come barreling down the road again, the deck empty and ready for more passengers. He watched the bare-headed driver rush out again through the fire, get the last of the wounded aboard, and take off a second time. It was incredible, McLaughlin thought. Who was that guy? Whoever he was, he felt like putting him in for the Medal of Honor.

The fire kept coming in, and some Australian advisors and ARVN recon troops moved up near the temple with a recoilless rifle, and joined in the cacophony aimed at the Palace. The sun was up, the weather was clear — and the Palace had finally been declared a legitimate target — so Captain Niotis got on the radio with Marine Air. A flight of Phantoms sliced in low, shrieking above the rooftops, and splashed napalm against the Palace wall. The canisters flew forward and down, wobbling end on end, the Phantoms pulled up, and a hundred yards in front of the Marines, the flames mushroomed, rolling up in red-yellow-black fireballs, shimmering hot and smoky across the battalion lines. The North Vietnamese fire slacked off and Lima Company secured its objectives.

While Lima pressed their target, Major Thompson organized a simultaneous attack by the rest of his battalion. Thompson, his CP group, and several grunts moved into the large administration building Alpha Company had taken during their night raid, and directed the fight that raged only a few hundred yards away. Thompson beamed; the attack was progressing well, a classic combined-arms effort — infantry, armor, and air — that couldn't have been better executed on a blackboard at Quantico. A tank, commanded by the unit's platoon sergeant, hunkered nearby, lobbing its 90mm rounds at various targets. In the excitement and confusion of the attack, Thompson noticed the sergeant suddenly orient the tank's cannon at the CP group. The barrel swung away, but then a second later, it was back on target — and suddenly, it fired. Thompson and the rest dove for cover. There was as explosion, but no one was hurt. They looked outside — a stone archway between them and the tank was a hunk of smoking rubble. The sergeant saw their faces at the window and opened up with his .50-caliber machine gun, raking the building. Everyone ducked for cover again until Maj. Lynn Wunderlich, the battalion operations officer — one of the coolest men Thompson ever saw in combat — grabbed a radio and asked the sergeant what the hell he was shooting at. The tank quickly turned to fire on the North Vietnamese.

Alpha Company, moving along with Lima on the southeast wall, prepared to attack. Waiting in the rubble under sporadic mortar fire, Lieutenant Polk found a battered guitar and began fiddling with it. His young radioman cracked, "Gee, Lieutenant, can I go up first on the wall?"

Polk kept playing. "Only if you carry a bayonet clenched in your teeth."

Then the word came to attack and they moved out against sporadic resistance. By 1:00 P.M., they had consolidated positions on the archway of the southeast wall. One of Polk's grunts, Cpl. James Avella, a twenty-one-year-old from New Jersey, produced an American flag from his pack. He wired it to a thin steel pole, climbed atop a tin roof, and fastened it to a telegraph pole.

Perhaps the happiest grunts that day were those in Captain Jennings' Bravo Company. With the battle almost over and Lima having moved in as reinforcements, Bravo — the first Marine outfit inside the citadel — was put on trucks for a well-deserved and much needed rehab in Phu Bai. Reporters described the Marines leaving as exhausted, undermanned, but undaunted. They were also lucky; Bravo had men killed and wounded their last day in Hue. The company left with sixty-one men still standing.

Lima Company was setting up along the wall for the night, when Staff
Sergeant McLaughlin sat talking with Corporal Collins, the young
squad leader who was in for a Bronze Star for his rescue attempt.
Collins told him about one of the wounded men, a 3.5 gunner, Lance
Cpl. Thomas E. Falk. When Collins had tried to patch him up, Falk
pushed him away, told him he was hit too bad to save, told him to go
help the others. By the time they got all the wounded back to the aid
station, Falk had died.

McLaughlin knew Falk for all the wrong reasons. He'd caught the
kid sleeping on guard duty a couple of times, and although he wasn't a
troublemaker, whenever there was trouble, Falk was always involved.
The kid might have been a problem before, McLaughlin thought, but
when things came down to the wire, he'd turned into one hell of a
Marine.

And that's what he wrote to Falk's mother.

Ten in the morning, and McLaughlin was with his platoon, up behind
three tanks which fired into the Imperial Palace. A recoilless rifle started booming, B-40 rockets zinged down and in seconds, all the tanks
had been hit. They roared back down the street and the grunts
followed, jogging back at a crouch, using the tanks for cover. Suddenly,
grenades started bursting around them — there were enemy troops
along the road flipping grenades over the courtyard walls. Everyone
started scrambling and shooting, running like hell. A grenade landed
at the feet of one Marine, and he instinctively jumped back, right into
the street — right into the path of one of the tanks hauling away. The
tread caught the kid at the waist, chunked over him with a terrible
smashing sound, and sped out of sight, probably not even knowing
what happened. The grunt lay smashed on the road, almost cut in
half, and tried to sit up, staring wide-eyed in shock at his mangled
body. The man's best friend, a corporal, crouched on the sidewalk, the
tears welling up in his eyes. Then the kid started yelling, saying he was
dead, that it hurt, telling him to put him out of it. The Marine was list-
ed in the records as having been killed by the tank, but McLaughlin
heard the corporal had done the only thing he could. He shot his best
friend in the head.

With the firepower restrictions concerning the Imperial Palace lifted
by General Lam, a tactical air controller circled the position in a light
observation plane. He controlled a flight of A-4s, employing bombs
and napalm against the northeast wall of the Palace — and then the

North Vietnamese shot him out of the sky. The Marines were able to rescue the wounded observer; the pilot was dead in the wreck. The remainder of the air strike had to be cancelled.

Lima Company started pushing through the rows of houses on their way to the Palace, prepping each building with a dozen grenades, then making fireteam rushes through the doors. They got inside one building and prepared to attack the house next door. McLaughlin set his rifle down, pulled two grenades off his flak jacket, and told the grunts to make their move as soon as they heard the explosions. He yanked the pins, clutched a grenade in each hand, holding the spoons down, and stepped out into the narrow alleyway separating the two houses. He was just reaching up to jam the frags through the wooden bars across the window, when he happened to glance over his shoulder — and there, down the alley, across the street, crouched behind a low wall was a North Vietnamese soldier. McLaughlin could see him clearly, visible above the wall from the waist up, with a B-40 over his shoulder sighted right at him. He jumped backward into the doorway, just as the rocket cracked down the alley and exploded against a wooden fence. McLaughlin backhanded his two grenades at the soldier, then ran to get his rifle.

The fight was on. The grunts kept moving, house to house, throwing dozens of grenades, hosing down the rooms with their M-16s, rushing to the next building. They caught several NVA soldiers running from a barber shop, sprinting away across the street, and everyone opened up. McLaughlin and a squad rushed inside the shop, firing from the hip, killing those NVA still holding their positions. More NVA fire suddenly started popping from fifty yards across the street. The marines rushed out the back, and hunkered down among the rubble, out of the way of the shooting.

They were safe, but at the same time, they couldn't get to the NVA in front of the shop. Finally, one of the platoon machine gunners, a muscular redheaded kid, dropped his M-60 and scooped up several grenades. He ran back inside the shop — in full view of the NVA through where the shop's plate glass window had been — vaulted up the stairs to the second floor, and started lobbing grenades across the street. All hell broke loose. McLaughlin and the rest kept down while shrapnel and ricochets, brick, plaster, and wood flew everywhere. When the dust settled, the machine gunner ran back to them, breathing hard, dusted white with plaster, and just flying with adrenaline, his eyes saying, I got those bastards! He grabbed another handful of grenades and ran back to the second floor. The firestorm broke out again. He came back, got more, then did the whole thing over for the third time. By the time he crawled back to cover, the shop had been shot to pieces and he'd come through without a scratch. The enemy fire ceased.

The platoon organized inside the barber shop and, about an hour later, McLaughlin was amazed to see a Vietnamese family come walking up through the rubble. The father cleared all the broken glass and debris off the counter, and started setting up his barber tools. The mother and kids simply started dragging the dead North Vietnamese soldiers out and laying them in back. McLaughlin was struck by their nonchalant attitude; they must have seen a lot, he thought.

The day before, on the 22nd, Sergeant Dye had been wounded. He'd been moving forward with Delta Company when they started taking tremendous fire from the Palace wall. He ducked behind some rubble with a Marine photographer, Corporal J. C. Pennington, when a B–40 exploded nearby, sending up a storm of rocks and shrapnel. Penny took a bad slice in his head, and Dye took fragments in his left hand, shoulder, and leg. They'd patched each other up and gone back and found a corpsman. Then Dye went back to the action.

Now he was hooked up with a Delta squad scouting toward the Palace. They cautiously moved forward through the blasted rubble of houses, getting right up to the Palace wall without being seen. There were holes blasted through the bricks by tanks and Ontos, and the grunts climbed through and spread out. Ahead of them was the inner wall and moat, around them narrow streets, tin shacks, and houses. They were searching through them when an old Vietnamese man popped out from a house with his hands up. The Marines gathered around him, asking, "VC? VC?" and the man pointed to the northwest, up where the ARVN were holding the line. Everyone had already been through the wringer and they decided not to go charging where the old man pointed.

Next was a large building on their side of the Palace grounds, with a tile roof and ornate carvings, and the squad warily filed up its staircase. They stopped outside the door, not really wanting to see what was on the other side. But Dye was curious. He poked his head through the door, couldn't see anything, and started to go inside. One of the grunts behind him whispered, "Shit, man, watch out for booby traps," but Dye crept in anyway. He just had to see what was inside; he was actually inside the Imperial Palace, it was like the climax to the whole battle. He quietly moved through the rooms, gripping his M–16, terrified, sweating like a pig. He made his way through the next doorway and there he was, right inside the vaulted throne room of the Palace. The walls were covered with golf leaf. Two thrones, one larger than the other, sat on a raised platform, and Dye stared in awe at the red and gold lacquer, the dragon and lion carvings, feeling mesmerized, wondering if that was how the knights felt when they stormed a castle. A shaft of light shone through a window on the left, and two North Vietnamese lay there. Dye walked over and poked them with the barrel of his M-16. They were stone dead.

Then he realized the rest of the Marines were inside with him. He smiled at the bodies, said something profane and funny, and the grunts grinned. Then they packed up and got back to their side of the lines.

By the morning of Saturday, February 24, Major Thompson's battalion was in position to finish up the North Vietnamese in the Citadel. Three days before, four battalions of the 1st Air Cavalry Division had swept through the NVA command and supply post west of the city in the La Chu Woods, with infantry, air strikes, Naval gunfire, artillery, and helicopter gunships. The Cav effectively wiped out the support for those last NVA soldiers still holding inside the Citadel. On the 23rd, the enemy command element, the 6th NVA Regiment, finally gave the survivors permission to retreat. They began pulling away from the Marine positions and fighting through the ARVN to the west, trying to escape and being pummelled by artillery along the way.

The only unsecured position in front of the Marines was the Imperial Palace. Lima Company was up on the southeast wall, getting ready to make their charge — all of them scared because there were two hundred yards of open ground between them and the wall, and they were convinced they were going to have another bloodbath like on the 22nd. But fifteen minutes before their push, word came down that the South Vietnamese were going to do it instead. Thompson had planned for the Marines to attack, but the RVN government wanted ARVN troops to make the final assault in Hue. It was a matter of pride. The Lima grunts watched as the Black Panther Company, led by Captains Coolican and Hue, moved up on their flank, then simply charged — running right at the Palace, shouting and firing, carrying ladders, climbing over the wall or vaulting through the holes already blasted in it.

The Marines sat watching from their perch, prepared to give support fire if any NVA appeared, and muttering among themselves, "Man, have those guys got balls."

"Yeah, but better them than us."

Many Marines liked to put the ARVN down, McLaughlin thought, but those Black Panthers were absolutely fearless.

The ARVN troops got inside the wall and were followed by three hundred more soldiers of the 2d Battalion, 3d ARVN Regiment. There was little firing. The NVA were gone, the last survivors retreating the night before, slipping away through the South Vietnamese lines, leaving only a few dud artillery shells, some equipment, and the carcasses of a horse and dog they had eaten in starvation. Also discovered were two soldiers from an ARVN reconnaissance company, who had been cut off from their unit and had spent the entire battle hiding within the NVA positions. The two men were haggard and broke down in hysterics upon their liberation by the Black Panthers. The Viet Cong flag, which had flown over Hue for twenty-five days, was hauled down and in its place, the Black Panthers raised the red and yellow banner of the Republic of Vietnam. The Marines and ARVN watching started to cheer. Major Thompson thought that if the ARVN were going to raise their flag, he was glad the Black Panthers did it — he had seen Coolican and his little soldiers in action, and he would go to war with them anywhere. But they had been the exception to the rule, Thompson thought: "The MACV records will reflect that the ARVN, assisted by the 1/5, took the Citadel. That was strictly public relations hogwash, like so much that MACV put out during the war. The 1st Battalion, 5th Marines took the Citadel. The ARVN were spectators."

Later that day, Thompson and his command group were visiting the infantry companies, when a leaderless mob of ARVN soldiers appeared along a business street. They began smashing into the shops, looting television sets, refrigerators, and such, ferrying the booty away in trucks.

On February 25, artillery pounded a last little band of NVA hiding in the southern corner of the walls, an ARVN ranger force secured the last patch of land known as Gia Hoi east of the walls, and the Citadel was officially declared secure. The fight was over and Lawhorn felt safe again. He could raise his head past a window without getting it shot off. He was exhausted, mentally and physically, but he marvelled over one thing: he was still alive. He was lucky, very, very lucky. Half the company dead or wounded, and he hadn't even been scratched. He prayed to the Lord every night over there. Lawhorn started walking around, looking through all the blown away houses, at the piles of dead North Vietnamese left behind, and when he started picking through the old NVA positions, he found something incomprehensible — dead civilians. They hadn't been killed by mortars or indiscriminate cross fire; they were all shot in the head and buried in shallow ditches. The Communists had simply massacred them. Lawhorn couldn't figure out why. He didn't give a damn about the NVA bodies he saw, but it hurt him to see all the dead and wounded civilians.

By Wednesday, February 28, 1/5 was being pulled out of the Citadel to conduct mop-up sweeps around the city. Mayer figured that since the battle was over, they were going to be sent to the rear for a little rest, but then he got assigned to one of the sweeps with Charlie Company. Oh well, he thought, it's always something. His buddies in the recoilless rifle section, H&S Company, loaded their personal gear and ammunition aboard three Mules, mounted with 106s, climbed aboard, and they took off down a dirt road outside the Citadel walls. They rumbled through an area thick with foliage, Mayer and the others sitting along the sides as if they were out for a ride in the country, until a sergeant shouted at them to jump down and walk flank security. They stopped at one end of a stone bridge, waiting for the Charlie Company grunts to move up on a parallel road and link up with them.

Mayer stood near his Mule, holding an M-16, and looked around, wondering what they were supposed to do. Something suddenly clanged against his vehicle, sounding like some joker throwing pebbles. He turned to see who the clown was — and then the cacophony abruptly welled up in his ears.

AK-47 fire was pouring across the bridge.

Everyone dropped down, grabbing weapons, running for cover, and Mayer rushed toward the stone pillars on their side of the bridge. Two Marines were already crouched behind them and one, a sergeant who had been shot in the foot, turned and shouted at him, "Hey, this is occupied!"

"Oh shit!"

Mayer went running like hell back towards the parked Mules, losing his helmet in his mad scramble, and dove flat behind one of them. All around, Marines were firing furiously. A B-40 shrieked out of the brush, flashing past like a giant white fireball. Mayer gripped his M-16 and tried to find a target across the bridge, but all he could see was a tangle of trees and bushes and vines. He never had the chance to fire a single shot. Suddenly, there was a sledgehammer blow against his foot and he yelled out, grabbed his calf, and spun down on his back. A second later, another burst of AK caught him across the legs, drilling a round through the flesh and muscle of both thighs.

A Marine jumped beside him. "C'mon, I'll take ya back!"

Mayer knew the man, a stocky 106 gunner, and all he could think was that the guy was going on R&R to Hawaii soon to see his wife. "No," he shouted, "you're married! Take a walk! Get outta here!"

Then his partner, the indestructible Howard, ran up out of nowhere and threw him over his shoulders. He ran towards a tiny, tin-roofed shed behind them — then tripped in a hole. Mayer tumbled to the dirt, screeching out in pain. The air still roared with fire and from the corner of his eye, he saw the dust of rounds hitting the ground puff up beside him. Howard picked him up again, stumbled a few more yards, then put him down for a quick breather. Mayer rolled flat and shouted at Howard, "Take off! I can make it from here!" Then he started crawling toward the little shed, dragging himself forward on his hands and elbows. He couldn't feel his legs. Oh God, he thought, I'm not going to make it. He could see two water buffalo tied to a tree beside the shed. One was shot to death and lay in a big clump at the end of his rope; the other was calmly chewing at the grass. Bullets kept snapping overhead, but he reached the shed, totally exhausted and covered in sweat. Two corpsmen were crouched timidly in back of the shed a couple of feet away. They yelled at him to roll over on his back. They reached out, grabbed his flak jacket, and hauled him to the back.

There were other wounded men collected behind the shed, and the corpsmen lay Mayer beside them in the row. One of them, a buddy, lay beside him, smoking a cigarette and calmly talking to the corpsman treating him. The man's arm was gone. Mayer looked down at his own foot; the jungle boot was frayed through and through, all torn and bloody. All together, three rounds had passed through him; the incredible pain of it had dulled to a throbbing ache. He lay there, fretting that either he was going to lose his foot, or they were going to patch him up and send him back to hell. Some grunts ran up, rolled the one-armed man onto a wooden door and hustled him past the water buffalo, through a thick hedgerow. Then they ran back with a stretcher and got Mayer. It was Brian Mayer's third Purple Heart. He'd been in Vietnam three months. He was going home.

Chapter 9

Mop-Up

While the so-called mop-up continued in the Citadel, the 1/1 and 2/5 Marines continued sweeping farther and farther out around the South Side. One of the biggest patrols started a little after midnight on February 26, when Lieutenant Colonel Cheatham picked up his whole battalion and went hunting. He left Major Steele at the apartments command post with the 106s for security, then accompanied Fox, Golf, and Hotel Companies on a night march down south through the city, across the pontoon bridge over the Phu Cam, then sweeping north to catch the NVA/VC stragglers between them and the canal. It was a dark, foggy night, but by morning, the sun was up and the Marines were in position.

They began pushing east towards the Phu Cam. Firefights erupted.

Cheatham and his staff hiked to an ARVN engineer compound atop a hill. No one knew about the South Vietnamese minefield, and the first Marines walking up to the gate were killed. Finally, the rest made their way through and the colonel set up shop inside. His Marines were finding the stragglers all right. Radio reports came in; three Marines KIA, thirty-seven NVA killed.

Major Steele was at the apartments when he got word to move up with tanks and supplies. They loaded up the trucks, then pushed out in a convoy, Steele riding up front in his jeep. They came around a turn in the road, and there was the spookiest sight Steele ever saw in Vietnam — a destroyed and deserted convoy. It was the one from the 11th Marines that had been ambushed at the beginning of the Tet Offensive, and no one had been by since. The trucks and Ontos were along the side of the road looking as if the people inside had left in a hurry. Doors were open, ammunition was still in the feed trays.

A few more meters down the road, the earth suddenly erupted behind Steele's jeep. The personnel carrier behind him had hit a mine. The whole front of the vehicle was gone, the engine blown away, metal torn up, and the driver sat there like a cartoon character, holding the steering wheel, his face black, his hair burnt away. The Marine was in shock and they got him onto a truck headed back for the BAS. Steele called up the engineers, but they had difficulty detecting the mines. The VC had placed them in wooden boxes before burying them, and the metal detectors couldn't always locate them.

Steele was off to the side of the road, talking with the first sergeant of the tank company, an old friend of his, when a Vietnamese truck packed full of ARVNs and civilians, pulled up. The driver went around the Marine convoy, drove a bit down the road — then another mine boomed, the truck went into the dirt, and the Marines had to get more casualties back. Finally, Steele gave the word and they went cross-country to the ARVN compound, cutting through a Vietnamese cemetery.

From the hilltop ARVN camp, Cheatham had a panoramic view of the valley below and the next hill. There were several old, concrete French blockhouses atop that hill, and the NVA were dug inside them.

Captain Downs and Fox Company swept across the valley towards them. Two heavy machine guns started pounding, and the Marines edged around to the back of the hill.

Lieutenant Harvey and Hotel Company hiked to the base of the hill on line, forming an "L" at the bottom with Fox. The NVA positions were about a hundred yards up. The whole area was covered with bushes and trees, and it was hard to see very far — especially being crouched down in the brush, trying not to get hit. The Hotel grunts got into a recessed trail and Lieutenant Harvey got on the horn for air strikes on the cement blockhouses. He was also on the radio with Downs, but with all the foliage, he wasn't sure exactly where Fox was. So, instead of directing the jet bombing runs parallel to the front line, as was prescribed by the book, he brought them in over his head, thus cutting down the chances of a jet overshooting the target and accidentally bombing Fox Company.

The USAF jets came on station and shrieked low, tumbling napalm canisters atop the hills. The NVA fire ceased.

With the shooting stopped, Harvey stood up to get a better look. He rejoiced; the position was smoking and burning from a near perfect hit.

Standing with his radio, he brought them in for another strike. Again, the Air Force made a direct hit.

Down on the trail, Gunny Thomas stared up at the jets, wondering why they were coming in over their heads, instead of flying parallel to their front. He didn't know about Fox Company. Harvey radioed the pilots to do another napalm drop.

One jet banked around, shrieked low over the treetops, and then four 500-pound bombs came flying down, wobbling end on end in their descent, hurtling down and forward while the jet shot back up. Suddenly, there was a tremendous roar and Harvey was slammed with a terrific concussion. He fell to the ground. He felt like puking. The ground trembled. When the explosions died away and the dirt stopped raining down, and he shook his head clear, Harvey realized that two of the explosions had come from behind him. Oh no, he thought, the pilot had pressed the button a second too soon. The grunts got up, shaken, stunned, looking around. What the hell happened? They stumbled around for a few minutes, trying to comprehend what the huge craters in the line meant. A couple of guys were wounded, and then they found four others — blown apart, arms and legs and intestines and brains smeared in the bushes. It must have been a direct hit. Guys were getting sick, turning away, not wanting to even look at the mess.

But Gunny Thomas didn't have any choice; somebody had to get the bodies, and he was the senior enlisted man. He started dragging them onto ponchos. He had to shout at the grunts, threaten them to get them to help.

On their flank, Fox Company was moving up to take the hill. They found twenty-one dead North Vietnamese in the demolished blockhouses. But, that particular body count didn't mean much to the Hotel grunts.

Lieutenant Harvey sat on the trail at the base of the hill. All this way, he thought, all ready to go up there and take that hill and then that jet drops a load of crap on them and four more of his grunts were blown away. He was absolutely crushed.

Corporal Allbritton was trudging along with his squad through the treelines. He was tired. Tired and beat and wasted. Four weeks in those Hue streets had done it. And now all this mop-up fighting. The day before, another man in his squad had been killed when a couple of mortar rounds had plopped in. Then there was the hill the jets had bombed right in front of them. Was that yesterday or the day before? He couldn't remember, too much had happened. He'd been wounded again, but he wasn't sure when. There was always something zinging around, and one day he noticed he had shrapnel in him. Or it could have been bullet fragments; no way to tell. Allbritton was so beat, he wasn't thinking. He started taking his squad across an open field. The NVA opened up.

Allbritton jumped down, rolled over and grabbed for a smoke grenade in his web gear. Gotta pop smoke, gotta get out of here! Then he heard the B-40 crack to his right. He jerked his head that way. Three little pine trees in a row snapped in half and there it was, small and black and flying towards him. It shot over his belly, moving so slowly he could see the yellow Chinese lettering painted against the olive-drab round. It missed him by maybe a foot then exploded a yard away. A big fragment dug into his left thigh, right above the knee. The rest of Third Platoon popped smoke to cover the squad's withdrawal, and Allbritton limped toward the truck that had come up to evacuate the wounded. His radioman, Moses, lay in back. Rocket fragments had caught him in the face, smashing his mouth so he couldn't talk.

Allbritton and Moses had been through a lot. They were the last of the original squad that had choppered into Hue. There had been some good moments, too. Back at the apartments, when the green replacements had arrived, some clean utilities had been brought in and Allbritton ended up with an extra-large set to drape around his short, 130-pound frame. The company had also latched on to one Gillette razor; being the leader of 3d squad in the Third Platoon, Allbritton was the last to get it. He hacked off as much of his beard as he could in cold water, then walked down the hallway, passing Moses and one of the new replacements. He went outside and a couple of minutes later Moses followed, grinning and laughing. He told Allbritton that when he walked by, the new kid asked who the new guy was, referring to his clean face and new fatigues. Moses said it was Corporal Arkie, and the kid guffawed, "My gosh! He looks so young and angelic."

Now that new guy was the veteran. And Allbritton and Moses were getting choppered out, leaving behind a squad completely different from the one they brought in.

Burghardt and Neas were survivors. They'd been through twenty-four days of it, weeks of running those streets, making it while half of Alpha Company got killed or wounded, and they started sending up the rear-echelon Marines as replacements. Now, they were leaving.

The company started out in the morning, sweeping south, house to house to a bridge on the eastern section of the South Side, along the canal. They were to leave the city over that bridge. The Marines found nobody in their sweep, and finally, Burghardt, Neas, and a couple of other grunts came around a small pagoda and stopped behind a low wall. The two of them stood behind the bricks, shoulder-close, and Burghardt waved two men across the bridge to secure the far side so the platoon could move over.

The first man got on the bridge and enemy firing commenced. The AKs roared from nowhere, mortars came in, and the man on the bridge went down, clutching his knee.

Then a burst raked over the wall. Burghardt saw a giant white flash expode in front of his face and he went flying back against the opposite wall, his helmet slamming down hard on his nose, crying out, "God forgive me!" Neas lay beside him against the wall, holding his arm. The same burst had put a round through it. He put his hand up on Burghardt's neck to let him know he'd been hit, and then he saw the blood. He couldn't believe his sergeant was wounded. A corpsman ran up and stripped off Burghardt's flak jacket. The bullet had gone through his neck and ploughed out his shoulder, so the doc tied a bandage around the exit hole and gave him a shot of morphine. Burghardt was scared, not because it hurt, but because it didn't. He couldn't move.

Neas started crying as he watched the corpsman work on Burghardt, as Burghardt kept calling to him by his nickname Alphie, asking him to find his wallet. Neas hardly hurt from his arm wound, but his heart felt like it had been ripped out as he stared at his good friend and trusted sergeant being loaded on a door for evacuation. Somebody dragged up the Marine who'd been shot on the bridge, and a Marine nicknamed Hoppy pulled up in a jeep. They laid Burghardt across the back on a stretcher, Neas and the other man climbed aboard, and Hoppy hauled off for the Hue stadium. Things started going fuzzy for Burghardt. They got to the stadium LZ and he could feel the cold mist in the air, and then he was being carried on an Army chopper. They landed at Phu Bai. Another short wait and he was in another helicopter. Within two hours of his being wounded, the corpsman aboard the hospital ship *Repose* in the South China Sea were pushing him into the operating room.

The next day, the doctors told him what had happened. The round had nicked his spinal cord, causing bone chips to sever some of the nerves. He was paralyzed. A quadraplegic. That second day on the ship, he was strapped to his bed with his head fastened in a brace, when an officer pinned the Purple Heart to the sheets.

During the third week aboard the hospital ship, a newspaper article about him appeared in *Stars & Stripes,* and some of the corpsmen taped it above his bed. The headline read "Marine Kills 7 in Hue Battles." By then, Burghardt could just barely move his left arm.

Lance Corporal Carter was tired of Phu Bai. When he'd first arrived at the hospital there were a leg full of shrapnel, they'd been short of Novocain, so the doctor simply jammed a probing rod up through the wound. He left the fragments in, stitched up the gash, and put a patch over it. It had been two weeks and Carter was sick of the hospital. He didn't like being in the rear to begin with; there was nothing to do, he missed his friends, and he was damn tired of rear-echelon gunnery sergeants telling him to fill sandbags. And it was more personal. He had heard an ugly story about his company first sergeant in the rear; he had taken four wounded Marines who were not supposed to be on duty because of their injuries, put them on a convoy to Hue as truck security, and three of them ended up getting killed. That's how the story went and Carter tended to believe it; there was a great feeling of hatred towards the first sergeant. Carter wanted nothing to do with noncombat Marines.

So, finally, he signed a waiver to get out of sick bay. He got his gear and his rifle, then rode back to Hue on a convoy. The truck bed was layered with bloodied sandbags; it must have been used in casualty evacuation.

There was no shooting up the road. The battle was all but over.

Carter found Fox Company down at the apratments CP, running platoon patrols across the canal to clear out the NVA still moving through the area. His first day back and he was with Third Platoon going out. They went through the treelines and civilians kept streaming by, headed back for the inner city now that it was secure. Pretty girls smiled and waved and flitted by as fast as they could, afraid that one of the bitter grunts might shoot them because they were Vietnamese. And the old men kept going by, not wanting to stop when the Marines tried to get information, just jabbering, "No VC, no VC!"

Finally, one of the grunts had enough. The next old papa-san who came by crying "No VC" was detained. The angry Marine, a tough corporal who liked to use his fists to settle arguments, grabbed him around the collar and shouted, "Okay, if there's no one out there, then you're going to get in front and you're going to be our point!" Carter stared impassively at the old man.

The corporal stormed to the front of the platoon, shoving along the old man, and the rest of the Marines followed. They went down a dirt trail, crossed a small bridge, got into the jungle, and a torrent of AK-47s suddenly burst from the side of the road. The old man took most of it and went sprawling dead. The corporal fell seriously wounded — then played dead as some NVA appeared from a trench and stripped off his watch, pack, and pouch full of M-79 rounds. The corporal survived.

The rest of the Marines scrambled for cover as fire slashed over their heads. No one could see a thing for all the foliage. Staff Sergeant McCoy was shouting for the 3.5-inch rocket launcher, and Carter and his A-gunner slid up belly flat. The NVA were down in spider holes and a trench in the brush. They crawled through the trees into a small pagoda opposite the NVA trench, and started blasting out shells. Captain Downs called for air support and two Marine Huey gunships came flying in. Carter felt like cheering as the gunships banked in, blowing hell out of the trench line.

The enemy troops started scrambling out, running for their lives. Everyone opened up, Carter kept firing his rocket launcher. He could see figures falling among the trees. An NVA machine gunner started firing, trying to cover his comrades' retreat. Carter stared into the green, trying to locate the gun. Then he saw the smoke rising from the muzzle and readied two LAW rockets. He fired the first LAW, it exploded past the gunner's position, and the man got scared and started climbing out of the trench. Carter saw the head and back pop into view, grabbed the second LAW, fired. The North Vietnamese soldier exploded.

That night, Richard Carter celebrated his birthday by sticking a match in some pound cake. He was twenty years old.

On midnight the next day, Operation Hue City was officially terminated. It had lasted twenty-six days.

Chapter 10

Aftermath

The battle left the city of Hue in a state of semiruin. On the South Side, the buildings still stood with little more than shell holes in courtyard walls, broken windows, and such — except along Le Loi Street where the heaviest fighting had taken place. The Citadel had been dealt a rougher blow with the air strikes, Naval gunfire, and artillery along with northeast wall and other places. The estimates tallied ten thousand houses either totally destroyed or damaged, roughly forty percent of the city. There was, however, simply no truth to early press reports that Hue had been pounded to a vast shambles by massive U.S. firepower (said *Life* magazine, ". . . the only way Hue could be won was by destroying it."). In retrospect, Hue got off rather lightly in comparison with fights like Monte Casino in 1944 where, indeed, a centuries-old monastery and much of the nearby city were pounded into a vast rubble heap by Allied shelling.

Soon after the battle, the South Vietnamese government initiated Operation Recovery, a 90-day relief and reconstruction effort aimed at the entire I Corps, but focused primarily on Hue. It brought food, clothing, shelter, and medical attention to that city's estimated 116,000 refugees (out of a population of 140,000). By the end of the year, life in Hue was relatively back to normal. As Major Swenson noted, "My final duties as liaison officer entailed taking visitors to Task Force X-RAY through the city on a guided tour. The city was not destroyed in the Tet Offensive. It was damaged, but still beautiful."

The war had finally come to the people of Hue — and they paid the price. As Hue pulled itself out of the mess, one bloody sidelight of the battle was uncovered, something worse than refugees and cross-fire deaths: the Viet Cong and North Vietnamese had massacred many of the people of Hue during their occupation. Over the years, the evidence was collected in bits and pieces; the discovery of mass graves, captured communist documents, statements by prisoners of war. It was learned that with the typical cold-blooded efficiency of the Communists, the VC had gone into Hue with lists of so-called Enemies of the People. Those marked included government officials, city administrators, intellectuals, teachers, college students, soldiers, foreigners — and their families — all those suspected of being potential enemies of the communist cause. There was one other category: all those who could identify the VC infrastructure now that it had surfaced for the Tet Offensive. That could include any innocent bystander. The people were rounded up and some were executed in the city. When the fight was obviously being lost by the VC, they marched their political prisoners outside the city to different sites and killed them. Some were buried alive. Great pains were taken by the Communists to conceal their work, and it took a year for the allies to put the pieces together. The South Vietnamese government finally recovered three thousand bodies in mass graves around Hue. Another two thousand people were still unaccounted for. The massacre, however, received little attention in the world news media because the revelation of the massive Hue killings coincided with the revelation of the My Lai massacre by one U.S. Army infantry platoon. There were others, in the anti-American sentiment of the time, who quite simply refused to believe the Communist Vietnamese were capable of such a heinous crime. For example, the photographer Griffiths wrote in 1971, that the Americans had invented the whole massacre scenario as a "propaganda campaign to present the [civilian] casualties of the fighting in Hue, most of whom were killed by the most hysterical use of American firepower ever seen, as the victims of a communist massacre."*

Since 1975, Hue and its people have, of course, been under Communist domination once again.

The individual North Vietnamese soldier fought bravely, but his leadership was lacking, and the Battle of Hue City proved another military defeat for the Communists in their militarily disastrous Tet Offensive. The records put the NVA/VC dead in Hue at 5,113, with another 89 captured, and no account of the number of wounded or those who died of injuries. The ARVN lost 384 killed and 1,800 wounded, most of them from the first week in the Citadel. The United

*Philip Hones-Griffith. *Vietnam, Inc.* N.Y.: McMillan, 1971.

States Marine Corps reported 147 men killed-in-action, and 857 wounded seriously enough to warrant evacuation to a hospital. Somewhere close to half of the Marine infantrymen committed to the battle were killed or wounded. As in all engagements during the Vietnam War, the U.S. casualty figures were somewhat lower than reality. In this case, they do not take into account those who died in hospitals from their wounds, those casualties among the Army and Navy helicopter, boat, and advisory support units, nor do they include those slightly wounded infantrymen who either were not evacuated, or who did not even bother to report their injuries.

Every Marine who fought in Hue was entitled to the Combat Action Ribbon (an award conceived more than a year later and awarded retroactively). Also, in 1969, those outfits that participated in Operation Hue City were awarded the Presidential Unit Citation. The units cited for their direct or indirect involvement in Hue included:

Task Force X-RAY Headquarters
Headquarters Company, 1st Marines
1st Battalion, 1st Marines
Headquarters Company, 5th Marines
1st Battalion, 5th Marines
2d Battalion, 5th Marines
L Company, 3d Battalion, 5th Marines
1st and 2d Battalions, 11th Marines
Provisional Platoon, 3d Tank Battalion
A and A-T Companies, 1st Tank Battalion
1st Engineer Battalion
1st and 3d Motor Transport Battalions
1st Shore Party Battalion
7th Communications Battalion
1st MP Company, 1st Marine Division
Combat Intelligence Team, Headquarters Battalion, 1st Marine
    Division
First Platoon, 3d Bridge Company, FMF
First Platoon, 34th Bridge Company, FMF
FLSGA
FLC
1st Force Advisory Team
Hue Ramp Detachment, U.S. Naval Support Activity
MCB-8 and MCB-121, U.S. Navy
River Group 521, U.S. Navy
D Battery, 1st Battalion, 44th Artillery Regiment, U.S. Army
97th and 329th Transportation Companies (Heavy Boat), U.S. Army

The Marine infantrymen who won the Battle of Hue turned the city back to the ARVN and continued the rice paddy–jungle war they had known before. There was no rear to pull back to for a rest; the companies went right on to further combat operations. And there lies one of the more grim realities of war. It might seem that an eighteen-year-old grunt who had endured the horror of a battle like Hue had a right to survive until his tour was over and it was his turn to go home. But there was no guarantee like that in Vietnam and many a man who was a Hue veteran survived the street fighting only to be killed several weeks or months later in just another firefight in the middle of just another rice paddy.

A combat infantryman couldn't help but be changed by the war in some way. For some, the change was bad; anxious memories, thoughts of dead friends, the absolute savagery and human waste they saw, the nightmares and mental wounds that wouldn't heal. For some, the change was good; the friendships, the pride in having been a Marine, the sense of maturity and confidence garnered from conquering a situation few could. For most, there is a mix between the two.

The grunt Jim Soukup, told about part of it: "The Marines have a tradition to uphold in any major battle and Hue City was no exception. I didn't know what was going on elsewhere or at the Citadel, but tearing down VC flags and raising Old Glory was an inspirational sight to savor. However, once again, you're just sending up a marker for Charlie to zero in on. But hell, after what you've gone through to earn that privilege, nobody really cares. Like the inscription on my Zippo lighter says, 'To really live you must nearly die.' Even today, the flag and anthem awaken a deep sense of pride for having served with those who gave their all for the honor and the privileges we enjoy.

"I am one of the lucky ones. I survived."

Lieutenant General Cushman (CG, III MAF) retired as a general after having served as the commandant of the Marine Corps. Brigadier General LaHue (CG, Task Force X-RAY) added the Distinguished Service Medal to his decorations before retiring as a lieutenant general to his home in Florida. Brigadier General Truong (CG, 1st ARVN Division) was in command of the I Corps Tactical Zone during the 1975 communist takeover, and it was his sorry duty to abandon Hue City and retreat. He was able to escape to the United States thanks to the sponsorship of a U.S. Army general. Lieutenant Colonel Khoa (Mayor of Hue) was quietly transferred to another post after the battle.

Colonel Hughes (CO, 1st Marines) was awarded the Navy Cross and Legion of Merit for his command in Hue, left Vietnam in June 1968, and retired soon after. Lieutenant Colonel Gravel (CO, 1/1) was slightly wounded after Hue, then in June 1968, he led his battalion to Khe Sanh where he was seriously wounded when his helicopter was shot down. He won the Legion of Merit and two Purple Hearts, retired as a colonel, and works for a Republican congressman in Long Beach, California. Major Murphy (1/1) was posthumously awarded the Silver Star and Purple Heart; his parents accepted the medals. Captain Batcheller (CO, A/1/1) reluctantly accepted the Navy Cross for Hue. His wounds left him with various physical problems, but through strenuous exercise, he was able to pass the USMC fitness requirements, and retired in 1983 as a lieutenant colonel. Captain Gallagher (1/1) is now a lieutenant colonel. Lieutenant Smith (CO, A/1/1) received the Silver Star for Hue, and a second Silver Star and Purple Heart at Khe Sanh. He went back as an advisor to the Vietnamese Marines and won the Navy Cross with them during the 1972 Easter Invasion. He is presently a lieutenant colonel. Lieutenant Courtney (A/1/1) was presented a Bronze Star after Hue, then was killed at Khe Sanh when he stepped on an unmarked U.S. land mine while walking point for his platoon. Lieutenant Donnelly (A/1/1) won the Silver Star, received his third Purple Heart at Khe Sanh, and is now a lieutenant colonel. Lieutenant Lyons (Chaplain, 1/1) won the Silver Star and Purple Heart for Hue. He had planned to make a career in the Navy, but was forced to retire in 1975 because of diabetes. At that time, he left the priesthood, subsequently married, and now lives in Chula Vista, California, and works for the sheriff's department as a counsellor in the county jail. Gunnery Sergeant Canley (A/1/1) won the Navy Cross for Hue and retired as a sergeant major. Sergeant Burghardt (A/1/1) received his third Purple Heart, a meritorious promotion to staff sergeant, and was medically retired from the Corps where he had hoped to make his career. He won the Bronze Star for Hue. His wounds left him in a wheelchair, but he learned to adapt, got married, and lives in Fountain Valley, California. Sergeant Gonzalez (A/1/1) was posthumously awarded the Medal of Honor. In 1976, his mother and Colonel Gravel participated in the dedication of the Alfredo Gonzalez Elementary School in his hometown. Corporal Jackson (A/1/1) left Vietnam in June 1968, when his brother arrived. (His brother was 100 percent disabled by a mine, and then his other brother arrived. All three were combat Marines.) Jackson now lives with his wife and three sons on Long Island, New York, where he is a registered nurse, police officer, and staff NCO in the Marine Reserve. Corporal Soukup (H&S/1/1) rotated home in April 1968, married, and is now an electric-power technician in Baltimore. Lance Corporal Neas (A/1/1) was sent back to the field after his wounds from Hue healed, then received his third Purple

Heart at Khe Sanh in April 1968. He is married and presently living with his family in Huntington Beach, California, where he is a telephone company systems-technician and a staff sergeant in the Marine Reserve.

Major Thompson (CO, 1/5) won the Navy Cross for Hue and retired in 1983 as a colonel. Captain Harrington (CO, D/1/5) received the Navy Cross and Silver Star for Hue, finished his tour, then returned to Vietnam, 1972-73, as an advisor to the Vietnamese Marines. He is presently a colonel. Lieutenant Green (D/1/5) is now a lieutenant colonel. Lieutenant Imlah (D/1/5) received the Bronze Star and Purple Heart and returned to the company after recuperating from wounds; he was killed in action in mid-1968. Lieutenant Polk (CO, A/1/5) won two Bronze Stars and three Purple Hearts, then was discharged in 1969. He married, divorced, then remarried and now lives in Nebraska where he is a sales manager with an automobile company. Lieutenant Williams (D/1/5) received the Navy Commendation Medal and Purple Heart and returned to the battalion. For his own safety, Harrington got him a rear job, but Williams talked his way back into the field one day; he ended up being wounded in a sudden firefight, and was finally sent home. Staff Sergeant McLaughlin (L/3/5) went back to Vietnam for a 1972-73 tour with the 9th Marines and retired as a master sergeant with two Bronze Stars and a Navy Commendation Medal. He now lives with his wife and family in Copperstown, Pennsylvania, and works for the state transportation department. Corporal Jackson (L/3/5) was killed several weeks after Hue when walking point on a platoon patrol; the NVA shot him three times in the chest in the first burst of an ambush. PFC Lawhorn (D/1/5) left Vietnam six months early when his brother arrived. (He ended up driving a jeep for an Army colonel in the rear). He married and lives with his family in Apollo, Pennsylvania, where he is an insurance agent and part-time deputy constable. Lance Corporal Mayer (H&S/1/5) was medically discharged with his three Purple Hearts. He lives in Medford, New York, with his wife and children and is a subway motorman.

Lieutenant Colonel Cheatham (CO, 2/5) came out of Hue with the Navy Cross and a promising career. He is presently a major general. Major Salvati (2/5) received the Silver Star, retired as a lieutenant colonel, and is an instructor with a Marine JROTC detachment in Round Rock, Texas. Major Steele (2/5) won a meritorious Bronze Star and is now a brigadier general. Captain Fine (2/5) is a lieutenant colonel. Captain Pyle (2/5) retired as a major, after twenty years of enlisted and commissioned service, and is an insurance agent in Virginia. Captain Christmas (CO, H/2/5) received the Navy Cross in an awards ceremony in which his father-in-law, Colonel Lownds, was also presented a Navy Cross. Captain Downs (CO, F/2/5) and Captain Meadows (CO, G/2/5) won Silver Stars. All three are now colonels. Lieutenant Hausrath (F/2/5) was posthumously awarded the Silver Star and Purple Heart; his parents received the medals. Lieutenant Harvey (CO, H/2/5) received the Bronze Star and Purple Heart, then went back to Vietnam as an infantry company commander, 1970– 71, where he earned another Bronze Star. He is presently a lieutenant colonel. Gunnery Sergeant Thomas (H/2/5) received a Bronze Star for Hue, a Navy Commendation Medal for his subsequent work on the battalion staff, and is now a sergeant major. Corporal Allbritton (F/2/5) was discharged with his three Purple Hearts, and now lives with his wife and children in Little Rock, Arkansas, where he is a mailman. Corporal Burnham (F/2/5) earned the Navy Cross for his exploit before Hue, won the Bronze Star for Hue — then went home when his brother was killed in action. He returned to Vietnam for a second tour, and is now a chief warrant officer. Lance Corporal Carter (F/2/5) won the Bronze Star and two Purple Hearts for Hue, then was seriously wounded by a booby trap about a month before he was due to rotate home. He was discharged the next year, married, later joined the Marine Reserve, then went regular again and is now a staff sergeant. PFC Kaczmarek (H/2/5) was seriously wounded after Hue and evacuated back to the United States. PFC McDonald (H/2/5) returned home to New Jersey and received the Silver Star years later, reportedly after petitioning his congressman about it.

Lieutenant Colonel LaMontagne (3d MarDiv) won the Silver Star for Hue, later assumed command of 3/9, and came home with the Legion of Merit, two Bronze Stars, and three Purple Hearts. He retired as a colonel and lives with his wife in New Hampshire. Dr. Hamilton (1st Med) won the Bronze Star, went back to his practice in Chicago, and retired from the Naval Reserve in 1982 as a captain. Major Breth (3d MarDiv) finished his tour with 3/9, earned three Bronze Stars and two Purple Hearts, and is now a colonel. Major Swenson (1st MarDiv) won the Bronze Star for Hue, finished his tour with the 3d Marines, and is presently a colonel. Captain Coolican (1st ARVN Division) left Vietnam with the Navy Cross, Navy–Marine Corps Medal, Bronze Star, and Purple Heart, and is now a colonel. Lieutenant Charbonneau (1st MTB) lives with his wife and children in Illinois, works as a customer service manager, and is a lieutenant colonel in the Marine Reserve. Lieutenant DiBernardo (AFRTVS) endured five years in a Hanoi POW camp before returning to his family in 1973. Then, for the first time, he saw the twin girls born soon after his capture. He was awarded the

Bronze Star, two navy Commendation Medals, three Purple Hearts, and retired as a major. Sergeant Berntson (ISO, 1st MarDiv) received the Bronze Star, two Purple Hearts, and a 70 percent disability after a year in and out of hospitals. Today, he lives with his wife and children in Tacoma, Washington, and is a partner in an insurance agency. Sergeant Dye (ISO, 1st MarDiv) left Vietnam in 1970, after three years in the war, with the Bronze Star, Navy Commendation Medal, and three Purple Hearts. He is presently a captain. PFC Landry (1/11) worked for the post office after being discharged, and today lives with his wife and family in West Lynn, Massachusetts. PFC Schamberger (1/11) married and divorced after the war, remarried, and now works for the phone company in Patchogue, New York. Greenway, Mohr, and Webb, the reporters who helped Berntson with his rescue attempt, were all awarded Bronze Stars in 1980 by the Commandant of the Marine Corps, the only civilians so honored by the Corps during the Vietnam War.

After being discharged from the Marines, Ed Neas contacted the VA about how to find his friend, Josef Burghardt. They put him in touch, and only then did Neas find out how badly he had been injured. In 1973, Neas and his wife stayed with the Burghardts for part of their honeymoon. Then, in 1978, when Neas was offered a job in California, he took it without a moment's hesitation. Today, he lives five minutes from the Burghardts.

In 1980, the two Marines and their wives attended the USMC Birthday Ball sponsored by Neas' Reserve unit. They were pleasantly surprised to learn that the guest speaker was Mark Gravel. They lost no time in reintroducing themselves to their old battalion commander, and began talking over their memories of that month in Hue. Whatever speech Gravel had planned to give was forgotten by the time he reached the speaker's podium. He spent his time talking about those streets and houses in Hue, about the valor of the young Marines like Burghardt and Neas, and all the others who didn't make it home. When he finished, the audience was standing, applauding those who had fought in Hue.

Glossary

A-gunner: assistant gunner.

AK–47 or AK: standard 7.62mm communist rifle.

APL: armored personnel carrier.

ARVN: Army of the Republic of Vietnam; a South Vietnamese unit or soldier.

B–40: standard, shoulder-fired communist rocket.

BAS: battalion aid station.

Basecamp: a unit's home base.

Bird: any aircraft.

Boot: a Marine recruit who is taught the rudiments by DI's.

Bush: any place outside a base where contact with the enemy is a real prospect.

C–130: large cargo plane.

CAP: combined action platoon; joint American Marine/South Vietnamese militia units set up to protect specific villages.

Cav: cavalry; specifically, the 1st Air Cavalry Division, U.S. Army.

Claymore: standard, fan-shaped, antipersonnel U.S. mine.

CO: commanding officer.

Concertina: barbed wire.

Corpsman: Navy medic.

CP: command post.

C rations, or C-rats, or Cs, or rats: combat field meals packed in metal cans.

CS: nonlethal tear gas.

DI: Marine drill instructors who train boots to be effective Marines.

DMZ: demilitarized zone, dividing line between North and South Vietnam at the 17th parallel.

Doc: common Marine nickname for their Navy corpsmen.

Duster: Army light tank of WW II vintage mounting twin 40mm Bofors air defense guns. Deployed as part of the Duster organization were quad .50 caliber machine guns mounted on trucks or directly on the ground.

E-8: tear gas launcher.

.45: standard U.S. pistol.

Field: any place outside a base where contact with the enemy is a real prospect.

Flak jacket: sleeveless armored vest designed to stop shell or grenade fragments.

FO: forward observer; man who directs artillery fire.

Gook: derisive, common American nickname for the Vietnamese.

Grunt: popular nickname for the Marine combat infantryman.

Gunny: Marine gunnery sergeant.

Hootch: any small building; specifically, the straw huts of the peasants.

Huey: nickname for the UH-1D helicopter.

H&S: headquarters & service unit.

HQ: headquarters.

In-country: to be in Vietnam.

KIA: killed in action.

Kit Carson Scout: former Communist who defected to the allies, was retrained, and volunteered to fight alongside the Americans; usually one was assigned to each infantry platoon as a scout and interpreter.

LAAW: light assault weapon; standard, shoulder-fired U.S. rocket.

LCU: landing craft, utility.

LZ: landing zone.

M-16: standard 5.56mm U.S. rifle.

M-60: standard 7.62mm U.S. machine gun.

M-79: grenade launcher.

MACV: Military Assistance Command Vietnam, overall U.S. command in Vietnam.

Mechanical Mule: small, flat-bed, four-wheel vehicle.

Medevac: a medical evacuation helicopter; to evacuate casualties.

MOS: military occupational speciality.

MTB: motor transport battalion.

Mustang: an up-from-the-ranks officer.

Nam: nickname for Vietnam.

NCO: noncommissioned officer.

NVA: North Vietnamese Army; a North Vietnamese soldier.

OD: olive drab.

Ontos: small tracked vehicle mounted with six 106mm recoilless rifles.

Payback: Marine term for revenge.

Phantom: F-4 fighter jet.

Piastre: Vietnamese currency.

R&R: Rest and Relaxation, a trip out of Vietnam that every serviceman was supposed to get once during his one-year tour.

Sea Knight: nickname for the Marine/Navy version of the CH-46 helicopter.

Short: soldier whose tour of duty in Vietnam was almost finished.

Spider hole: nickname for enemy foxhole.

Spooky: nickname for plane mounted with rapid fire mini-guns.

TAOR: tactical area of responsibility.

Tet: the Vietnamese lunar new year; specifically, the massive communist offensive launched during the 1968 Tet celebrations.

TOC: tactical operations center.

III MAF: Third Marine Amphibious Force; overall Marine command in Vietnam.

USAF: United States Air Force.

USMC: United States Marine Corps.

VC: Viet Cong; a South Vietnamese guerilla.

WIA: wounded in action.

World, the: anyplace but Vietnam.

Bibliography

BOOKS

Bartlett, Tom, et al. *Ambassadors in Green.* Washington, D.C: Leatherneck Association, Inc., 1971.

Braestrup, Peter. *Big Story: How the American Press and Television Reported and Interpreted the Crisis of Tet 1968 in Vietnam and Washington.* Garden City, New York; Anchor Books, 1978.

Herr, Michael. *Dispatches.* New York: Avon Books, 1978.

Jones-Griffith, Philip. *Vietnam Inc.* New York: The Macmillan Company, 1971.

McCullin, Don. *Hearts of Darkness.* New York: Alfred A. Knopf, 1981.

Oberdorfer, Don, *TET!.* New York: Doubleday, 1971.

Palmer, Dave Richard, *Summons of the Trumpet.* Novato, Ca.: Presidio Press, 1978.

Pearson, Willard, Lt. Gen. *The War In The Northern Provinces 1966–1968.* Washington, D.C.: Department of the Army, 1975.

Simmons, Edwin H., et al. *The Marines in Vietnam 1954–1973, An Anthology and Annotated Bibliography.* Washington, D.C.: Headquarters, U.S. Marine Corps, 1974.

Tolson, John J., Lt. Gen. *Airmobility 1961–1971.* Washington, D.C.: Department of the Army, 1973.

Westmoreland, William C., Gen. *A Soldier Reports.* Garden City, New York: Doubleday and Company, Inc., 1976.

Young, Perry Deane. *Two of the Missing: A Reminiscence of Some Friends In the War.* New York: Coward, McCann & Geoghegan, Inc., 1975.

PERIODICALS

Bartlett, Tom. "Tet; Bloody Tet. . . ." *Leatherneck,* February 1973, pp. 16–21.

———— . "They Have Borne the Battle." *Leatherneck,* July 1973, pp. 16–23.

———— . "In The Highest Tradition." *Leatherneck,* September 1980, p. 63.

Christmas, G. R. "A Company Commander Reflects on Operation Hue City." *Marine Corps Gazette,* April 1971, pp. 34–39.

———— , "A Company Commander Remembers the Battle for Hue." *Marine Corps Gazette,* February 1977, pp. 19–26.

"Fight For a Citadel," *Time,* March 1, 1968, pp. 20–21.

Herr, Michael. "Hell Sucks." *Esquire,* August 1968, p. 66.

Leroy, Cathy. "A Tense Interlude with the Enemy in Hue." *Life,* February 16, 1968, pp. 22–29.

"Man On The Spot." *Newsweek,* February 19, 1968, pp. 33–43.

Martin, Bruce. "House to House." *Leatherneck,* May 1968, p. 54.

Olson, John. "The Battle that Regained and Ruined Hue." *Life,* March 8, 1968, pp. 24–29.

Smith, George W. "The Battle of Hue." *Infantry,* July/August 1968, pp. 16–26.

Thompson, Paul, "Hue." *Leatherneck,* July 1968, p. 22.

"Up From the Ranks." *Marine Corps Gazette,* November 1970, pp. 44–45.

"Victory At Hue." *Army Journal,* pp. 3–20.

White, Peter T. "Behind the Headlines in Viet Nam." *National Geographic,* February 1967, pp. 149–193.

DOCUMENTS

"After Action Report: Battle of Hue."

"After Action Report: Headquarters, 1st Infantry Division Advisory Detachment, Advisory Team 3."

Beavers, Richard W., Sp5, and Walker, Miles D., Maj., 31st Military History Detachment, "History Study 2-68, Operation Hue City," August 1968.

"Command Chronology, 1st Battalion, 1st Marines, January 1968."

"_____ , February 1968."

"Command Chronology, 1st Battalion, 5th Marines, February 1968."

"Command Chronology, 2d Battalion, 5th Marines, January 1968."

"_____ , February 1968."

"Command Chronology, 3d Battalion, 5th Marines, February 1968."

"Command Chronology, 1st Battalion, 11th Marines, February 1968."

"Command Chronology, 1st Tank Battalion, February 1968."

"Operations of U.S. Marine Forces, Vietnam, February 1968."

"Task Force X-RAY After Action Report."

"U.S. Marine Corps Oral History Program/Interviewees: Lt. Col. Ernest Cheatham, Majors Ron Christmas, Mike Downs, and Chuck Meadows, 23 July 1973."

"_____/Interviewee: Lt. Col. Marcus J. Gravel, 17 July 1973."

FILMS

CBS News videotape of Hotel 2/5 raising colors over Province Capitol.

Neil Davis, documentary.

Index